TRIUMPH

POWERFUL STORIES OF ATHLETES OF FAITH

PAT WILLIAMS
with Ken Hussar

SHILOH RUN PRESS

Print ISBN 978-1-62836-970-0

eBook Editions:
Adobe Digital Edition (.epub) 978-1-63058-556-3
Kindle and MobiPocket Edition (.prc) 978-1-63058-557-0

Cover image © Faceout Studio, www.faceoutstudio.com

Published by Shiloh Run Press, an imprint of Barbour Publishing, Inc., P.O. Box 719, Uhrichsville, Ohio 44683, www.shilohrunpress.com

Our mission is to publish and distribute inspirational products offering exceptional value and biblical encouragement to the masses.

ecpa Member of the
Evangelical Christian
Publishers Association

Printed in the United States of America.

DEDICATION

....

I dedicate this book to Ken Hussar,
my friend of thirty-four years.
We have worked together
on over sixty books.
I write them down, and Ken works them over!
PAT WILLIAMS

This book is also dedicated to
two beautiful mothers:
Anna N. Hussar, who celebrated
her ninety-sixth birthday as this book was
being completed,
and to
Carolyn J. Hussar,
my loving wife for forty-four years
and mother of our three children,
Caryn, James, and Stephanie.
And grandmother
of Gabriel and Camilo Hussar,
and Carter and Camryn Baxter.
KEN HUSSAR

CONTENTS

....

Honoring

INTRODUCTION

The late sportswriter Grantland Rice wrote, " 'It doesn't matter whether you win or lose, it's how you play the game,' was first said by someone who lost."

I have been involved (more correctly, *deeply immersed*) in sports for the majority of my seventy-four years. I have spent fifty-two of those years in professional sports (baseball and basketball) as a player, general manager, and senior vice president. As a noncasual observer, I emphatically submit that in the sports world, winning really, really matters.

What matters most to you and me, however, is how we as individuals play and win in life. It is tempting to say "in the *game* of life," but life is not a game. It is a serious business.

The book you are about to read, *Triumph! Powerful Stories of Athletes of Faith*, contains dozens of stories submitted by athletes, coaches, and sports observers who have experienced ultimate victory as a result of their faith in God. With a winning theme in mind, my coeditor, Ken Hussar, and I have organized these inspiring submissions using the acronym TRIUMPH: *Trusting, Rejoicing, Inspiring, Understanding, Meditating, Praising, Honoring.*

May these stories bless your soul, bolster your faith, and motivate you to boldly and victoriously serve our omnipotent God.

PAT WILLIAMS
SENIOR VICE PRESIDENT, ORLANDO MAGIC
MARCH 2014

TRUSTING

....

1. Winning Ways

> *Uzziah sought God during the days of Zechariah,*
> *who taught him to fear God. And as long as the king*
> *sought guidance from the LORD, God gave him success.*
> 2 CHRONICLES 26:5 NLT

Ever since I've been in a leadership position, my focus has been the model of Christ as the Servant-Leader. There are different ways to lead, but I've always felt it is better if people follow me because they *want* to follow, not because they *have* to. To lead like that, you have to earn people's trust and respect. The way to do that is to show them you are there to help them.

As a coach it was my job not necessarily just to win championships, but to help all players, everyone in the organization, to do their jobs as well as they could. I really tried to, number one, be a role model and, number two, serve my team spiritually. I wanted to teach the players as much as I could about football and how to be better players, but I also wanted to help them be better people, to do well in the community, and to do well after football. I wanted them to know that they are, first and always, servants of others.

I hope my players saw consistency in my life no matter what happened. . .good or bad, up or down. I hope they saw someone who tried to live his Christianity every day.

With anything that comes across my desk, if I pray about it and ask the Lord's direction, He's going to work those situations for His glory. It will be for the best and it will succeed—maybe not the success the world will see, but success in His eyes.

Remember, you don't have to do everything the way the

world says. You don't have to buy into the belief structure that is popular right now. You need to be your own person. Young people are so tempted to follow the crowd, but standing firm in what you believe gives you significance. I believe the true path to significance is helping people and doing things that benefit others and not just yourself. Sure, I'm happy that I had the honor of winning the Super Bowl as a coach, but I'm happier that I helped fifty-three guys win the championship.

Sometimes along the way, we encounter roadblocks. During our Super Bowl season, we lost to Jacksonville 44–17—one of our worst losses since I became coach at Indianapolis. Fans were saying, "The Colts are falling apart," but we dug in as a team and figured out what happened and learned from it. The end of the story is that we went on to win the Super Bowl that year. You usually learn as much or more from a loss than you do from a win. In life, you have the chance to learn from any negative situation, be it an illness, the loss of a job, or whatever comes your way.

You're never going to get anywhere in sports or in life until you become convinced of the truth of the gospel of Jesus Christ.

Oh sure, you may become a professional athlete and have nice cars, houses, and a lot of money, but what you will find is that all that stuff goes away pretty quickly. You have to understand that Christ died for your sins, and that He died not just to be your Savior, but so that He could be the center of your life. And if you understand that, then you have to be committed to it. You have to be sold out to it—regardless of the role God wants you to play.

Being "sold out to Jesus" means you must be steadfast...and a little stubborn. First Corinthians 15:58 says, "Stand firm. Let nothing move you," and that's even when it's not popular.

I know I've lost some jobs because the owners who interviewed me asked me, "Is getting to the Super Bowl the most important thing in your life? Can I count on you to be there twenty-four hours a day and be available around the clock to do whatever it takes to win a Super Bowl?" And my response was, "No, you can't. Because if that's what it takes to have this job, then I don't want it."

The stands God calls you to take may not be popular. They may not always get you ahead. But you have to stand firm in your convictions, because being steadfast and handling adversity well is what a winner does.

It all starts with the gospel of Jesus Christ. It starts with asking Jesus to be your Savior and then living for Him no matter what.

Tony Dungy

2. Heaven Is Already Mine

Yet to all who did receive him, to those who believed in his name, he gave the right to become children of God.
John 1:12

As far back as I can remember, I had one dream in life: to become a pro athlete. I grew up in the old steel mill town of Bethlehem, Pennsylvania, where I competed in basketball, baseball, football, and track at Liberty High School. I attended Temple University in Philadelphia, where my dream of being a professional athlete was narrowed to football.

In 1981 I signed my first pro football contract. I could bench press more than five hundred pounds, drove a nice car, and had attended a university. However, there was still something missing in my life. I was from a wonderful home and had been brought up going to church, but if someone were to ask me if I was going to go to heaven when I died, I would reply, "I don't know. I hope so." When I thought about eternity, I was very insecure. I honestly had no idea where I would end up when I took my last breath.

Most people hope they have done enough good things to outweigh the bad things they have done. This is how I thought and lived my life for twenty-five years. But I never knew if the good things I did would take care of all the bad things I had done the night before.

That all changed on April 30, 1983, just before a game in Tampa, Florida. I was in my third year of professional football, and I took part in what had become somewhat of a pregame ritual for me. I went to "church"—also known as pregame chapel. That day I sat in a hotel room with twenty other players and coaches.

I had done this plenty of times before. But it was different this time. A man called "Doc" came to speak to us, and his message was one I had never heard before. He called it "The Difference between Religion and Biblical Christianity." He said that religion was man's greatest effort to reach God and that it was all about *doing*. Biblical Christianity, on the other hand, was *done*.

He said that biblical Christianity was not about attending a certain church or about how many good things you had done in a lifetime. Biblical Christianity is about a real person named Jesus Christ—about who He is and what He did. Jesus, God's Son, had left heaven and come down to earth, where He lived a sinless life for thirty-three years. He never so much as disobeyed His parents or had a bad thought. At the end of His life on earth, Jesus said, "No one takes my life. I lay it down." Jesus Christ paid the price for all humanity by dying on the cross of Calvary, and three days later He showed Himself to be God by rising from the dead. Jesus' last words on the cross were, "It is finished." He had done something that humanity could not do for itself. He paid for our sins with His precious blood.

I knew the Good Friday and Easter story. However, that day Doc shared a Bible verse I had never heard before: John 1:12, which says, "Yet to all who did receive him, to those who believed in his name, he gave the right to become children of God." He said that means that a person has to individually and by faith receive what Jesus did for him/her on the cross two thousand years ago.

Receive means to *appropriate*, to take to one's self and call one's own at a specific time. That day, by the grace of God, was my day, and by faith I put my trust in what Jesus Christ did for me on the cross of Calvary. Now I know that I am going to heaven when I die, not because of what I have done or what I haven't done, but because of what Jesus did for me.

My faith in Jesus motivates me to live for Him and to tell others about Him—not because I am trying to work my way to heaven but because heaven is already mine.

RICH GARZA

3. It Was His Doin'

> *The LORD has done this, and it is marvelous in our eyes.*
> PSALM 118:23

When I was a boy growing up in a two-sawmill central Alabama town, the ladies would say, "Wayne, you are going to be a preacher like your daddy."

Daddy was a street preacher, tent revivalist, radio preacher, and bivocational pastor-evangelist. At seven I would ride with him on Saturdays in our 1945 Chevrolet with two loud speakers atop to six small towns. He would play a gospel song, preach for fifteen minutes, and give those who came to town the opportunity to receive Jesus as Lord and Savior. Then we would move on to the next town.

I was proud of my daddy and loved going with him. I was raised on evangelism. Playing football, baseball, and basketball captivated my interests also. Evangelism and sports were my two loves.

It was beyond comprehension that my journey in life would lead to four highly privileged careers across America, and that it would take my family and me to Kansas City, Indianapolis, Richmond, Tuscaloosa, Colorado Springs, and Charlotte.

Being small in stature, my dream of playing football for the University of Alabama never came true. Instead, I decided to attend Samford University, a Baptist college in Birmingham, confident that God would reveal to me His plan for me to be a minister. As a student sports information director, my writing and public relations skills were my ticket through college. Our football coach was thirty-five-year-old Bobby Bowden, who would go on to become one of the nation's finest.

Although I was passionately committed to walk with God, I never felt God's call to preach.

After graduation my path led me to the University of Alabama, where I worked as a graduate assistant in sports information. The football coach, Paul "Bear" Bryant, was already legendary, as was the quarterback, Joe Namath. The Crimson Tide won the national championship both of my years (1964 and 1965) there. As a boy who had just left the sawmill town, I was awestruck. But this "was the Lord's doin'."

My favorite Bible passage back then was Proverbs 3:5–6: "Trust in the LORD with all your heart and lean not on your own understanding; in all your ways submit to him and he will make your paths straight."

It was during my time at Alabama that the college campus captured my fondest interests for a vocation in athletics. I also was introduced to the Fellowship of Christian Athletes (FCA), an organization just ten years old at the time.

At my first FCA camp, in 1964, I found the guys I'd been searching for, those whose interests were Christ and athletics. One year out of graduate school, I was asked to join the national staff of FCA in Kansas City. The twelve-hour drive in my brand-new 1967 Ford led to a highlight reel life beyond my wildest dreams.

Over the next twelve years, my life was a divine major league experience of serving the Lord from coast to coast, working with high school, college, and professional athletes and coaches in FCA camps and Weekend of Champions, and facilitating seven Final Four FCA coaches' breakfasts. All that while heading up the national high school and college programs.

I was humbled to be one of a dozen staff members to see this ministry launch. Over the past fifty-five-plus years, it has had a mighty impact for Christ, with hundreds serving on staff and millions reached with the gospel.

For one who is still easily impressed with people, places, and things, it was exciting to me to be closely associated with men like Tom Landry, John Wooden, Tom Osborne, Dean Smith, Roger Staubach, Carl Erskine, Bob Pettit, Ray Berry, Archie Griffin, and dozens more elite people in athletics.

When God directs, you must be ready for the next assignment. Seventeen years after departing from Alabama, I returned to my dream job in athletics as the University of Alabama's sports information director. New York Giants coach Ray Perkins took over for the retired Coach Bryant and brought me home with my wife, Barbara, and our two young daughters, Elizabeth and Amy.

What an incredible twenty years in college football at Alabama we enjoyed. Eighteen of those years I served as FCA adviser, putting together 550 programs—one each Wednesday night at nine. What a ministry God gave me as the FCA athletes used their sports venues as their platform to serve Jesus Christ. Again, it "was the Lord's doin'."

No one leaves big-time college football unless they get fired or die, I've always said. But I departed because the Lord said, "Your time is up here, and I have something else for you to do." Longtime friend Jerry Jenkins, of *Left Behind* fame, came for a visit in 2002 and invited me to join his Christian Writers Guild staff in Colorado Springs. In the next two months, the Lord gave me fifty signs that I was to assist Jerry in raising up a new harvest of Christian writers across the nation and throughout the world. It was a glorious experience of almost four years in picturesque Colorado Springs.

Then one day, I received a call from the Billy Graham Evangelistic Association, asking if I would consider interviewing as director of the new Billy Graham Library in Charlotte, North Carolina. After two interviews, Franklin Graham hired me as the first library director. It was such a high honor for one born into evangelism. I wanted to call my parents, who were by now in heaven, but a friend gave a soothing explanation, "Wayne, they knew about it before you did."

Welcoming almost four hundred thousand guests from seventy-five countries in the first three years has become the dessert of my career. The best part is seeing several hundred invite Christ into their lives and thousands rededicate their lives to Christ.

As I look back over four careers, I realize was asked to serve in each one. They were gifts from almighty God. Seldom does a day go by that I don't think of Maplesville and tell someone that my daddy was a street preacher and tent revivalist. In those early boyhood days, God was preparing me to be where I am today.

God is sovereign, and He can view our lives from beginning to end in one glance. My hero, Eric Liddell of *Chariots of Fire* fame, made this scripture verse well known: "Those who honor me I will honor" (1 Samuel 2:30). My life is an example of the truth of that verse.

Perhaps the ladies were right. From humble beginnings, I grew to be a preacher like daddy, but with a different platform. I have learned that little is much in the hands of God. To Him be the glory alone because "it was His doin'."

WAYNE ATCHESON

4. Pine-Tuning: What God Taught Me on the Bench

Commit to the LORD whatever you do,
and he will establish your plans.
PROVERBS 16:3

Since my early high school years, it was my dream to play baseball at the United States Military Academy at West Point. After being recruited to play catcher for Army's baseball team, I, like many athletes, found that I had to "pay my dues" and wait for a starting position to open up. Having been my high school's baseball team captain and home run leader, I was eager to play at the collegiate level. During my "plebe" (freshmen) year, I had a few plate appearances but mainly served as the bullpen catcher. I told myself that my time would come. My "yuk" (sophomore) year provided me with more appearances on the field, but, once again, I had to continue to bide my time.

During this period, I remained faithful and active in West Point's Fellowship of Christian Athletes (FCA) program. The weekly Bible studies were engaging and provided me a great opportunity to get to know my teammates in a spiritual setting. However, as time went on, I found myself asking God if my time with the baseball team was being wasted. I still wasn't playing much. Could I be better utilizing my time?

In my "cow" (junior) year, I became the baseball team's Bible study leader and was a part of West Point's FCA student leader board. During the fall and winter of that year, those of us on the baseball team who were involved with FCA developed quite a bond. Many of our members were from the freshmen or sophomore class; as a junior, I felt I was there to provide spiritual leadership. Little did I know that I would face one of the most difficult decisions of my life that upcoming spring.

Going into our main season that spring, I had the second-highest batting average among returning players and served as the second-string catcher. Later in the season, the senior catcher tore his rotator cuff in a game against Navy, our biggest rival. I never wished to have personal gain over someone else's misfortune, but I knew that this was my time to step up and fill the role I thought was rightfully mine. After the countless hours of practice over the past two and a half years, it was my time to lead the team from behind the plate in the biggest regular season games of the year. My parents even flew in from Florida to see the weekend games, so this was a chance for them to see me play at the collegiate level.

As I gathered my gear to get ready to take the field, my head coach yelled out across the dugout, "Scottie, you're catching!"

What? I thought. *Coach is putting the freshman in?* I was crushed. After all those years, after all those practices, I was unexpectedly pushed aside. My friends on the team understood the significance of the coach's decision. I put my gear down and attempted to suppress my feelings. I needed to support the team, right? I thought, *Maybe Coach is just going to play Scottie this game and he'll start me in our doubleheader tomorrow.* I could only wait.

The next day proved to be no different than the one before: Coach started the freshman. I sat on the bench those two games, outwardly cheering on the team against our primary rivals but inwardly thinking, *What is my purpose on this team?* I had always been a leader on the teams I had played for. Darkness clouded my dreams of playing baseball at the Academy.

After that weekend, I thought I would wait to see how things played out. Even though I felt insulted that the head coach started a freshman over me, a junior, in our biggest regular season games of the year, I thought that just maybe he would start me the following weekend. He didn't. Having thought through things the past week or so, I decided that I was finished. *We all have to hang up the cleats at some point,* I thought.

Before practice on Monday, I met with the head coach and told him that I was turning in my uniform. He accepted my resignation. I couldn't just let him run over me like that, right? I had given so much to this program already. The countless late-night practices down in the field house, the lost spring breaks, and a majority of my weekends at West Point forgone to play baseball. *What was I working for?*

Monday afternoon I sat studying in my bedroom in the barracks, attempting to work on the biggest paper of my academic career at West Point. As I tried to concentrate on what I was typing, I could hear the ping of the bat outside my window, which I had opened to let in the cool New York spring wind. I shut the window. Thoughts of baseball continuously flowed through my head. *Baseball withdrawal,* I initially thought. The problem was that every day that week I could still hear the ping of the bat through my closed window. It was as if the game was trying to call me back. I couldn't get baseball out of my heart.

On Wednesday, my thoughts drifted to the guys on the team that participated with FCA. Who was going to lead the Bible studies? I wondered. Was the baseball FCA program going to fall through now that I wasn't there to lead it?

The next few days, I went through some extreme torment about not leading the baseball team's FCA program or being on the team. I prayed to God and asked Him, "What am I to do?" The pain was so great that I ended up not finishing my paper on time and had to receive an automatic grade reduction for turning it in late that Friday.

Something is wrong, I thought. *I don't think God wants me to quit playing baseball.*

On a rainy Friday afternoon that same week, the team was preparing to board the bus for some out-of-town weekend games. About thirty minutes before the players and coaches loaded themselves and their gear, I swallowed my pride and walked over to the baseball field to talk with the head coach in his office at the clubhouse.

"Coach," I said, "I made a mistake in resigning. I want to be back on the team. I'm okay with whatever decision you make as to whom the starting catcher will be. I just want to be on the team. In practice, I will lead the two freshmen catchers in the drills that we have to do, and whoever you decide to start, then that is best for the team. I just want back on the team."

He responded, "If I allow you to be on the team again, I might decide to never play you again. Are you okay with that?"

"Yes," I said, without blinking an eye.

He asked me to step outside of his office while he talked it over with his assistant. After what seemed like an eternity, he called me back in and let me know that I could stay on the team. I was overjoyed.

I didn't play in one game the rest of the season. I continued to lead the team's FCA meetings and held true to my word as I pushed the freshmen catchers during practice.

My "firstie" (senior) year started out no different than my junior year had ended. The coach continued not to play me. Eight games into our season (1–7), before our annual spring break trip to play down in Florida, our head coach resigned for personal reasons. During the trip, the former assistant and now acting head coach gave me a chance to start against the University of South Florida, which was then nationally ranked. I did a horrible job catching (literally the worst defensive game of my life) but did superbly at the plate—going 3 for 4 with a double and two runs batted in. From that point on, I never caught again but later became the starting designated hitter.

Despite breaking into the lineup midway through my senior year, by the end of the regular season I led the team in home runs, was second in runs batted in, and fourth in total bases. More importantly, despite entering the Patriot League tournament ranked third (we were known as the Cardiac Cadets due to our eighteen come-from-behind wins), our team won the tournament and, for the first time in West Point's history, made it to the NCAA regional playoffs.

In our league tournament, I was able to slap a clutch three-run double to lead the comeback win in the elimination game against Bucknell and added a crucial two-run double in the series-clinching victory against Navy.

As I moved from the United States Military Academy into my active-duty military career as an Airborne Ranger with the 82nd Airborne Division, I found myself leading soldiers in combat and applying those valuable lessons I learned while playing baseball with the Black Knights at West Point. These lessons include the importance of being a team player, of selfless sacrifice, and, most important, of trusting the Lord despite not seeing what His purpose is at a certain point in my life.

BOBBY BROWN

5. Benefiting from God's Moving Experiences

The eyes of all look to you, and you give them their food at the proper time.
You open your hand and satisfy the desires of every living thing.
PSALM 145:15–16

I truly believe God has a purpose for each of our lives. One of our responsibilities is to trust Him, seek His wisdom, and find out what He has in store for us.

I have enjoyed an incredibly blessed twenty-three-year (and counting) career in university administration. As the director of athletics for the Iowa Hawkeyes, I often humbly wonder why God has allowed me this privilege. I have my health, a beautiful family, and an awesome job.

I grew up in the Twin Cities area of Minnesota. My parents divorced when I was four years old, and for as long as I could remember, we were a family of little means (we were poor!). My mom worked several jobs at a time. My younger brother, sister, and I shared a tiny apartment bedroom, and Hamburger Helper and powdered milk were regular parts of our diet.

College was not a part of my extended family's culture.

None of my grandparents or parents had ever attended. Because of my surroundings and our economic standing, there was no reason to believe I would break the cycle.

As a youngster, I played sports every day. You name it, we played it. Later in life, we joined organized teams, but prior to that we would simply head to the park, choose sides, and play. I didn't have any grand plans or expectations to earn a college scholarship or to play professional sports—I simply loved to play. I still have that passion for sports today.

I attended a large high school (more than three thousand students in tenth through twelfth grades) in Burnsville, Minnesota. Mostly because of the numbers—and probably because of my limited athletic ability, although I choose not to remember it that way—it became necessary for me to pick one sport and specialize. I chose football.

We won the Minnesota state high school football championship my junior year. I had the opportunity to play in an all-star game, and—with all that team success—I began receiving letters from colleges and universities inviting me to come to their school to earn a degree and play football. Some of them were even offering to pay for my education. Because of my family's lack of post–high school education, we didn't really know what all this meant, nor did we know how to go about the process. It was both exciting and overwhelming.

In the end, I was offered and accepted a full-ride scholarship to attend North Dakota State University. I wasn't a great college football player, but I played on some great (three-time national championship) teams. It was clear I wasn't destined to play professional sports, but I had a world-class college student-athlete experience.

I began my professional career working for the Ford Motor Credit Company in Fargo, North Dakota. I'm wired in such a way that within a day or two of starting my entry-level position, I was setting goals to one day become president of Ford Motor Company.

Fortunately, God had other (and better) plans for me. Out of the blue, I received a call one day from Jim Miller, the head of the North Dakota State University Foundation. He wanted to know if I would consider coming back to my alma mater to raise money. I spent three years at NDSU learning that business and trying to make the Bison better.

My next stop was a seven-year stint working in athletic development and external relations at the University of Northern Iowa in Cedar Falls. It was there I met my future wife, Connie.

In 1996, I was offered the senior associate athletic director position at the University of Washington in Seattle. This was another incredible seven-year run, with another pair of amazing blessings: our son, Luke, and daughter, Madison, were both born during our time in the Pacific Northwest.

The University of Wyoming came calling in 2003, and I had my first opportunity to run a department as the athletic director. We loved Laramie, the mountains, and the incredible friendships we built. I could have easily spent my entire career working for the Cowboys.

Come to think of it, I've been happy at each stop during my career. Every day isn't simple, and there are certainly challenges along the way, but I pray every day that God will use me for whatever purpose He has in store. Part of my prayer is, "Lord, I'm going to do the best I can. Bless all that I think, say, and do. If my best isn't good enough in this situation, lead me to where You want me to be."

Fast forward to 2014. We've been blessed to be back in Iowa since 2006, when I was offered the opportunity to become the director of athletics for the Iowa Hawkeyes.

One night I was standing on the field in Landshark Stadium (now Sun Life Stadium) in Miami at the conclusion of the 2010 FedEx Orange Bowl. The Hawkeyes had just capped a magical season by defeating the Atlantic Coast Conference champion Georgia Tech Yellow Jackets. I was on the stage with our president, head coach, and a pair of our student athletes as our team was presented the Orange Bowl Championship trophy. We were all so proud of Kirk Ferentz, his assistant coaches, and the student athletes for all they had accomplished. I was soaking in the moment and thanking God for how truly blessed I am and have been for so many years.

So what is God's purpose for me? I'll keep trusting and keep seeking, because I know He's not finished working in my life. But for now, I am in a profession doing what I love to do, in the place I'd most like to do it—offering young men and women the same opportunities I was afforded nearly thirty years ago.

God is so good! Follow your passion. Trust and seek the Lord's direction every day.

GARY BARTA

6. Trust and Obey

Trust in the LORD with all your heart and lean not on your own understanding; in all your ways submit to him, and he will make your paths straight.
PROVERBS 3:5–6

I have been a believer in Christ since I was a child, but I truly learned to trust in Christ when I found myself sitting on the bench for the Auburn Tigers football team in the middle of my sophomore year of college.

After a stellar freshman year under then head coach Terry Bowden, I thought my college career was going to be nothing but smooth sailing. Well, my father always told me that smooth sailing doesn't make a great sailor. Well, I guess a life without trials doesn't make a strong Christian, either.

After my freshman year, Coach Bowden was fired and Tommy Tuberville was brought in to replace him. At the time,

Coach Tuberville didn't think I had what it took to play in the Southeast Conference. For a while, I thought he had selective memory issues or maybe the early stages of Alzheimer's, because during my freshmen year, I nearly beat his Ole Miss Rebels singlehandedly. During our faith walk with Christ, things in the human realm may not always make sense. It took me almost eight full weeks before I got an opportunity to show what I could do for the 1999 Auburn Tigers.

One rainy October day in Arkansas, the Lord saw fit to give me an opportunity to display the talents and ability He had given me. We were down 31–0 late in the third quarter, and I was put in the game at running back. About 85 yards and a touchdown later, I was the starting running back for the team the rest of the year. I went on to lead the team in rushing after starting three games that year at running back. During the course of those eight weeks on the bench, I was even moved to defensive tackle at one point. That's right: all 235 pounds of me playing defensive tackle in the SEC, where the smallest offensive linemen are usually just a biscuit shy of 300 pounds. I did not know what God had in mind for me, but when you decide to trust God with your life, you just keep trusting, even when things around you may not make sense.

On the bus ride to play Arkansas that day, I had surrendered all my hopes, dreams, goals, and visions to the Lord Jesus Christ. I told Him that day that if He wanted me to be done playing football, then I was done. Whatever He wanted for me was what I wanted to do. In this life of faith, all God wants is all of us.

Fast forward about six years. I just started my fifth year in the National Football League, and I was the starting fullback for the Miami Dolphins. As far as I knew, I was playing pretty well, and the coach's grade sheets of my performance had reflected that. We had just finished the sixth game of the year—against the Kansas City Chiefs in a game played on a Friday night because a hurricane was supposed to make landfall in South Florida sometime Sunday.

I was putting up hurricane shutters early in the afternoon that Sunday when the phone rang. My life was about to change in a big way. It was my agent calling with the news that, for the first time in my life, I had been cut from a team. Not only did I have a hurricane getting ready to touch down on top of my home in South Florida, but I also had an unexpected personal category five storm making landfall on me. I was a twenty-six-year-old husband and father, and I cried my eyes out in front of my wife and daughter. I recall Beth, my wife of just over four years, asking me what my life's verse was. What an awesome woman! She had just reminded me of the truth that was going to set my mind and heart at peace.

For as long as I can remember, I have signed "Jeremiah 29:11" under every autograph. This verse tells me that the God of the universe has a special plan for my life, and that plan is to bless and prosper me, not to harm me. At that very moment, I felt a sense of all-encompassing peace I had never felt before washing over me. The Lord had allowed a trial in my life that was going to draw me closer to Him, and I never could have experienced that type of provision from God if I had not walked through that particular test.

Remember, earlier I mentioned God's plan is always to bless and prosper us. Later that week, after the phones started working again in South Florida, guess who had called and left a message asking me to join his football team. Bill Belichick, the very best head coach in the NFL, a coach who had won three out of the past four Super Bowls.

Little did I know that because of the contract language, the Dolphins also had to pay me for the whole year. In addition, the best team in football signed me, so I collected a check from them as well. The Patriots also went two weeks deep into the playoffs that year. In the end, I was blessed financially, professionally, and, most importantly, spiritually.

Perhaps the best part of the whole scenario was that two weeks after I got picked up by the Pats, we took a road trip to

South Florida to play those Dolphins who had just cut me. Let's just say that God showed up again. Corey Dillon went down with an injury on the first play of the game, and I was given the opportunity to play the entire day at running back, not fullback.

What did Jeremiah tell us about being blessed and prosperous if we trust in the plans of the Lord? I totaled more than 120 all-purpose yards and helped lead my new team to a win against a conference opponent.

My encouragement to you is to know that the way of the Lord is not always easy or expected, but He promises it will be blessed and prosperous. Just trust and obey. When you live for the Lord, He takes you to higher places every day. Life is full of ups and downs, but when you take the Lord's way, He will make your path straight.

HEATH EVANS

7. What Got the Turtles to the Ark

> *Therefore, if anyone is in Christ, the new creation has come:*
> *The old has gone, the new is here!*
> 2 CORINTHIANS 5:17

Early August of 1963 was the start of a month and a year I will never forget. I was on my way to Henderson Harbor, New York, for my first-ever Fellowship of Christian Athletes (FCA) national conference with my dear friends Danny and John Lotz. Ted Youngling, a football coach at rival Duke University, had asked me three years in a row to attend one of these conferences, but I had an excuse each time as to why I could not go, such as, "I'm too busy, Ted," or "I can't leave my business for a week," or "My wife and boys say I am already gone more than I should be."

This time, however, he approached me with a different strategy. "Hey Albert, I know you can't go, but I wanted to let you know that this year we will be going to Henderson Harbor, New York, for our first-ever FCA conference there on that beautiful island. Just thought you'd like to know about some of the great professional athletes who will be there. All-Pro Bob Pettit of the St. Louis Hawks; college basketball coaches Ben Carnevale, Dean Smith, Johnny Orr, Bob Davies; football coaches Paul Dietzel and Biggie Munn; baseball greats Carl Erskine and Dave 'Boo' Ferris—just to name a few."

That's all I needed to hear—the names of so many athletes and coaches I had idolized. Now I *wanted* to go so I could have a chance to hang around with them for an entire week.

Just one week in a place where there was no cussing, no dirty jokes, no bragging about how many girls you had made out with. . .I knew these guys had something I did not have, and I most certainly wanted it. When I returned home, I was a brand-new person and understood for the first time in my life what 1 Corinthians 5:17 is all about. I still have the letter I wrote to my wife, Jackie. She knew a different husband was coming home to her and our boys. I still thank the good Lord on a regular basis for James Jeffrey, long-time director of the FCA, praying that beautiful prayer of salvation with me as we joined hands that next-to-last night there on that island.

Oh yes, the story gets even better. When Jackie saw the changes in my life, she knew my newfound faith was real, and she, too, wanted what I had. For almost fifty years, we have been blessed as we kept Christ first in our lives. Ten years after returning from that island, I left a very lucrative life insurance business to go out on faith to start a ministry that lasted from 1973 to 1998. Yes, Ted Youngling never gave up on me. Is there a lesson here? Absolutely! Perseverance is what got the turtles to the ark. Don't ever forget that.

ALBERT LONG

Editor's note: Albert Long is a graduate from the University of North Carolina in Chapel Hill and the only four-sport letterman in Atlantic Coast Conference history—football, basketball, baseball, and track.

8. No Pain, No Gain

Be on your guard; stand firm in the faith;
be courageous; be strong.
1 CORINTHIANS 16:13

It was March 14, 2002, and the Cave Spring Knights were playing in their first Virginia State basketball final four since 1969. Led by Duke-bound superstar J.J. Redick, Cave Spring was enjoying its best season in school history.

Although the season had been a good one, it hadn't happened without some struggle. Midway through the season, Redick had suffered a potentially season-ending foot injury—a tear of the plantar fascia tendon. The Knights struggled without their leader, losing four of the six games they played without him. However, just as the postseason approached, the team got some unexpected good news: J.J. had been cleared to start playing again.

With their star player back in the lineup and all the other guys having expanded their roles in his absence, the Knights were ready to make some noise. Pulling upset after upset, they won their district tournament and regional tournament. After surviving a near loss in the state quarterfinals, the team refocused and set its sights on the Final Four.

The whole community was pulling for this team. People waited in line for hours to get tickets to the big game. It was something right out of *Hoosiers*. The Knights would face the mighty Hayfield Hawks in the semis. The Hawks were 26–1 and heavy favorites heading into the game. The atmosphere at the Liberty University Vines Center was electric. Thousands of fans filled the seats, waiting to see if J.J. Redick was as good as advertised, waiting to see if the Hayfield Hawks rugged man-to-man defense could wear him down.

The game was close during the first half. Cave Spring Coach Billy Hicks urged his team to stay confident and aggressive. The Knights came out in the second half and took control. Behind the outside shooting of Redick, Adam Trumbower, and Andrew Davison, the Knights took a commanding lead. Late in the fourth quarter, as Coach Hicks was getting ready to put all the substitutes in the game, J.J. broke away on what appeared to be a basic layup. It turned out to be much more. As he dropped the ball in for his final two points of the evening, he felt something pop in his foot as he landed. As he ran back down the floor, he could feel the pain in his injured foot. Coach Hicks caught his eye and knew something wasn't right.

In the locker room, the Knights celebrated their victory and the fact that two days later they would be playing for a state championship. Not wanting his teammates to know anything was wrong, J.J. put a smile on his face, but deep inside he was crying. He knew he had reinjured his foot. After all the hard work, all the sweat, all the sacrifice, he wouldn't be able to play in the game he had always dreamed of playing in. He knew it was out of his hands.

Jonathon Clay (J.J.) Redick was the third of five children raised by Ken and Jeannie. They had instilled a deep belief system in their children. They believed in the wonderful power of healing that only God could accomplish. They believed in the power of prayer, and that would serve their son well in the coming days.

As the team made the hour-long trip from the arena to the school, the coaches huddled in the front of the bus. The players were loud, so the coaches could talk openly without being heard. They were already working on a game strategy to implement what might give them a chance in the state championship game without J.J.

It was Friday afternoon, less than twenty-four hours before tipoff. Coach Hicks talked to the players as they stretched and loosened up before practice. The mood was good. The players and coaches all had smiles on their faces. No one even noticed that J.J. wasn't on the floor with the team. He was in the training room getting therapy on his injured foot. He had asked his coaches not to tell the team about his injury. He was so unselfish; he didn't want his teammates to lose heart. Since first injuring his foot, it was customary for him to spend the day after a game with the trainer getting the soreness out. None of his teammates suspected that he might not play the next day.

After practice, the team gathered at the Redick's house for one last team meal together. The next day, the Cave Spring Knights would take the floor at Liberty University and face the George-Wythe (Richmond) Bulldogs, a team that was 29–1 and boasted several college basketball prospects. The winner of this game would be the Virginia AAA State Champions.

The day of the state championship game started out as a beautiful spring morning. It had just stopped raining and the sun had come out. Dr. Hugh Hagen, father of Cave Spring's standout Tom Hagen and an orthopedic surgeon, had just finished his morning bike ride along the Blue Ridge Parkway. As the rain stopped and the sun came out, he noticed a colorful rainbow across the sky. He stopped and thought about the team and the challenge they faced that day. He said a prayer for the team and for J.J., who had been a lifelong friend of his son. Dr. Hagen had examined J.J. after the semifinal game and knew how much pain he was in.

Later that morning, Coach Hicks and J.J. were the first two to arrive at the school. The bus wasn't scheduled to depart for two hours, but they both wanted to get there early and prepare. Coach Hicks asked J.J. how he felt. His response was, "Coach, it hurts. I can hardly walk, but *I am* going to play today."

It seemed as if everyone in southwest Roanoke had made the trip to Lynchburg to see the Knights take on the favored

Bulldogs. Eight thousand–plus screaming fans filled the arena. The coaches went through the pregame talk, and the Knights took the floor to a thunderous roar. All the coaches' eyes were on J.J. as he went through warm-ups. He barely left the floor when he shot. His moves were deliberate. He winced in pain each time his injured foot hit the floor.

Coach Hicks reflected on how hard the team had worked, all the obstacles they had overcome, and how unfair it was for J.J. not to be able to play. As the team gathered in the locker room one last time before the start of the game, Coach Hicks told the guys how proud of them he was. He told them they would remember this day for the rest of their lives—win or lose. They came together, recited the Lord's Prayer, and ran out onto the floor. J.J. stayed back in the locker room. He dropped to his knees and started to pray. He asked the Lord to take away his pain so he could play: "Lord, just take away the pain during the game. I will gladly take it back when the game is over. It is in your hands, Lord. I cannot do this without You."

As J.J. limped out onto the floor for the jump ball, he was keenly aware of the pain in his foot. He was also aware of the thousands of cheering fans. He was aware of all his classmates who had packed the student section behind the Cave Spring bench. He was aware of his teammates who took the floor with him. All had been friends since childhood. He was also aware of his parents, who had empowered him with the belief that through God, anything was possible. Then, as the ball was tossed into the air to start the game, a miracle happened. All the pain that J.J. Redick had felt in his injured foot suddenly disappeared. Over the entire course of the game, his foot never hurt. As a result, the Knights, behind J.J.'s career high 43 points and eight three-pointers, upset the mighty Bulldogs 70–62 and claimed the school's first boys' basketball state championship.

With God, anything is possible!

BILLY HICKS

9. Being on the Receiving End

For we are God's handiwork, created in Christ Jesus to do good works,
which God prepared in advance for us to do.
EPHESIANS 2:10

I learned a very hard and costly lesson during my senior year at Southern Methodist University. I fumbled twice in the key game against Texas, costing our team a championship. From that experience, I learned that when you're a pass receiver in football, it doesn't do any good for the defense to get the ball, for the quarterback to throw you an accurate pass, or for you to catch it if you then fumble the ball away. I learned what is basic, what is a priority. To borrow a Latin phrase, *sine qua non*—"without which it is nothing."

In the bigger and more important picture of life, I was also too long in learning what I believe is a *sine qua non* of life—what is priority, what comes first. It doesn't do any good to be successful in many areas of life if we fail to do what I believe is the most important thing in life—have a right relationship with God. We are not here by accident. We have been created for a purpose. We are creatures of choice, and that means we can choose to turn our attention toward a personal relationship with God. For me, this is basic. This is a priority. The result is that we won't be fumbling away our lives on meaningless activity.

There was a tremendous drive and need in me to play football. I could really catch a football, and the opportunity to play was there. As I grew spiritually, it became clear to me that God was the source of my abilities and any opportunities that came my way.

My friend and longtime teammate on the Baltimore Colts Don Shinnick helped me to pray, "God, I'm going to trust Your Son as my Savior; will You help me?"

I had questions: About death—what happens at the end?

About purpose—what I am here for? About the burden within me—what does it mean? Soon after that prayer, the burden was gone, and I knew why. I had been forgiven because Jesus paid the penalty for my sins on the cross. He also made eternal life after death a free gift; He had already paid for it. No one can earn a ticket to heaven. We receive it by faith.

Finally, I know my purpose. Jesus lives in me—in all of us who love Him. He has the power to fulfill our purpose, which is to do God's will. Our job is to let Him do it; let Him take the reins and guide us where He chooses. Without Him, life is nothing.

RAYMOND BERRY

10. Football Business and God's Business

For just as each of us has one body with many members,
and these members do not all have the same function,
so in Christ we, though many, form one body,
and each member belongs to all the others.
ROMANS 12:4–5

Football is a very emotional, stressful, and, at times, volatile business. To be able to rely on someone else when things get tough is very important because you truly can't do it all yourself.

A lot of things in life are out of our control. That is why it's so very important to keep your life in perspective. That's what my Christianity does for me. My faith keeps me grounded and focused on what is really important in life. What Jesus did for us—for me—it's the most beautiful thing that has ever happened—and there are no strings attached.

My football and career journey has taken me down many paths. I have coached at Brigham Young University and assisted with the San Francisco 49ers, and have been head coach with the Green Bay Packers and Seattle Seahawks. Three of my teams have made Super Bowl appearances, winning against New England and losing to Denver and Pittsburgh.

My wife, Kathy, and I married in 1971, and we have four daughters. God has led and richly blessed our lives together. Prior to our marriage, God used Kathy through letter writing to encourage me spiritually. She influenced me to focus on my relationship with Jesus Christ during some transitional and transformational times in my life.

The key verses in my life are from Proverbs 3:5–6: "Trust in the LORD with all your heart and lean not on your own understandings. In all your ways submit to him, and he will make your paths straight."

Sometimes the National Football League world gets really complicated. I take a great deal of comfort in knowing that God is in charge of where we are going. He's someone I can rely on.

MIKE HOLMGREN

11. Catching On

May the Lord make your love increase and overflow for each other and for everyone else, just as ours does for you.
I THESSALONIANS 3:12

One of my favorite stories of faith in sports isn't about an unknown athlete, a player who comes out of nowhere to perform some incredible feat. In fact, "The Kid" is quite well known. Gary Carter is one of the best catchers ever to play baseball in the majors—an eleven-time All Star, a World Series hero, and a Hall of Famer.

But Gary's story is one of the most amazing I've ever heard as it relates to persevering through adversity, finding God, and being faithful in glorifying Him on one of the largest platforms in the world—national television after winning the 1986 World Series. This is a story about a superstar who lost his mother at a young age and who would later lean on his Savior through the tumultuous and rigorous years in professional ball and who would come to grips with his mother's death because of Christ's love for *him*.

I met Gary in West Palm Beach, Florida, where the Montreal Expos held training camp. As pastor of First Baptist Church of West Palm Beach, I led a Bible study for various players from the Expos and the Atlanta Braves, who also trained there. Gary was among those players. We became friends, and I soon became his pastor.

Gary and his family settled in the area, and I was privileged to baptize him, his wife, and his three children on the same day. He was so excited about that moment. In fact, I saw the same exuberance in the baptismal that day as I saw in Gary when his Mets won the World Series. He was "The Kid," grinning ear-to-ear as he took in the significance of that special day with the most special people in his life—his wife and kids.

Gary got his nickname because he played the game with high energy, with the exuberance of a kid. He is perhaps best known for his gritty, two-out, two-strike base hit that ignited a three-run rally in the bottom of the tenth inning for the New York Mets in game six of the 1986 World Series, against the Boston Red Sox. The Mets went on to capture the World Series the following game. And in an interview with NBC's Bob Costas, Gary first and foremost praised his Lord and Savior, Jesus Christ.

But before that high-profile platform, before the major leagues, before adulthood, Gary was a young boy struggling with the loss of his mother, Inge, to leukemia. Just twelve years old at the time, Gary wondered how God could allow his mother to die. He found refuge in playing—and excelling—in all sports. Athletics were the sanctuary that kept the pain at bay, and the baseball field, especially, was his home. Later in life he realized that when he got out there to play, he was really playing for his mom. She had been a gifted athlete who loved sports and kids and who had worked with the parks and recreation department before she died. Gary found the joy of playing had come because he was her son.

And the joy of giving back, Gary would say, also came because he was Inge's son. He began his fight against leukemia by donating money generated from memorabilia sales and golf tournaments to the Leukemia Society. And, now, through the Gary Carter Foundation, he gives to various charities, including to less fortunate children in the West Palm Beach area, by providing funds and supplies and giving of his time.

In 2009, Gary was named head baseball coach for the Palm Beach Atlantic University Sailfish. Though winning was and is important to Gary, what is most telling about this man is what he said upon accepting the job.

"I am looking forward to becoming a Sailfish," Gary said. "My goal is to make Palm Beach Atlantic's baseball program the strongest Division II program in the country. But my primary goal is to help these young athletes become better Christians and prepare them for life, not just baseball."

Inge Carter became the motivator in the life of her young son. He played for her. . .and lived for Christ until losing his battle with brain cancer and gaining eternity with his Lord and Savior in 2013.

JACK GRAHAM

12. Handling Life's Curveballs

This is what the LORD says: "Stand at the crossroads and look;
ask for the ancient paths, ask where the good way is,
and walk in it, and you will find rest for your souls."
JEREMIAH 6:16

Pro sports careers often travel like a roller coaster ride. The glory of winning championships, of personal achievement, and of overcoming adversity make for incredible highs. The agony of losing seasons, being cut from the team, and injuries can make for difficult lows. One athlete, Pat Combs, experienced some "mountaintop" highs and some extremely painful lows during his collegiate and professional baseball career, which lasted from 1986 to 1996.

The tall, left-handed pitcher from Houston played his way into the collegiate record books while at Rice University in 1986 and then Baylor University in 1987–88, establishing several Baylor and Southwest Conference records, which led to his being selected to play on the USA National Baseball Teams for two successive summers, in 1987 and 1988.

While at Baylor, Pat was recognized as a leader both on and off the field, as indicated by his selection as an Academic All-American with a 3.8 grade-point average. All these achievements supported his being the Philadelphia Phillies' first selection in the 1988 Major league Baseball Draft and his being given a chance to represent the United States on the Olympic baseball team that summer.

Unfortunately, Pat was the last player cut from the United States Olympic team. He received the bad news immediately before the team's plane left for Seoul, South Korea. He had pitched well in the Olympic trials, going 5–1 with a team-leading 2.62 earned-run average on a pitching staff loaded with future major league talent, including Jim Abbott and Andy Benes. But with only twenty roster spots available, the coaches determined that their pitching staff could be trimmed. Pat was the odd man out and was sent home to watch his team win the gold medal in Seoul.

In the aftermath of the Olympic setback, Pat was motivated to get to the big leagues quickly as he turned his attention to beginning his professional career with the Phillies. He rose quickly through the Phillies minor league system, and in 1989 he became the first player in major league history to be promoted from every minor league level (A, AA, AAA) and into the major leagues in his first professional season. In September of 1989, Pat won his first four major league games as a starting pitcher, and his career seemed destined for greatness.

In 1990, Pat's first full season with the Phillies, he led the team in wins, strikeouts, and earned-run average, and became the anchor of the Phillies pitching staff. Media and fans began making comparisons to Phillies Hall of Fame greats Steve Carlton and Robin Roberts. Pat found himself on top of the world, or at least on top of Philadelphia, where Phillies fans were clamoring for success not seen since the glory days of the early 1980s, when the team featured Carlton, Mike Schmidt, Pete Rose, and Tug McGraw.

The 1991 season started out well for Combs. He went 2–0 in April, but just after pitching a shutout against the Houston Astros in May, he developed a sore and swollen elbow. After many attempts to get the elbow to heal, it was determined that Pat had a bone spur and would need surgery. Removing bone spurs is normally considered a minor surgery, but in Pat's case it became more complicated, as the spur affected a tendon in the back of his pitching arm. Following the so-called minor surgery, Pat never regained the same velocity and control that had made him a dominant starting pitcher when he first arrived in the majors. He spent the next four seasons attempting to regain his form, but it became apparent after spring training in 1996 that Pat's best pitching days were behind him.

After playing with such tremendous passion for twenty-four years of his life, Pat retired from the game he loved in the summer of 1996. From the highs of a stellar college career, to the lows of being the last player cut from the 1988 US Olympic team, to the highs of getting off to a rocket start in his major league career, to the lows of a career-ending injury that ended his playing days before his prime, life as an athlete was clearly an extreme roller-coaster ride for Pat Combs.

You have probably seen the T-shirts bearing the message SPORTS IS LIFE. This is not entirely true, though Pat can attest to how sports can mold and make a life worth living off the field. In the competitive field of athletics, life lessons of hard work, determination, responsibility, courage, overcoming adversity, and perseverance gave Pat what he needed in his daily living after his playing days ended.

Today Pat is a leader in his community, in his business, and as a follower of Jesus. He has been a faithful husband to Christina since 1989 and is the devoted father of three sons—Carson, Conner, and Casey. Pat has coached youth sports in Richmond, Texas, and in his current home of Southlake, Texas, for the past fourteen years. He also serves on the board of directors for many ministries in and around the Dallas–Fort Worth metro area, and devotes much time to the mentoring and discipleship of men. In his professional life, Pat serves many families, foundations, and companies as a financial adviser with Morgan Stanley Smith Barney.

"As I look back on my sports career, I am so thankful that I had the chance to compete at the very highest level in baseball," he says. "Sure, I would like to have pitched twenty years in the major leagues and won a World Series, but God had a different plan for me—and I fully trust that God wanted to use me in a powerful way after baseball. Everything I learned on the ball field, especially the teamwork and servant leadership skills, has helped me to be a better husband to Christina, a better dad to my boys, and a better adviser to the people I serve. My hope is that I can use what I have learned from my baseball career to help people go where God wants them to go so we can make an eternal difference together."

Pat's story teaches the lesson that we can continue to get up and move forward, even after extreme disappointment. When our plans don't go exactly as we would have liked, we can rest assured that God still has a plan for us that includes a tremendous purpose. . .as long as we follow Jesus and live for Him.

TALMAGE BOSTON

13. At What Point Do You Hit Rock Bottom?

I have seen something else under the sun: The race is not to the swift or the battle to the strong, nor does food come to the wise or wealth to the brilliant or favor to the learned; but the time and chance happen to them all.
ECCLESIASTES 9:11

At what point do you hit rock bottom? Is it when you are trying to find shelter in the night inside a storage garage or slouching down inside a 2000 Impala, knees to your stomach, hoping a policeman doesn't bang on the window in the middle of the night?

Is it when you pass by the arena in which the masses cheered you on as an NBA player, and suddenly you are stunned by the silence that now surrounds you?

Is it when you lose the six cars—a Mercedes-Benz, a GMC Yukon, a Range Rover, a Lexus, a Corvette, and another Yukon—or the two homes?

Is it when your wife, tears in her eyes, kicks you out of the house and files a restraining order, fearing that you might harm her or your two children?

David Vaughn didn't stop to take inventory of his life and

how it all unraveled. He was too busy trying to survive day by day. But through all the chaos, he would remember his favorite verse from the Bible: Ecclesiastes 9:11.

Put into his own words and perspective, David thought to himself: *Everyone can fall and can make mistakes, but through your faith in God you can be restored and survive the troubled times you go through.*

Now in his early forties, David Vaughn has survived troubled times. There's been a trail of tears and much heartbreak and pain, but his spiritual compass allowed him to find his way home.

But he would need to travel a lot of hard miles to get there.

The inventory of what Vaughn lost is staggering: Two houses, six cars, and a closet full of fancy clothes—expensive trinkets of self-indulgence—are all gone. The professional basketball career is over too. A guy who made $2.2 million over four NBA seasons was reduced to scraping by on $260 a week, his state unemployment check.

He bears the scars of homelessness, of an estranged husband and father, of a guy who nearly had a foot amputated and ended up in a nursing home because it accepted indigent care.

There was no seminal moment when it all unraveled for Vaughn, just a patchwork of mistakes, naïveté, and sins for which Vaughn now holds himself accountable.

Vaughn grew up poor in Nashville. His mother died when he was fifteen. His father, a marginal professional basketball player, couldn't care for him. After a brief stay in state foster care, Vaughn ended up with his paternal grandparents. His world was one of hand-me-downs. The only time he got new clothes was at Easter and Christmas.

He ditched school at the University of Memphis as a junior to apply for the NBA Draft. Looking for a backup big man, the Orlando Magic selected Vaughn, a 6-feet-9, 250-pound power forward, with the 25th pick in the 1995 draft.

It seemed like a nice fit. Vaughn would join his former college teammate, Anfernee "Penny" Hardaway, on one of the rising teams in the NBA.

The good times, for both the Magic and for Vaughn, would be short-lived. The Magic began to unravel when Shaquille O'Neal left in the summer of 1996. Vaughn's world began to unravel the day he signed his first contract.

The poor kid from Nashville was suddenly a rich man. Having no sense of fiscal responsibility, he squandered much of the money. It escalated when he met Brandie, his wife-to-be, in 1997—more responsibility, more mismanagement.

He bought a home in Orlando and another one in Nashville. He paid $25,000 to a contractor recommended through a friend of the family to put in new bathrooms and turn a bedroom into a closet. Vaughn just cut him a check, no contract. The work was never done. His collection of cars grew to six.

But the money to pay for all of this would soon disappear. In 1999, the New Jersey Nets, his fourth NBA team, cut him. Career over. Vaughn hung on for a while, playing in Europe before that dried up too.

He came back to the States unemployed, with no college degree and lacking strong vocational skills. He finally found work driving and unloading trucks for a furniture store.

Overcome by lack of self-worth, Vaughn did his best to blow up his marriage. Domestic violence and drugs became his combustible cocktail. In May of 2008, a restraining order bounced Vaughn out of the house and onto the streets.

He found solace reading books at the downtown public library or at bookstores like Borders. He squeezed in to sleep at the Salvation Army or, if he could afford it, cheap hotels. Other nights, he slouched down inside his Impala.

He took showers at health clubs, where he had memberships and where he worked out, stretched, and tried to stay in shape. He had an underlying purpose as well: burn hours to stay off the streets as much as possible.

He would eventually end up in a hospital, suffering the consequences of multiple bites from a brown recluse spider, which forms an ulcer that destroys soft tissue. Doctors considered amputating his left foot before various drugs finally kicked in. Unable to pay a penny of the cost of care, Vaughn was transferred to a local nursing home for the remainder of his convalescence.

The healing process manifested itself in other ways. Brandie rushed to his side, ignoring the restraining order, when she heard of her husband's condition.

"There was something in me that could not let go of him," Brandie Vaughn said. "I knew the things he was going through and whatnot. That wasn't my husband. It was something he was dealing with.

"When I got the call about him being in the hospital, I took that as God telling me 'you need to go back.' Our vows say, 'in sickness and in health, richer or poorer, till death do us part.' He was still my husband, and he had no one else, and if I wasn't there for him, I don't know where he would be. I had to take him back in the condition he was in and pretty much nurse him back to health to the person he is now."

Newspaper accounts of his situation have helped lead Vaughn to a better place.

Vaughn has a job now, working with Florida's Department of Children and Families, in a unit that establishes eligibility for food stamps and Medicaid applicants. Brandie has a part-time job in a restaurant in Orlando. They now live in a two-bedroom condo in Orlando. The family went to see the Orlando Magic play several times during the 2009–10 season, tickets courtesy of the front-office staff of his former team.

"A lot of people stepped forward and gave from their heart," Vaughn said. "I don't take anything for granted these days. I thank the Lord for putting me in a position to have a new beginning."

The six cars and the two homes are gone, but that doesn't matter to David. His most precious gifts now are found in the smiles in the faces of his wife and two children, and in the strength he draws spiritually every day.

David Vaughn, once a lost soul, is home again.

GEORGE DIAZ

14. Staying the Course

You will keep in perfect peace those whose
minds are steadfast, because they trust in you.
Isaiah 26:3

When we see guys on the Professional Golf Association Tour who have done well, we might assume that it was easy for them to get to this point. Not so with most—including Ben Crane. There was a time when Ben was so completely discouraged that he could easily have given up.

He had no caddy, no regular golf coach, and no network. He was filled with self-doubt and at wit's end. Crane graduated from the University of Oregon, where he didn't have a standout college career. But he passionately loved golf and wanted to make a career in it. Ben says that since graduation from college and turning pro, he has learned that his only hope is in God. He knew he couldn't make it without Him.

Crane was engaged to his future wife, Heather Heinz, and she knew his heart's desire. Having missed three cuts in a row, he wondered if he was good enough to make it on the tour. He was playing at Hilton Head that weekend. His parents and Heather were there for the tournament, and he missed the cut.

When Ben considered that just a few guys even make the cut each week, it occurred to him that the tour was really a place for failure. But since the age of ten, he had a dream of playing professionally. He had to share his disappointment and discouragement with his parents and Heather, and he did so in a family meeting. There was a sharing of hearts, hugs, and also some tears. Heather knew how much Ben loved golf.

Ben's mom gave him and Heather a book their pastor, Ron Mehl, had written: *A Prayer That Moves Heaven*. Ben read these words, which spoke directly to his heart:

> *It's easy to worship after the battle has been won, after*
> *the spoils have been gathered. It's easy to praise God after*

you've received the answers to your prayers. . . . I've seen
lots of people praise God when the promotion comes. . .
when the cancer tests come back normal. . .when the
marriage is restored. . .when the unexpected check comes
in the mail. . . . But it's not as common to hear those same
songs of praise from a throat constricted by weeping.

Something strange happened to Ben after reading those words. He was almost glad things were bad. As they discussed the ideas from Pastor Mehl's book, the gloom that was in Ben's heart left him and he began to thank and praise God. Together they prayed for a good caddie. Ben relates that he slept better that night than he had in a long time.

From there, Ben traveled to Greensboro, but things didn't go well there, either. Another cut missed. Next came New Orleans and yet another missed cut. On and on it went. He missed five cuts in a row.

One of Ben's favorite quotes from basketball coach Rick Pitino is "Success is a choice," but after that fifth cut, he was bummed. Heather talked to him by phone and told him she was concerned about him. He felt better after they spoke, and again he voiced his commitment to choose success and to persevere and not give up. That's easy to say but hard to do.

At the Byron Nelson Tournament in Los Colinas, Crane played poorly at first, but he had peace. He recalled a phrase from Eric Liddell in the movie *Chariots of Fire*: "God made me fast, and when I run I feel His pleasure." That statement resonated with Ben. He felt God's pleasure when he played golf.

The match began ordinarily for Ben. It took some time for him to find his sweet spot, but when he did, his game just came together. Suddenly he realized that he was doing really well. At one point, he was in close contention with Tiger Woods. In fact, he was two shots ahead. The next day he was paired with Ernie Els, a two-time U.S. Open Championship winner.

Crane played well. He kept giving God the glory and wasn't

nervous. God was doing something infinitely more than he ever could have asked or thought. Paul Stankowski told him he looked like a ballet dancer when he headed toward his ball.

After a few strokes, birdies, chips, and putts (and a lot of sweat), he was at the PGA Media Center talking about his game. He had finished. Not only that, but he earned his PGA card for 2003 by coming in second in that tournament.

Ben garnered a sizable check that week—$518,000. When asked how he did it, he was at a loss for words, except for one thing. He lifted both hands up toward heaven and thought to himself, *God has done infinitely more than I could have asked or even dreamed.*

The message here is to follow your dream regardless of how tough it might be to get where you know God wants you to go.

J. B. COLLINGSWORTH

15. Flying in a New Direction

Consequently, faith comes from hearing the message, and the message is heard through the word about Christ.
ROMANS 10:17

I was playing for the Anaheim Angels in 1994, and one day our team was flying from Texas back to Anaheim. It was during that time that I knew I was coming to a crossroads in my career. A young ballplayer faces everyday struggles and confronts the fear that the team is going to send him back down to the minor leagues and that he may never get called back to the majors again. I was no exception.

During our return trip to Anaheim, I could hear a couple of guys in the seat behind me talking about Christ. One of the guys was Chad Curtis, one of my teammates. As they spoke, I started to think about my own church background. When it came to church, my family were basically holiday Christians—you know, those who only attend church on Easter and Christmas. Sure, I believed in God, but I didn't know much about Jesus and who He is, nor did I think that I needed a personal relationship with Him.

It was then that I heard Chad ask the other player a truly important question. He said, "If this plane were to crash, do you think that you would go to heaven?"

That question certainly got my attention, and I sat up in my seat. I relocated to an empty seat near Chad, and he asked me if I knew who Jesus Christ is. "No," I told him.

Chad then related the gospel of Christ to me. He explained to me who Jesus Christ is and that we have to turn away from our sins, repent, and acknowledge that we are sinners. He told me that through Christ's death and resurrection, He has paid the full penalty for our sins. He then asked me if I wanted to accept Christ as my Savior, and I said, "Sure."

It was a decision I had to make. Right then and there on the plane bound for Anaheim, I prayed to accept Christ as my Savior.

I am grateful for guys like Chad, guys who are not afraid to share their faith with their teammates. It is not an easy thing to do, but had it not been for him sharing the gospel of Christ with me, I might not be a Christian today. I learned from Chad how important it is to share Christ with others and how we should never take for granted that our friends know about the gospel message.

DAMION EASLEY

16. Get Off the Couch

*"I will forgive their wickedness and will
remember their sins no more."*
HEBREWS 8:12

Sometimes Christian athletes live their beliefs in quiet ways, far removed from the cheers of the crowds or the microphones of sideline reporters. Though their faith may be private, their lives speak volumes about where they've set their eyes and their goals.

Only two days after his eighteenth birthday, everything was looking good for Warrick Dunn. One of Baton Rouge, Louisiana's, most extraordinary high school athletes, he was being recruited by several major universities—a tremendous source of pride for his single mother and five younger siblings. But that hope was turned to tragedy on January 7, 1993, when Dunn's mother, Baton Rouge police officer Betty Smothers, was shot and killed in a robbery as she provided protection for a grocery store manager making an after-hours bank deposit. Suddenly Dunn's world was turned upside down. Not only had he lost his mother, who he'd always described as his best friend, but he was now responsible for his brothers and sisters.

With the help of his grandmother and the support of the community, Warrick eventually decided to attend Florida State University on a football scholarship. It was the school his mother had most wanted him to attend because she admired Coach Bobby Bowden's faith and character. Bowden and FSU's senior star quarterback, Charlie Ward, agreed that Ward and Dunn should room together so that Ward could serve as a kind of older brother to help Dunn through his first year. Ward, a young man of tremendous faith himself, felt that it was his responsibility to reach out to his new teammate and help him feel God's presence and comfort.

Emotionally, Dunn was struggling, but on the field he was absolutely dominant. He set several rushing records for the Seminoles, was part of a National Championship team, and was the first-round pick of the Tampa Bay Buccaneers in the 1997 NFL Draft.

As soon as he signed his first professional contract, Dunn knew that he wanted to do something meaningful with the blessings he'd been given. Building off of his mother's unrealized dream of buying a house for her family, he quickly established the Warrick Dunn Foundation, whose Homes for the Holidays program assists single parents to purchase, furnish, and maintain their first homes.

As Dunn's career progressed, so did his work. When he was traded to the Atlanta Falcons, he began the program in that city too. As of 2009, Homes for the Holidays has helped close to a hundred families in Baton Rouge, Tallahassee, Tampa, and Atlanta. It is Dunn's way of giving back to each of the communities that has supported him. He is also one of the founding members of Athletes for Hope—along with Lance Armstrong, Jackie Joyner-Kersee, and Cal Ripken Jr., among others. This organization is dedicated to helping professional athletes, as well as fans, plug into charitable causes and opportunities to serve.

Despite the tragedy that changed his life forever, Dunn fought through the pain to extend help and hope to families much like his own. He gave of himself, opening himself up to healing until he was able to offer the greatest gift of all: in 2007, he visited Louisiana's death row to meet with his mother's murderers.

I was with him that day, and the strength he showed was incredible. He had brought with him a notebook full of questions he wanted to ask about the night of the crime—what the men were thinking and anything else that might help him understand it all and give him some closure. But instead, as we sat there in the visiting room, Dunn put down his questions, looked into the face of one of the men who had murdered his mother, and said quietly, "I forgive you. I forgive you."

On the drive home, I asked him what had enabled him to reach into his soul and find such forgiveness for those men who had hurt him so badly. Dunn's answer was simple: In the face of all of the pain in the world, in the face of anything he had seen that he didn't like, his mother had always told him that the responsibility to do good lay within him. "You don't spend a moment on the couch," she'd taught him. "You get up and you do something about it."

DON YAEGER

REJOICING

....

1. Climbing Quarterback Mountain

Not to us, Lord, not to us but to your name
be the glory, because of your love and faithfulness.
PSALM 115:1

"What a catch by Jerramy Stevens for a touchdown! And the Bucs have the lead on a touchdown pass from McCown! How about Luke McCown in this game today? He showed a lot of moxie. Thick-skinned today."

Those words from FOX Television commentators summed up more than just the first win of my NFL career.

The real story began nine months earlier.

As February of 2007 drew to a close, I drove toward Tampa with my growing family.

My wife, pregnant with our second son, sat next to me. Our one-year-old boy, Jonah, rode behind me, content as he watched Elmo and *Go, Diego, Go!* Our two dogs, Judge and Tess, lay in the back of our SUV.

With a full day's drive ahead of me, my thoughts circled around the task at hand. I looked ahead to the upcoming off-season workouts with the Tampa Bay Buccaneers. I entered my third season with the Bucs but missed the entire 2006 season with a torn anterior cruciate ligament (ACL). In the process, I fell to the bottom of the depth chart. I had a mountain to climb.

By the end of April, we had seven—count them, seven!—quarterbacks on the roster. Considering that most teams keep three signal callers at the most, that mountain grew steeper with each new addition.

As the first spring practices began, I took zero snaps under center. Every now and then I'd get one rep at the end of practice. No one talked to me. No one talked about me. In this hype-driven league, that's never good. My agent prepared me for a year without a job.

My friends and family urged me to speak up. Demand my shot. Fight for my opportunity. But I took a different approach. God's Word says, "In quietness and trust is your strength" (Isaiah 30:15). So I kept my mouth shut and worked hard, confident that God controlled my fate. If I had one snap, I ran the play better than anyone else on the field.

Then one day, one rep turned into two. I made sure I ran those two plays the best they could be run. A week later, two reps became three. By the end of training camp, I had worked my way into the number two spot. I had climbed the mountain and survived. What a view! I took a deep breath and smiled at the thought of what I had accomplished.

Wow! The valley seemed so far away. But it was closer than I realized. The Buccaneers opened the 2007 season in Seattle. I played one series as our starter, Jeff Garcia, shook off a hard hit on the sideline. We lost the game and failed to score any offensive points. The next week, my coaches demoted me to third on the depth chart with no explanation.

Frustration set in as I fumed over the hard work that seemed all for nothing. We don't always know why God does what He does, but this time I would get a glimpse.

My wife called me at work a few weeks later. She cried as she spit out the words, "It's a tumor."

Our newborn son, Elijah, had a tumor in the bone of his skull. Alarms sounded in my head. You hear the word *tumor* and instinctively panic. When you face something like this, everything else grows very dim. Even football takes a backseat.

We scheduled surgery and started planning. We went to pre-op visits with both the surgeon and Elijah's pediatrician. A long two weeks later, we walked into the hospital just before 6:00 a.m.

The surgeon assured us the procedure would be minimal. He told us Elijah would be in surgery for three to four hours and said the tumor would almost certainly be benign. But "almost" wasn't good enough. We needed to hear something definite.

After only two hours, the doctor came to tell us the news. We rejoiced when we heard that our son would not be facing cancer. Our hearts were overwhelmed with the outpouring of love and encouragement we received. The understanding from even the unlikeliest of places left us stunned.

In a profession where players double as products and men are oftentimes treated as merchandise, the Buccaneers' organization stepped to a personal level with me. Without hesitation, they put the game aside. They encouraged me, talked to me, and supported me so that I could do the same for my family. Business is business and will always be, but for a brief moment this team became more like a family.

We left the hospital the day after surgery with a happy, healthy boy. Elijah had so much bandaging on his head that he looked like he was wearing his daddy's helmet. Surprisingly, it didn't seem to bother him. Maybe he's destined to wear the real thing one day.

I left the hospital with a renewed strength and relentless heart. It was time to take back my job.

God's Word tells us, "Those who hope in the Lord will renew their strength. They will soar on wings like eagles; they will run and not grow weary, they will walk and not be faint" (Isaiah 40:31). Eight weeks later, it was time to soar.

We were on the road, facing the New Orleans Saints in the Louisiana Superdome. The week thirteen game carried huge playoff implications. A win would all but clinch the National Football Conference South title for us.

I started a game for the first time in three years and completed my first fifteen pass attempts. Head coach Jon Gruden flung open the playbook. I threw quick slants and deep balls, and I ran for close to 40 yards.

Much like my year, the game had its ups and downs. I had moments to be proud of and those I wanted back. With less than four minutes left in the game, I took a sack in the end zone, giving the Saints two points and putting them up by three. They kept possession of the ball. With each second that ticked off the clock, a chance to win slipped further away. I shook my head in disgust, but my teammates assured me we'd have one more chance.

They were right. Seconds later, the Saints fumbled, and our defense recovered the ball. This was it. We had our chance.

I handed the ball off four times as we inched our way closer to the goal line. With 17 seconds left, I walked to the line of scrimmage, three yards away from victory.

I knew the play. I was prepared. My center snapped me the ball, and I threw it up to my tight end, Jerramy Stevens. He made a great catch and. . .well, you know the rest.

We won the NFC South that year. I brought home the victory and the game ball.

I had climbed another mountain and again stood with a smile, singing praises to my God and King. "Not to us, LORD, not to us but to your name be the glory, because of your love and faithfulness" (Psalm 115:1).

What love God showed me when He rescued my son. What faithfulness He showed me as He raised me up to become more than I could be on my own.

LUKE MCCOWN

2. One Fan I'll Never Forget

*Dear friends, do not be surprised at the fiery ordeal that has come on you to
test you, as though something strange were happening to you.
But rejoice in as much as you participate in the sufferings of Christ,
so that you may be overjoyed when his glory is revealed.*

1 PETER 4:12–13

This story is not about an athlete, or a coach, or a well-known sports celebrity. It's about a fan—a baseball fan. Not long after I became the public relations director of the then Philadelphia Athletics, a sportswriter for *The Germantown Courier*, Ralph Waters, whom I had met at a couple of press conferences, stopped by my office one day to ask if I could arrange for a special friend of his to meet Connie Mack. "His name is Owen Young and he has been an A's fan all his life," Ralph told me. "He's getting up in years, and it would mean everything to him."

As a newcomer to the organization, I thought I'd better find out if anyone in the front office knew Mr. Young. As soon as I mentioned his name, one of the secretaries groaned and rolled her eyes. "Yes," she said, "we know him. He's a nuisance—always calling up and bothering us. He's wacko."

The woman's callous attitude startled me, but I thanked her for the information. Since it was the offseason and things were not yet as hectic for me as they eventually would become, I decided I should find out more about this Mr. Young, so I telephoned him. My call surprised and delighted him, and he proceeded to relate his long-standing interest in the A's, which spanned the entire forty-nine seasons Mr. Mack had owned and managed the team. I learned that Owen had lost a leg to cancer and that he was now totally blind.

Owen never troubled the office staff again after that, and his occasional phone conversations with me were always brief and to the point. All he had wanted was for someone to listen to him. Soon after that initial conversation, I spoke to Mr. Mack about Owen, and the grand old gentleman most willingly agreed to meet with him. Owen was thrilled, and on the appointed day, his friend Ralph drove Owen with his wheelchair to Shibe Park.

Mr. Mack could not have been more cordial to this one-legged blind man, who was not many years his junior, as the two of them reminisced about the great teams of the Athletics' storied past. Owen had his picture taken with Mr. Mack, and Ralph saw that it appeared in *The Germantown Courier*. For Owen, it was a dream fulfilled.

Owen and I continued to keep in touch throughout my years in Philadelphia. I learned from Ralph that Owen was poor, but I didn't realize how poor until I called on him one day, shortly before my family and I moved to Baltimore. I wanted to take him some clothes, which I knew he could use. He lived in a one-room "apartment," and he kept up with the news of the world through an old box radio and a dial phone, with which he could call the numbers he had memorized. He slept on a cot, and the rest of the day he spent in his wheelchair.

That part of Germantown had deteriorated, and the kids took pleasure in harassing the old man. They would ring his bell, and when he came to the door, they'd pull him out to the sidewalk and spin his chair around so he would become disoriented. Then they would run off and leave him there trying to find his way back to his front door. Owen was sad to hear that I was leaving town, and when we said good-bye, I had the feeling I would never see him again.

Fast forward about six years. I had graduated from Princeton Theological Seminary, having resigned my position as public relations director of the Baltimore Orioles in order to study for the ministry. I was now serving a church in Philadelphia. One night I was the guest on a late-night radio talk show, during which my controversial host was accepting calls from listeners. Imagine my amazement when a voice on the line said, "Reverend Armstrong, this is your old pal Owen Young!" We had a great reunion on the air.

I called on Owen a few days later, not knowing what to expect. I was shocked by his appearance. He had no eyes in his sockets and his nose had been completely eaten away by cancer. He had only partial hearing in one ear. His remaining leg was cancerous and very odorous, and the smell was intensified by four cats and their unchanged litter box.

Owen wanted to talk baseball. His beloved Athletics had moved to Kansas City, so he was now rooting for the Phillies, though not uncritically. In response to my questions, he was forthcoming about his situation. He assured me that he had everything he needed, but he had no medical insurance, no Social Security, and his only income was the $71 a month he received from what he called his "pension for the blind." Out of that, he paid $25 a month for rent and paid his food bill, which he said was minimal. I later learned that his friendly grocer was absorbing some of Owen's food costs, and a caring doctor was paying his phone bill.

At the next meeting of our church diaconate, I told the deacons about Owen and asked if they would be willing to take him under their care. The following Saturday, a couple of them called on Owen and were completely dismayed by what they saw—but totally smitten with him.

In the days that followed, teams of church members cleaned and painted Owen's apartment, provided him with new linens, and established a standing order with the grocer to cover Owen's food costs. Someone called every Sunday afternoon to play the tape of the morning service. In the course of each visit, Owen would invariably offer the most beautiful prayers, in which he never failed to thank God for "me health." He was an inspiration to everyone who called.

One day I received a phone call from Owen, asking if I would stop by to see him. When I arrived that afternoon, he wasted no time getting to the point: "I want to join your church. Now, mind you, it's not because you're me pal. It's because your people have been so kind to me. They've welcomed me into their hearts."

"But you're a Roman Catholic, Owen. How would your priest feel about that?"

"We all worship that same God and we all have the same Savior," he said. "I have nothing against the Catholic Church, but nobody from my parish ever calls on me like your people do. They really care."

Owen was unable to attend the six-week series of membership preparation classes for those who would be joining our church. I therefore arranged to meet with him in his apartment, each time bringing one or more of the elders with me. He took those sessions very seriously. On the Sunday afternoon before the final Wednesday night of the classes, the entire board met in Owen's apartment to hear him reaffirm his faith and to receive him as a member of the church. Every one of us was inspired by Owen's testimony, and he was moved to tears he had not the eyes to shed.

Much to our surprise, as well as concern, Owen announced that he wanted to come to church on Palm Sunday, when the new members were to be publicly recognized and welcomed. The deacons agreed to make that happen. They bought him a new suit and matching tie. One of them, with the help of two others, took him to his home and gave him a bath. Owen splashed around in the tub like a little boy, singing lustily.

The next day, there he was in his wheelchair at the end of the front pew, wearing his dark glasses and plastic nose, almost like the ones you find in a costume store, to mask his disfigured face. He couldn't see, and he couldn't hear well, but he knew he was in church and he made a joyful noise to the Lord when the hymns were being sung. Everyone in the congregation greeted him, along with the other new members, following the service. Owen was in seventh heaven.

That was the only time he was able to attend the church. It was simply too much of an effort. But he listened to the tapes of the sermons and shared his comments with me regularly. Owen had taken his vows with great seriousness. Out of his meager income, he pledged two dollars a week, divided equally between benevolences and current operating expenses, as the congregation had been challenged to do. Every Sunday afternoon, one of our callers would collect Owen's weekly offering, which was always ready and waiting, two envelopes with a dollar in each. (Owen had torn off the upper corner of the benevolence envelopes so he could tell the difference.)

Some months later, we launched a fund-raising campaign for a major renovation of our physical plant. Teams of callers were assigned to call on every family in the church on a certain Sunday afternoon. Knowing his situation, the committee did not assign someone to visit Owen. The next day, I received a phone call from a very indignant Owen, wanting to know why no one had come to collect his pledge. I apologized and arranged for a trustee to call. Owen wanted to pledge three hundred dollars over a three-year period. The trustee was dubious but filled in the amount as directed by an adamant one-legged blind man in a wheelchair.

When I saw his pledge card, I called Owen right away and gently asked if he was sure he could afford such an amount. I was severely rebuked. "You've been saying we should put God first," he said indignantly, "and that's what I'm doing!" What could I say? Owen practiced the principle of sacrificial giving because he trusted God to provide.

But that's not the end of the story. Owen insisted that I suggest some service he could do for the church. I was totally nonplussed. Then an idea popped into my head: "If I give you the names and numbers of a few of our elderly shut-ins, would you be willing to call them every day to visit and pray with them on the phone? That would be a wonderful ministry, Owen." He was delighted with the suggestion. Two days later I stopped by to tell him about five persons, whose names and numbers he easily memorized. They became his little "flock."

Owen continued that ministry until he finally lost his agonizing battle with cancer. There were many tears at his passing.

Not long thereafter, I called on one of his telephone companions, a woman in her nineties who was terminally ill. A sweet but lonely person, Miss Lou had no close relatives. As I sat by her hospital bed, she whispered softly, "Oh, Mr. Armstrong, if only I could have met Mr. Young face-to-face so I could tell him how much his calls meant to me. He made my life worthwhile."

Let it never be said that there is not something everyone can do to help others. I knew a one-legged, cancer-ridden, deaf, and blind octogenarian who proved otherwise. If the Philadelphia Athletics Historical Society should ever want to choose the most courageous A's fan, I would nominate "me pal" Owen Young. He was one fan I'll never forget.

DICK ARMSTRONG

3. Put on a Happy Face

But even if I am being poured out like a drink offering on the sacrifice and service coming from your faith, I am glad and rejoice with all of you. So you too should be glad and rejoice with me.
PHILIPPIANS 2:17–18

The voice of Detroit's childhood is in its sunset. But the last thing Ernie Harwell wanted from those whom he loved—and who dearly loved him—was pity as he approached the closing chapters of a glorious story. There were many communal tears since Harwell publicly acknowledged on September 4, 2009, that doctors diagnosed him with incurable cancer of the bile duct, but he looked upon it as the ultimate challenge man can face—his own mortality.

Ernie taught us how to die with not just dignity, but with a spiritual certainty that our tangible being serves as mere prelude to a greater, more existential destination.

The mornings turned more difficult; the physical discomfort became greater. The timbre of that once deeply soothing baritone lost its sturdiness. He no longer had an appetite, another symptomatic casualty of this cruelly indiscriminate disease. Harwell's body was telling him that he should sleep and rest, but there were letters from well-wishers that he wished to answer. He stayed busy writing a regular column for the *Detroit Free Press*.

Harwell still planned, still prepared, still lived.

He accepted an invitation to appear at Fordham University in May. He was scheduled to receive the Vin Scully Lifetime Achievement Award at Fordham with Tigers great Al Kaline presenting him with the award. That time frame contradicted the doctors' dire diagnosis, but Harwell looked at this test as an opportunity to validate the limitless bounds of one's faith.

"He's the most gentle, the most tolerant, the most patient man I've ever known," Harwell's former radio partner, Paul Carey, told the *Free Press* in February 2010. "He's just one of a kind. . . . What a wonderful person. What a remarkable person."

We still marvel at his indefatigable optimism and ability to put a smile on even the dourest of faces. In a *Free Press* column he penned regarding his early fears of public speaking, Harwell quoted a Jerry Seinfeld standup bit in which he cited a poll listing public speaking as the United States' number one fear. Number two is dying. And the joke goes, if you go to a funeral, you're better off in the casket than delivering the eulogy.

He wrote about how, during his early days as a baseball broadcaster in Baltimore, the team's sponsors would dispatch him for various local speaking engagements if they couldn't land a better known ballplayer, coach, or, as Ernie put it in his dry wit, "any kind of belly dancer."

Readers thanked Harwell. He was the one suffering, yet he could still make us laugh and make us forget what he was going through. What he was going through takes a special individual, buoyed through incredible strength.

The first time I met Ernie Harwell, he introduced himself to me.

Shouldn't it have been the other way around?

I was a first-year columnist with the *Free Press* in 1999, and he was. . .well. . .he was Ernie Harwell.

He was a member of every native Detroiter's extended family, a source of comfort and optimism through the vibrant images he conveyed through decades of Tigers radio broadcasts. And there was that distinctive voice saying how he wanted to meet one of his favorite columnists.

I initially looked around to see if he was talking about somebody else. Let's just say, I could've flown home that night without need of an aircraft.

He was too modest to understand the impact he's had on so many people simply through the sheer sincerity of his spirit. They don't erect statutes for that, but it's nonetheless the greatest legacy any of us can leave behind.

Ernie would often email me, saying how much he liked a column. And the first reaction for some might be that it's a nice gesture, but he's a radio man. But Ernie always loved the written word. He was a sportswriter for the *Atlanta Journal-Constitution* and also contributed to the *Sporting News*, which, back in the 1940s, was baseball's biblical tome.

Ernie was a great writer, which helps explain why he was a great broadcaster. It's all about communicating with your audience. His advice was invaluable to a young columnist finding his voice. Like everything else, Ernie kept it simple. Just tell the story. Let the progression of the details reported spur the readers' emotions, be it excitement or exasperation.

Don't just "be yourself," he told me, but more importantly, "be comfortable with *yourself*."

Ernie remains Detroit's communal uncle. He symbolized home and the reassurance that embodies it. It didn't matter if you were driving several hundred miles away. When nightfall came and the radio signals bounced just right, you could still clearly catch him sitting in amazement at Mark Fidrych's 1976 rookie season or the Tigers racing to their 35–5 start in 1984.

And, suddenly, you were transported back to your back porch with your brother on a summer's evening, when your only concern as an eight-year-old was whether Kaline could recover from his broken arm in time to play in his first World Series in 1968.

We'll always cherish the stories he told on the radio.

But there's also a treasure of written tales spun that we'll appreciate just as much.

It's always hard saying good-bye to a loved one, but celebration eclipsed sorrow on a memorable early September evening last year at Comerica Park as Harwell thanked the Tigers and Detroit for a life well lived with absolutely no regrets. But the roles quickly reversed and Ernie found himself the deserving recipient of a city's love and appreciation for his simple kindness and genuine humanity.

He never bailed on Detroit and was always one of its stronger advocates. Such devoted friends are scarce now. That's why it was impossible for those my age and older who've always called Detroit home to fully repay Ernie for all the joy he provided us through the decades.

A heartfelt "Thank you" was a good start.

"I'm truly humbled by the blessings the Tigers and the people of Detroit bestowed upon me," he said prior to the game.

We could say the same.

Ernie courageously accepted the consequences of his cancer. He happily embraced whatever time remained, determined to cherish every moment. He refused to turn Wednesday's tribute into a somber affair. A reporter hugged him following his short press conference, and Ernie reassured him that he would be all right.

"I'm talking to him," said his former radio partner Jim Price, "and he says to me 'Why are you so sad?' He's just an amazing man with an incredible outlook on things."

Ernie briefly spoke to the Comerica Park crowd following a two-minute video presentation. Every so often a "We love you, Ernie" from the audience punctuated the overall celebratory tone.

"It's a wonderful night for me," he said. "I'm very lucky to be here."

And when he left the field to another standing ovation, the organist played "Put on a Happy Face." He didn't want us crying.

DREW SHARP

Editor's note: The great and beloved Ernie Harwell passed away on May 4, 2010, at age ninety-two, to spend eternity with the Savior he loved and served so faithfully.

4. Drilling Home a Point

"I have raised you up for this very purpose, that I might show you my power and that my name might be proclaimed in all the earth."
EXODUS 9:16

The 1963–64 season at Tulsa University was not my best individual year when you look at the per-game scoring and rebounding averages. But it was the best season for our team because of a couple of teammates who made it happen.

As a point guard who was the team's leading scorer and rebounder the year before, I found it much more fun to have other players on the team I could share the ball with and help us win. I was happy to be the team's second-leading scorer and rebounder in exchange for a winning season. There were so many great articles written about my role as the leader of our team, but at times I felt my teammates were not getting the recognition they deserved. Although I felt I could do a few more things than most of my teammates, I never understood how anyone could see those differences.

Throughout the season, Coach Joe Swank would tell me after the games that an NBA scout from the St. Louis Hawks or from the New York Knicks was there and wanted to say hello. I don't remember how many times the scouts were there, but these two teams seemed to be the only teams interested in my services. In those days, there were only a few teams in the NBA. Besides those two, there were the Boston Celtics, the Baltimore Bullets, the Philadelphia 76ers, the San Francisco Warriors, the Los Angeles Lakers, and the Detroit Pistons.

The league draft was done by telephone conference call. I was very interested in the draft because I wanted to see if I was going to be drafted by the Hawks or the Knicks, but because it was not a public conference call, I just stayed busy and waited to find out in the paper.

I felt that I had a great option if I didn't get drafted. Phillips 66, located just fifty miles from Tulsa in Bartlesville, Oklahoma, had offered me a contract to play for their AAU team that completed in the Industrial League, along with the Denver Truckers, the Akron Goodyear, and several others. They also played college and university teams and could qualify for the Olympic team. Each of the players was employed by the Giant Oil Company and could stay with the company after their playing days were over. This was great job security to anyone. There was only one problem: if I tried out for a professional team, they would consider me a pro and I would lose my amateur status. Therefore, I would have to make the pro team or my playing days were over. This was a time in my life that my Christian faith was the only thing I could turn to.

Finally, the call came from the newspaper telling me that the Los Angeles Lakers had drafted me in the second round. I was stunned. Not knowing much about the NBA in the first place, but even less about the Lakers, I knew God must have a plan.

When the Lakers called to tell me they had drafted me, they

told me that Hot Rod Hundley was retiring and they needed a guard that could cover other teams' best guards so Jerry West didn't get into foul trouble. Here was my chance; there was an open spot on the roster, and I had a chance to get it.

Later in my career, Lakers owner Bob Short told me how I was drafted. The Minneapolis Lakers had become the Los Angeles Lakers just three years prior, but Mr. Short still lived in Minneapolis. He explained that one of his best friends and business partners had a son on the Tulsa University track team who sent him all the articles from the Tulsa newspapers. During the telephone conference draft, Mr. Short was listening in when the commissioner said it was the Lakers' turn to draft their second round pick. From Los Angeles, the general manager asked for more time and it was granted. However, from Minneapolis came, "We are taking King from Tulsa," then came from LA, "Who the heck is King from Tulsa?" From Minneapolis came, "It's my team, and I'm taking King from Tulsa." From LA, "Okay, it is King from Tulsa."

A few days later a call came from Lakers general manager Lou Mohs, who wanted to come in and offer me a contract. Since there were no agents in those days, I, along with my future wife, Tonya West, met with him. Tonya and I had planned to get married after my first year with the Lakers. The meeting was very businesslike, and he was offering me $9,500 with a $500 bonus.

I asked him for a no-cut contract, and he told me they didn't give no-cut contracts because the coach wanted everyone to have an equal opportunity. I thought that was a fair way of doing things and was actually impressed with that attitude. He said rookie camp would be at Loyola in Los Angeles and that I needed to be there on Sunday and check into the motel where they would issue our per-diem of $27 a day for meals. He left me the $500 bonus, and Tonya and I bought a $130 engagement ring. I also got my 1955 Ford engine overhauled for $125 so I could drive to LA.

I practically lived in the gym during the next two months

in one of the hottest summers I can remember. Then, knowing that it was going to take me a couple of days to drive to LA, I called and asked Mr. Mohs if I could come in a few days early to rest up from the trip. He informed me that I was to get there on Sunday, like everyone else. I said, "Yes, sir," and hung up.

I left Tulsa about 4:00 p.m. and headed west on historic Route 66 so that most of my driving would be at night when it was cooler (my car had no air conditioning). My first stop was about 4:00 a.m. the next day in Gallup, New Mexico. I stayed in a budget motel and hoped to sleep until noon, get up and run a mile or two, and then eat and hit the road again. However, I didn't know that the trucks were going to be running all night right outside my window, so I was awake and too pumped up to relax and sleep. I went out behind the motel and ran across a field for about a mile. I was exhausted. I thought I was in great shape, but I couldn't get my breath and was sure I had lost my conditioning overnight. But as I was driving out of town, I saw a small sign that indicated that the altitude was almost a mile high.

My next stop would be after midnight in Needles, California. In an all-night Denny's, I had breakfast and read a story in the *Los Angeles Times* titled LAKERS TO OPEN ROOKIE CAMP. There were going to be eight guards vying for the position created by Rod Hundley's retirement. Then there was speculation as to who would make the team. Three of the players had played on other teams and had been released. The number one draft choice had led the country in scoring with more than thirty points a game at Jacksonville. Another player was from a small college in western North Carolina and was the player who would make the team because he had a no-cut contract. When I read that line, I was angry. I was disappointed in the organization for lying to me. But when things like this happen to me, I have always been a fighter instead of a quitter. I was more determined than ever to prove that the Lakers were going to need to pay two of us.

I rolled into LA the next day and found the motel. I was

in the lobby checking in when I met the number one draft pick. He was a 6-feet, 5-inch guy who seemed very confident. I introduced myself and asked him when he got in. He informed me that he had been there thirty days working out with the regular team. I excused myself and went to my room. It was another disappointment, but I felt a confidence in myself that I had never had before. I spent some time thinking how all of this had come together and how my commitment to this goal would be an opportunity for me to share my faith in a way that I would never have again. It was a peace and confidence that only God could give.

I could hardly wait for practice to start. But we didn't start until Monday at 10:00 a.m. I was at the Loyola gym at 8:00 a.m., and no one else was there. I waited for an hour and was very concerned that I was at the wrong gym. Then, about ten minutes after nine, a car drove up and parked near the front door. I got out and walked up and asked the driver if he was with the Lakers.

He said, "Yes, I am, son. I'm the coach." Seeing that he didn't know me from film or from seeing me play, I introduced myself to coach Fred Schaus. I liked him when I first met him and learned to appreciate him as a man. He was a teacher first and a coach second. When we were able to get into the gym, I accomplished my first goal of being the first person on the court. Thirty minutes later, practice started with all eight guards. The first hour consisted of drills. I knew then that God was involved in this. I had been blessed with a high school coach who won more state championships than anyone in the state of Arkansas. Two of those titles were while I was playing for him. He was the ultimate coach of drills.

In fact, every drill Coach Schaus ran was one that Coach Gayle Kaundart taught me in high school. Not only could I do them full speed, but I could do them with my right or left hand.

After watching several players who could not do the drills without causing disruption, Coach would ask me if I knew how to do the next drill before we started it. And each time it was another drill I had been taught in high school. It was obvious to me that God was in control of this event.

My confidence was growing. During that first hour, the windows were opened in the gym so we could get some fresh air. But instead of fresh air, smog rolled through the windows. In fact, the Los Angeles area was having a smog alert. We were not able to get a deep breath without our lungs hurting. So when Coach Schaus blew the whistle and said to take a five-minute break and get a drink, each player just dropped to the floor and tried to catch his breath.

Even though I wanted to do the same thing, I had never had a coach who would allow me to even sit down during practice, let alone lie down on the floor. Instead, I ran to the other end and shot free throws and worked on my ball handling and never got a drink.

Later, when Mr. Mohs met with me and told me they had decided to keep me, he asked if I knew why I made the team.

He said, "Do you remember the first day of practice when we had the smog alert?"

I said, "Yes!"

He said, "Well, Jerry West and I were sitting together watching practice, and during the break, when everyone laid down except you, he turned to me and said there is only one guy out there that can make us better."

I didn't respond to him for a moment. I could hardly believe it. I had made the team for one reason. I knew that God was there the whole time giving me the strength and confidence I needed.

God always gives us what we need when we need it.

JIMMY KING

5. All Thumbs (Again!)

> *"'No one will be able to stand up against you all the
> days of your life. As I was with Moses, so I will be
> with you; I will never leave you nor forsake you.'"*
> Joshua 1:5

May 15, 1985, was a day I never will forget. How could I? It was the day my hockey career hung in the balance.

I was twenty years old and had just finished a successful season playing for the New Jersey Devils. My National Hockey League career had just begun and I was off to a great start. I was considered one of the league's rising stars.

My dad operated a farm in Wyoming, Ontario, and I planned to spend the summer helping him with his work and playing in a senior baseball league, as well. On May 15, I was in a hurry to get to a ball game and trying to get my work done. I saw a piece of paper blow into a machine—one of our corn planters—and I automatically reached in to pull the paper out. As I made this move, I was a little off balance and slipped, forcing my hand right into the machine. In a split second, the thumb on my right hand was severed three-quarters of the way down. I successfully pulled my hand from the machine, but as I examined my hand, I saw that my thumb was gone. I was in a state of shock and total disbelief. My initial thought was, *If only I could get those two seconds back.*

I cried out to my father for help. He helped me into his truck and rushed me to the hospital. Then he drove back to the farm, searched through the machine, found the missing part of my thumb, and rushed it back to the hospital and got it into the hands of the doctors.

My dad had taken me to University Hospital in London, Ontario. By divine appointment, I believe, the surgeon on duty had been trained in the specialty of body part reattachment.

At the time, he was very honest with me, telling me there was a 25 percent chance that the surgery would be successful. He explained that enormous damage had been done to my thumb.

The surgeon's most important step was to take a vein out of my foot and transplant it into my thumb, but he had a difficult time getting the blood to flow freely. Finally, the blood flowed successfully, and six weeks later I had a regular-looking thumb.

As I went through this emotional ringer, I thought my career had been ripped away from me before it even had a chance to develop. I had gone to church as a young boy, but now my faith was really tested. I knew the healing of my thumb was literally "out of my hands," and I prayed to God that He would work it out. I was worried that my hand would never work the same way, but I knew I had to let it go. I said to God, "It's in Your hands."

The big question on my mind was if I could still score goals in the NHL; that's what I loved to do more than anything else. The following season was my best year to date. My hockey performance kept escalating as the years went on.

Through this crisis, my whole outlook changed. The Lord taught me to slow down. I was not as impatient as I had been. On the ice, I began to play with more intelligence. God had taken a disaster and taught me patience and tolerance.

There comes that moment when all of us face adversity. We get to make a choice—either to go in the right way or in the wrong way. I think God rewarded me for having faith in the face of adversity. He allowed me to have a twenty-year career in the NHL. That career continues in my scouting duties for the Detroit Red Wings. I thank Him every day for showing me the way through the toughest time of my life. Place your trust in Him, and He'll do the same for you.

PAT VERBEEK

6. Live to Be Happy after the Games

> *I have fought the good fight, I have*
> *finished the race, I have kept the faith.*
> 2 TIMOTHY 4:7

"Rollie," Chuck would say to me, "did you make the calls? We want to be happy after the games." It was 1972, and I was a young man serving as an assistant coach at the University of Pennsylvania, just getting my shoes laced up, as it were, in the world of college basketball coaching. I couldn't have asked for a better mentor than head coach Chuck Daly.

In those early days, I did a lot of recruiting for Chuck. I mean, I worked hard. Making calls, talking to students and their families, tap-dancing a little—anything I could do to get those good players for our teams. And always, at day's end, it was the same question: "Rollie, did you make the calls? We want to be happy after the games."

After I left the National Collegiate Athletic Association circuit, I moved to West Palm Beach, Florida, but it didn't take long before I was "seduced by the competition," as Chuck might say. I soon became head coach for the new Northwood University National Association of Intercollegiate Athletics basketball team. Many of my old friends lived nearby, and they would come to the games to cheer us on—NBA Hall of Famers Billy Cunningham and John Havlicek, Bobby Orr, Bill Raftery. . .and Chuck Daly. It was the greatest thing to have them all rooting for us. I'd never stopped thinking of Chuck as my coach, and he never stopped giving us pointers.

In 2009 Chuck was diagnosed with pancreatic cancer. This turned my world upside down. Toward the end, I began visiting him every day in the hospital. It was rough, watching this awful disease eat away at my friend, the man known for so long as "Daddy Rich," because of his beautiful suits and his thick, wavy hair.

One day as I sat by his bed, Chuck turned and said to me, "Rollie, did you make any calls?" It was as if a time machine had catapulted me back more than thirty years, and I was his young assistant coach all over again.

"Did you make any calls, Rollie?" he said. "Did you get any players today? We want to be happy after the games." With almost his last breath, he was saying to me, "Rollie, you'd better get out of here. You'd better go sign some players. Because all of your famous friends are going to be a lot happier over their lobster dinners after a win."

Chuck understood that real happiness in life—whether you're playing basketball or scoring your next contract—comes with winning. That was the theme of his seventy-eight-plus years, and the more I've thought about it, the more I realized what a profound idea those words communicate. What does it mean to win in the game of life? I believe it means that when all is said and done, when that final whistle blows—as it will one day for us all—that we enter the courts of heaven knowing we've done all we were created to do, that we lived the life God had in mind for us from the beginning.

When it's your turn to stand before the Lord, when you leave this earth and are ushered into His presence, will you be happy "after the games"? How can you know you are right with God before that moment comes? As I see it, the best way to make sure that will happen is to make every day count here on earth. Make sure you have trusted in God and His Son, have turned your life over to Him, and are living your life in a manner that pleases Him.

None of us knows how many days we will have. I'm sure my friend Chuck Daly had hoped for a few more than he got. But I also know that, because of the quality of life he lived—a life of integrity, modeling leadership excellence to everyone he ever met—that there is little doubt Chuck is at long last "happy after the games."

I hope and pray that you, my friends, are living your lives in such a way that you'll know that eternal happiness, too.

ROLLIE MASSIMINO

7. Here's to You, Mr. Robinson

In the same way, you who are younger, submit yourselves to your elders. All of you, clothe yourselves with humility toward one another, because, "God opposes the proud but shows favor to the humble."
1 PETER 5:5

I am a blessed man. I was asked to coauthor the autobiography of Coach Eddie Robinson with Coach Rob in 1996. I did not know him personally before that but enthusiastically agreed to take on the project because of the incredibly high regard in which I held him after following his legendary career as a college football coach. Eddie Robinson was a rare gift to humanity.

We first met in April 1997. It was the night Major league Baseball paid tribute to Jackie Robinson on the fiftieth anniversary of his breaking baseball's color barrier. We watched the lobby television. As I watched, I realized these were two men named Robinson who helped change America because they stood up and because sports has the power to bring people together.

Never a public crusader for civil rights, Coach courageously challenged racism in his own way. He proved that a black man could be a great football coach and simultaneously build the tenacity and determination of those in his charge as he led adolescents into manhood. I think of Coach Robinson as every bit the barrier breakers that Jackie Robinson and Muhammad Ali were.

He loved his wife, Doris. They always held hands, even after nearly seven decades of marriage. He wanted his players to see the example of a happy home so they could envision this setting as the center of their future lives. This was a real-life love affair.

His career at Grambling lasted through eleven US presidents and three wars. Grambling was home to Coach and his wife for more than sixty-five years. They were married that long, and he coached for fifty-six years—all at the same institution. In the end, he had more wins than any other coach, sent more than three hundred players to NFL camps, had a graduation rate of 80 percent (when football graduation rates were around 50 percent), and never had a player get in trouble with the law until his fifty-sixth year of coaching.

Eddie Robinson was a proud American. I saw him sign hundreds of autographs. Below each signature he always added, "A Proud American." He confronted segregation in his life. But Eddie and Doris Robinson would stand still for the national anthem, their eyes fixed on the flag. Often one would see tears in his eyes when the singer hit "the land of the free." This was a great American leader who happened to be a coach and happened to be African-American.

Coach proved the power of an individual to make a huge difference in the lives of young people. I spoke at his funeral in 2007. I will always remember that when his former players in the crowd of nearly ten thousand were asked to stand up, nearly twenty-two hundred players got on their feet. They were players from the 1940s, '50s, '60s, '70s, '80s, and '90s. They came to pay tribute to this man of faith who had a passionate commitment to make this a better world. He had positively influenced each of their lives. Eddie Robinson left a gigantic legacy.

Coach Robinson had a great life. He loved his God, and now he is with Him. May God bless you, Coach.

RICHARD LAPCHICK

8. An Unbeatable Pair:
God's Blessing and Old-Fashioned Hard Work

Do you see someone skilled in their work? They will serve before kings;
they will not serve before officials of low rank.
PROVERBS 22:29

As a child growing up in Grand Rapids, Michigan, my only claim to fame athletically was serving as a cheerleader for the basketball team at Christian High. Oh, I could get the crowd stirred up and put on a show, all right. One game, my antics really brought down the house—right in the middle of one routine, I split my pants. My old high school cronies laughed about that one for years.

When I graduated from high school, my religion teacher, Dr. Leonard Greenway, signed my yearbook with the message, "With talent and leadership potential for God's Kingdom." I had never looked upon myself as a leader, but that little message registered with me. Could I be cut out for a life of leadership? Me, the cheerleading pants-splitter?

I was blessed to develop a friendship in high school with Jay Van Andel. We struck up a business partnership in which I paid him twenty-five cents a week to ride with him to school in his Model A Ford. We shared a dream of going into business together and plunged right into the business world after short stints in the military and college.

We tried our hand at a number of ventures—a flight school and a drive-in restaurant, among others. We later learned about Nutrilite, a food supplement company in California, and we became distributors. It was the catalyst that triggered the birth of Amway, which Jay and I started in our homes in 1959. Little did we know what lay ahead.

I'm often asked how Amway grew into a $9 billion

worldwide enterprise. I tell people God has been involved from the beginning and, in my case, gave me many gifts, including confidence and persistence. I wanted to be an entrepreneur and I was willing to risk failure. And then there's the fact that Jay and I got up and went to work every day and added another product, another distributor, another country. There were no great miracles, just good old-fashioned hard work—every day.

In the midst of launching our company, we both started families. Our household of six shared a love of sports. We got into the sailing world and competed at a very high level. We supported Baseball Chapel and other sports-related ministries. Our son Doug played football at Purdue University.

Over the years, our family occasionally considered purchasing a sports franchise. We flirted with the Dallas Cowboys, but my wife, Helen, was concerned that NFL games played on Sundays would disrupt our church attendance.

Then, in August of 1990, our professional sports involvement moved to another level when Pat Williams, who had helped found the Orlando Magic in 1987, began pursuing a baseball expansion team for central Florida. He needed an owner, so a mutual friend, Billy Zeoli, brought us together for an hour at my office on the Friday before Labor Day. The National League, Pat told me, had set a $95 million price tag on an expansion team. He sold me on our involvement. Just like that, we were in the big-time sports world.

As it turned out, the baseball team was awarded to Miami over Orlando. However, when the Orlando Magic founding owners decided to sell the team in the summer of 1991, we were first in line with our checkbook open, ready to acquire it. That decision launched a wonderful family venture that has helped to unite our extended family around a common athletic cause.

Since that thrilling moment when we became owners of the Orlando Magic, the DeVos family has viewed the world of sports as an opportunity to promote strong family values, community pride, good sportsmanship, and our Christian faith. I have never been ashamed to speak up about my belief in God. In fact, every time I receive a flowery introduction before speaking, I just tell the group, "I'm just a sinner saved by grace."

God has been very good to me. Years ago I began to have serious problems with my heart. The doctors told me I would need to have a transplant. Because I was over seventy at the time, I was not considered a viable candidate to have the surgery done in the United States.

My family and I spent five months in London waiting patiently for the right heart to become available. Would you believe that heart was in a woman in the same hospital who needed new lungs? In such cases, it's best to transplant a new lung and heart as a unit. It turned out the woman's heart matched up with mine, so she received a new heart and lungs from me, and I received her heart. That was in 1997, and as of this writing, I am eighty-eight years old.

Over the years, I have often thought of my high school teacher who predicted that I, as an eighteen-year-old boy, would become a leader in God's kingdom. In honor of my old teacher—and my God—living up to that challenge has been my life's mission.

RICH DEVOS

9. Don't Worry, Be Joyful!

Do not be anxious about anything, but in every situation, by prayer and petition, with thanksgiving, present your requests to God.
PHILIPPIANS 4:6

During the early 1980s I was really struggling with my game. I'd had a number of pretty successful finishes through the years, but for some reason my game had started to deteriorate, and I found myself in something of a slump. One particular season had not gone well for me, and as fall approached I realized I was in danger of losing my card. There were only two tournaments left for the year, and I had to make a good amount of money during those rounds in order to gain a spot for the next season. Otherwise I'd have to go back to qualifying school and try to get back on the tour. It was not a great feeling.

My chances came down to the last day of the season at Pensacola. I knew I needed to shoot at least a 69 for the day to put me far enough up on the money list to keep my card. By the eighth hole, I was already two over par. It didn't look promising.

Walking toward the ninth tee box, I found myself completely exasperated. I began thinking to myself, *What am I going to do now?* I was convinced there was no way I could recover before the end of the round, so I began to go over my options. *I don't want to face another year of qualifying school,* I thought. *Maybe I should just get a job at a club somewhere. Or maybe I need to go into another line of work. I'm obviously not cut out for the PGA tour.* I was at the end of my rope and emotionally beaten to the ground.

Then, as I stood on the ninth tee box, a strange thing happened. For some reason, a clear and distinct thought popped into my mind: *What's the difference between a birdie and a bogey a hundred years from now?* The thought seemed to come out of nowhere, but it really got my attention.

I told my caddy, Buzz, about it, and he said, "That's a good way to look at it. Just do your best. A hundred years from now, no one will care what you shot."

I knew I had ten holes to go, and I committed that moment to stop worrying about what would happen and just play my best. I stood on the tenth tee box before my shot and said aloud, "What's the difference between a birdie and a bogey a hundred years from now?" Then I took my shot—a beautiful drive right down the middle. My next shot was a 9 iron, and as I stood over the ball, I said the phrase again, this time a little under my breath. "What's the difference between a birdie and a bogey a hundred years from now?" Then I took my swing, and the ball sailed right into the hole for an eagle.

I was playing with two great guys that day, Larry Rinker and Gary Hallberg, and they were thrilled for me. We high-fived each other on the green and then made our way to the tenth hole. For the rest of the day, I made a habit of repeating that statement before each shot. My game turned completely around. Larry and Gary had already earned their cards for the following year, and they spent much of the round rooting for me. Their encouragement, along with my fresh outlook and perspective, allowed me to relax and play the way I knew I was capable of playing. I ended up shooting a 67 for the day, and that was all I needed to regain my spot on the tour.

In golf, as in life, it's easy to get caught up wallowing in self-pity when things don't go our way. We spend a lot of time fretting over things that are not that important in the grand scheme of life—usually things that we have little control over anyway. Every now and then we need to be reminded that, regardless of what happens, God is in control. He is right beside us, whispering in our ear, *You're right where you're supposed to be. Just trust Me and it will work out.*

Besides, what's the difference between a birdie and a bogey a hundred years from now anyway?

WALLY ARMSTRONG

10. Hammered by the Fans, Armored by God

Finally, be strong in the Lord and in his mighty power. Put on the full armor of God, so that you can take your stand against the devil's schemes.
EPHESIANS 6:10–11

It was the spring of 1981. I was a transfer student who dreamed of walking onto the Auburn University football team.

My journey began with a visit to assistant football coach Wayne Hall's office early one morning. Coach Hall, who had just been hired by the new head coach, Pat Dye, was watching film in his office. He was tough, stern, and to the point. "Come back at noon with shorts, shirt, and shoes," he grumbled. "If you last two weeks, I'll give you a locker. If you last two more weeks after that, I'll give you a uniform."

Coach Dye, who grew up on a farm, played at Georgia, and later coached under the legendary Paul "Bear" Bryant, had been hired to turn around an Auburn program that had struggled in recent years. He knew he had to change the culture, and that change started that spring with the longest and hardest practices any of us had ever endured.

Players who were bigger and stronger than me were quitting every day. It was the hardest few weeks of my life. Those were the days before the National Collegiate Athletic Association put limits on practice time, and Coach Dye pushed us farther than we ever thought we could go. I wanted to walk away, too, and I almost did.

I woke up one morning and decided I was finished. I walked into offensive line coach Neil Callaway's office and announced that I was quitting. But Coach Callaway and Coach James Daniels, both assistants on Coach Dye's first staff, would not let me give up. They encouraged me to stay and fight through the adversity.

That was a pivotal moment in my football career and in my life. I didn't quit, even though playing on the offensive line in the Southeastern Conference as a walk-on was even more farfetched than I realized at the time.

After almost giving up on my dream, I made the team and lettered for two seasons at Auburn. I started at left tackle in 1982 and 1983 and blocked for the great Bo Jackson. My playing career ended at the Superdome in the 1984 Sugar Bowl, which Auburn won 9–7 over the University of Michigan.

The hard lessons I learned from Coach Dye would serve me well in my career and in my life. Coach Dye used to say that it was his job to develop his players mentally, physically, and spiritually. Coach Dye used football to teach us about life. He put us through the fire and made us physically and mentally tough.

After my playing career ended, I returned to Auburn as a graduate assistant, then as conditioning coach, administrator, and, finally, athletic director in 2004. Had I walked away and quit when the going got tough that first spring, none of that would have happened.

Perseverance and persistence got me through those tough times, but it was only later in life that I learned that being mentally and physically tough alone would not be enough. Just as my physical and mental toughness had been pushed to the limits as a player, my faith was also tested.

Tommy Tuberville, a popular and successful head coach who had won an SEC championship at Auburn in 2004, resigned shortly after the 2008 season. I was cussed and called a liar by critics who did not want to believe that Coach Tuberville had simply decided it was time to step down. It didn't get any easier when my heart led me to hire a coach with a 5–19 record in his two years as a head coach.

I was skewered and mocked, even booed and heckled at the airport in a scene that was replayed countless times on the

Internet. Hundreds of stinging emails flooded my in-box. Some questioned whether I would even be around for the next football season.

However, I had seen Coach Gene Chizik up close during his highly successful tenure as defensive coordinator at Auburn from 2002 to 2004, and I knew him to be a man of faith, great integrity, and a tremendous work ethic. I saw how his former players revered him and knew he was the right man for the job, even though he was not the popular choice. It was during that dark and difficult time that the lessons I had learned from Coach Dye—to never quit and to do what is right even when it isn't popular—really paid off.

Proverbs 29:26 says, "Many seek an audience with a ruler, but it is from the LORD that one gets justice." That verse, which I had quoted at my introductory press conference after being named athletic director, has inspired me to do what I know is right no matter what the consequences are. Ephesians 6:10, a verse I try to visit every day, has also sustained me through tough times. If we "put on the full armor of God," as the scripture says, we have nothing to fear.

A year after the controversial hire, Auburn won a New Year's Day bowl under Coach Chizik with a team that had won five games the year before. Less than two months after that victory, Coach Chizik and his staff assembled one of the best recruiting classes in the country.

Storms will always come for you and for me. I haven't seen the last or probably even the worst storm that will come my way, but I know that God will cover and protect me, that I have nothing to fear if I suit up daily in the full armor of God.

I often think back to that day in 1981 when I wanted to quit. I think about all I would have missed and opportunities I would have squandered. That experience taught me that the best way to get through tough times is to push through them, not walk away from them.

When challenges arise and adversity comes, never give up. Persevere. Keep the faith. Do what you know is right, even when it isn't popular. Adversity, after all, only makes triumph that much sweeter.

JAY JACOBS

11. Beating the Odds in Sin City

You may say to yourself, "My power and the strength of my hands have produced this wealth for me." But remember the LORD your God, for it is he who gives you the ability to produce wealth, and so confirms his covenant, which he swore to your ancestors, as it is today."
DEUTERONOMY 8:17–18

It was a Saturday morning, and I was coaching my son's Little League team in the heat of the Las Vegas sun. I was supposed to be thinking about baseball. But suddenly my mind was consumed with memories of the NFL.

I'm from the South, where football is like a religion. So when I gazed across the field on this particular morning, I recognized a sports hero from Sunday afternoon NFL games on TV and the covers of countless magazines. It was Randall Cunningham, the retired quarterback of the Eagles, Vikings, Ravens, and Cowboys. I remembered how he single-handedly changed the quarterback position in the professional ranks. I loved him because he was a great player, but I appreciated his testimony even more.

You never know what it's going to be like to meet one of your sports heroes. As the Little League game went on, I got excited. Would meeting Cunningham live up to my expectations?

Being in Vegas had already been a wild ride for my family, and I hadn't even met any NFL superstars yet. I'm a pastor, and my family was in Vegas to plant a church. I had never planned on moving to Sin City. I had been perfectly content serving the Lord in the South, in a great church that was growing and heavily involved in missions. I thought I was right where I was supposed to be, doing exactly what I was supposed to be doing.

But God interrupted my life. Through a series of events, He relocated my family, along with two other families, to launch Hope Baptist Church in Vegas. God has a real sense of humor. You couldn't have picked three families who knew less than we did about church planting in a city like Las Vegas. When people heard our Southern accents, their first two questions were, "Where are you from?" and "What are you doing here?"

But our inability made us the perfect candidates. We were totally dependent on the Lord. Our rally cry became, "If God is not God, then we are sunk!" In February 2001, we held our first public gathering in my home. There were eighteen adults at the gathering, and we united our hearts together, realizing that God had invited us to get in on the great things He was doing in our city.

We prayer-walked through the city for five months, ultimately praying over fifty thousand homes in five zip codes. While we prayer-walked, God increased our little fellowship, and by May 2001 we had more than seventy adults at our home meetings. Each week we carried the furniture outdoors and filled rooms with folding chairs. People sat in rows on the kitchen counters. I could tell by the look in my wife's eyes that this new faith community needed to find a new meeting place. We huddled as a group and prayed for God to open the door for us to meet in a new place.

That was right before the Saturday morning when I saw Randall Cunningham. When I saw him, I couldn't resist the temptation to go and introduce myself to him. As we talked, I thanked him for standing for Christ in the public arena. He was faithful to the platform God had given him, and God was using him in a great way to impact many young lives.

Like everyone else, he asked me, "Where are you from?" and "What are you doing here?" and I told him the story of our blossoming church.

"Where are you meeting?" he asked.

"Funny you should ask," I replied. "We've outgrown my home and actually prayed this last week that God would open a door for us to find a new place."

Cunningham then told me about a small dance and recording studio he owned. It had a meeting room he used for Bible studies during the week.

"Would you like to use it for your church services?" he asked.

No more moving furniture at the Pitman house! We were having church at Randall's place!

Since that Saturday, our church has seen more than two thousand people come to faith in Christ. We've launched nine new churches and established missions partnerships on four continents, where thousands of national pastors are trained and tens of thousands of people come to Christ annually. Cunningham has also planted a new church here in Vegas that is impacting our community, and we partner together to see God transform lives.

Isn't it interesting how God works? He takes three families from the South and an NFL quarterback from Philly and connects them in "Sin City" to join in His activity of transforming the world. That is a living testimony that we serve a big God who is at work in a big world and who invites us into a big life of joining in His activity.

VANCE PITMAN

12. Mickey's Last-Inning Win

And this is the testimony: God has given us eternal life,
and this life is in his Son. Whoever has the Son has life;
whoever does not have the Son does not have life.
1 JOHN 5:11–12

Mickey Mantle never expected to pay—or, to put it more precisely, Mickey Mantle never expected to be around when the bill collector came looking for him. He lived with a sense of approaching death. Because his father, grandfather, and two uncles had died of Hodgkins disease, all before the age of forty-two, Mantle came to believe that he, too, would be dead soon. So he played hard and partied harder.

Unable to, or afraid to, confront his fears and share them with his wife and children, he lived a hollow life that seemed to be what Hemingway had in mind when he said, "Whatever makes you feel good is good," which for Mickey Mantle translated to baseball, women, and booze, a combination first revealed by a Yankee teammate, Jim Bouton, in his book *Ball Four*. Bouton praised Mantle for his boyish charm and warmth to his teammates while at the same time suggesting he might have had an even more spectacular career if he had slept more and paid fewer visits to bars and nightclubs.

All of it was so much "boys-will-be-boys fun" until Mantle's weary, worn, and woeful face showed up on a magazine cover under the headline I WAS KILLING MYSELF: A CONFESSION TO ALCOHOLISM.

He once had a dream in which he could hear the public address announcer saying, "Now batting, number 7, Mickey Mantle," only he was outside the stadium, the doors locked, the fences and gates locked, Casey and Billy and Whitey all looking for him, waiting, and he couldn't get in. A recurring dream, night after night. . .the dream of failure, of banishment, maybe even of death.

His numbers speak for themselves—536 home runs, 1,509 runs batted in, seven world championships, three Most Valuable Player awards—statistics compiled in spite of the fact that he battled chronic injuries during his eighteen-year career with the Yankees.

In 1995, Mantle, no longer a tower of power, was battling cancer. He sat behind a mass of microphones and honestly told the world, "Don't be like me. I'm no role model." "The Mick" confessed that alcohol had kept him from reaching his full potential as a player and as a human being. He was living proof that a man reaps what he sows.

In 1994, after rehabilitation at the Betty Ford Center, Mickey was finally able to beat his alcohol addiction. In 1995, however, doctors discovered that cancer had ruined his liver. He received a liver transplant that gave a glimmer of hope, but cancer remained in his body and he underwent chemotherapy.

Knowing that his life was wasting away, Mickey called his friend and teammate Bobby Richardson, a committed Christian, and asked him to pray for him over the phone. Several weeks later, Mantle's family called Richardson and asked if he could come and visit with Mickey.

When Richardson entered the hospital room, he fixed his eyes on Mickey and said, "I love you and want you to spend eternity in heaven with me."

Mickey flashed that All-American smile of his and said, "Bobby, I have been wanting to tell you that I have trusted Jesus Christ as my Savior." Mickey had received the salvation and forgiveness that we all so desperately need.

When Bobby Richardson asked Mickey on what he based his assurance that he would spend eternity in heaven, Mantle quoted John 3:16: "For God so loved the world that he gave his one and only Son, that whoever believes in him shall not perish but have eternal life."

At Mickey's funeral, Bobby Richardson was able to tell the thousands of mourners and a national television audience that Mantle could be counted as one who had said yes to Jesus. Richardson went on to say that there are only two groups of people: those who say yes to Christ and those who say no. There is no "maybe." He quoted John 3:36: "Whoever believes in the Son has eternal life, but whoever rejects the Son will not see life, for God's wrath remains on him."

Mickey had saved his best life choice for his last at-bat.

PAT WILLIAMS

13. Ahead of the Competition: Running with Jesus

Therefore, since we are surrounded by such a great cloud of witnesses, let us throw off everything that hinders and the sin that so easily entangles. And let us run with perseverance the race marked out for us.
HEBREWS 12:1

It is sometimes strange how things happen in life. I started out just wanting to be part of an athletic team. Somehow that became the benchmark when I was a young boy. I tried out for the baseball team, and I went from the outfield to the infield to the bench and was cut—and it was the church baseball team.

Then I tried out for the junior high track and field team and did not make it for three years. By the grace of God, I went out for the high school cross country team, and that's when this all started. I got a letter jacket. I thought I would get a girlfriend.

In the course of the year, my running times decreased dramatically. In 1962 I ran the mile in 5:38. The following spring, I ran it in 4:07. I can't explain how that happened. I have to go back now and pinch myself to be sure that it actually *did* happen. For those of you who aren't runners, a minute and a half off is a phenomenal turnaround in just one year.

When I ran well, I had a hard time believing it was actually happening. Before the next big race, I would sit down and watch films of my previous races and think, *That's me. I think I can do it still.* All I can tell you is that God gave me some wonderful talent and a great coach.

I confess that I did have some grueling workouts. We ran as many as forty quarter miles in practice. My high school track coach was also the swimming coach, so we took the concept of swimming—short intervals with very little rest—and applied them to track and field. I became one of his guinea pigs. We overworked but had great success. I was one of those rare guys who did not break down under the physical load.

For ten years, running was my god. In 1964, I became the world's first high school athlete to run the mile in under four minutes and qualified to compete in the Tokyo Olympics. I owed it all (I thought) to my god—running. I gave my god the best of everything. . .my time, my energy, my love.

In July 1966, I set my first world record at 3:51.3. I was the fastest miler alive. Following that race, I was pretty exhausted. I barely notice the pretty girl outside the stadium who stopped me to ask for my autograph. "I am sorry," I moaned, "but I'm tired. I'll give you one later." I escaped to the dorm, assuming I'd never see her again, and promptly forgot about the incident.

Later that year, as a college sophomore, I received a *Sports Illustrated* Sportsman of the Year award, one of the world's most coveted prizes among professional and amateur competitors. I also received the Sullivan Award as best amateur competitor in the United States and gained worldwide recognition as a runner.

In the midst of the glory, I became aware of a gnawing emptiness in my heart. "If I'm so successful," I reasoned, "why am I so dissatisfied?" Regardless of what I achieved, I was always pressed to get better.

Around Thanksgiving of 1966, a friend arranged a blind date for me. "Remember the girl who wanted your autograph after you set the world record?" my date prodded. "Well, I'm here to collect!" I was embarrassed, but we enjoyed a good laugh together. Her name was Anne. We began dating. I soon grew to love her more than I loved running.

In 1967, I set another record for the mile at 3:51.1. The record stood unbroken for eight years. I competed in the 1968 Olympics and took home the silver medal in the 1,500-meter race.

But—the emptiness remained.

Anne and I were married in 1969. For the first time in my life, running lost its place of supremacy. I began losing races, and sportswriters blamed her. I told them, "Look guys, I'm married now. I want to spend some time with my wife." I was so frustrated I walked off the track at the national championships. Shortly after, on camera with Howard Cosell, I announced my retirement.

I thought I had finished running in 1971, and then I decided I should return to competition. Running again became an obsession. The following months were the most frustrating of my life. One week I would be running great, the next I finished dead last.

Around this time, I began meeting people who said they were "born-again Christians." Like me, they were going through personal trials. Yet they emerged saying, "Praise the Lord!" *What kind of response was that?* I wondered. They had something I wanted.

When individuals have a lot of success, we tend to think they are people who are really happy inside. But I wasn't. Instead, I had the sense of, *There has to be something more.* In the spring of 1972, my wife and I were attending a Bible study, and an older couple (Bernie and Clara) began sharing with us, even though I was already *churched*. My family had gone to church Sunday morning, Sunday night, and Wednesday night. I even went to youth group. Whatever was happening at church, I was there. But Bernie and Clara began sharing with me what it was to really *know* Jesus Christ in a personal way—as opposed to just being *churched*. Anne and I realized that what was missing in our lives was not world records or gold medals; we needed a relationship with Christ.

Shortly before the 1972 Munich Olympics, Anne and I had a racquetball date with Bernie and Clara. After the game, they invited us to their home for a glass of lemonade. "I have a story to tell you," Bernie said. He explained that while he also had been *churched*, he had only recently invited Christ into his life and been baptized in the Holy Spirit. Our curiosity heightened.

Anne and I began to study the Bible. After about thirty days of study, we concluded Bernie (or rather, the Bible) was right and we both needed to be born again and baptized in the Holy Spirit.

On May 18, 1972, we knelt with friends to receive the Lord into our lives and be filled with the Holy Spirit. As we prayed, the empty place in my heart, never filled by the successes of running, was filled with an overwhelming peace.

I was America's hope for the gold medal in the 1500 meter race at the 1972 Olympics in Munich. That hope died when I fell just 500 meters short of the finish line in my qualifying race. Though the video proved I had been fouled by a runner who bumped me, the Olympic Committee refused to reinstate me because they had never made such a ruling before.

I admit I was bitter. After all, the medal had been "stolen" from me. The old Jim Ryun wanted to express his anger to each committee member with a swift kick of his size 12½ track shoe. But how was the new Christian Jim Ryun going to handle the situation?

I struggled for years with hurt and bitterness over that event. One night I knelt and said, "Lord, forgive me for the bitterness in my heart." I knew the Lord had forgiven me, but I still felt unable to forgive those who had wronged me.

I continued in prayer, pursuing complete forgiveness. Then

one day I became aware of an amazing thing—I was no longer bitter. God allowed me to be disqualified from the world's most prestigious athletic competition to show me how to be a real winner.

During the coming years, my plan is to speak, to run camps, and to share Jesus Christ every opportunity I have. Jesus has made a difference in our family's life, and with only so many years left to live, these are the priorities I will focus on until the Lord calls me home.

Anne and I, along with our children, Heather, Drew, Ned, and Catharine, and their families (including ten grandchildren) continue to run the race of life with Jesus as our Lord. We daily experience His grace and discipline, and His guidance and leadership permeate our lives.

Running with Jesus will fill a void in your life and give you the peace and joy you long for.

JIM RYUN

INSPIRING

....

1. Seeing the Light

> *When Jesus spoke again to the people, he said, "I am the*
> *light of the world. Whoever follows me will never*
> *walk in darkness, but will have the light of life."*
> JOHN 8:12

There is a story—most likely an urban legend—of a university student who was a diver on his school's swimming and diving team. The student, Robert, was training for the 1988 Olympic diving competition.

His roommate Larry was a committed Christian who would speak to him for hours about how Jesus Christ had saved him. Robert had grown up in a secular home with no church affiliation, so Larry's spiritual journey intrigued him. Robert even asked questions about the forgiveness of sin.

The day arrived when Larry "called for the question." He asked Robert if he sensed his need for a redeemer and if he was ready to trust Christ for his salvation. Robert blanched at the question and returned an emphatic, "No!"

In the weeks that followed, Robert seemed distant and sullen. Then one night he phoned Larry and asked where he should look in the New Testament for verses that related to salvation. Larry passed along some scripture references and offered to meet with Robert, but Robert declined. Larry knew Robert was troubled but did not know how to reach him.

Because he was training rigorously for the Olympic tryouts, Robert had obtained special privileges to use the university's pool. Sometime between 10:30 and 11:00 that night, he decided to go to the pool to practice a few dives. It was a clear November night, and a full moon bathed the glass-enclosed pool. Light shone brightly on the upper wall of the pool area.

Robert ascended to the highest platform to practice his first dive. As Robert stood backwards on the platform to make his dive, he spread his arms to gather his balance and looked up at the wall. He saw his own shadow cast by the moonlight. It was in the shape of a cross. He stopped his dive. At that moment, he felt a convicting spirit and was burdened by his sins. All of Larry's hours of witnessing and the scriptures he had read about Christ spoke to his heart.

Suddenly the lights in the pool area came on. The custodian, who had come to check the pool, looked up and saw Robert on the edge of the diving board. He yelled upward toward Robert, "*No-o-o-o-o-o!* Don't jump! We drained the pool this morning for repairs!"

Robert looked down from his platform and was startled to see an empty pool. He had almost plummeted disastrously, but the cross had stopped him from diving to his death.

Robert could bear the burden of his sins no longer. He sat on the platform and asked God to forgive and save him. He trusted Christ some twenty feet above the pool level.

Like Robert, we all sit on the edge of eternity and must decide whether to accept or reject the gift of salvation offered through Jesus Christ, the Light of the world. We need to make sure we do it *before* we take the final dive.

JOE ANDRADE

2. The Stat That Matters Most

Jesus answered, ". . .whoever drinks the water I give them will never thirst. Indeed, the water I give them will become in them a spring of water welling up to eternal life."

JOHN 4:14

In my job at the Billy Graham Evangelistic Association (BGEA), I have the privilege of meeting with many special people around the world who are striving to use their time, talents, and treasures to reach others with the good news of Jesus Christ.

As a kid who grew up in small-town America (Hobbs, New Mexico, population 28,657), playing baseball was a passion of mine that eventually paid for part of my undergraduate degree.

Fast forward a few decades, and you can imagine the increase to my heart rate when I received a call from our International Ministries team asking if I would "mind" reaching out to Albert Pujols to invite him to partner with us in our efforts to reach the people of the Dominican Republic through our World Evangelism through Television Project, My Hope.

Pinch me! I must be dreaming.

After regaining my composure, I agreed to take on the job and to do the "heavy lifting."

As you may know, many experts have referred to Albert Pujols as perhaps "the greatest baseball player of all time." As of the end of the 2013 season, Albert had 492 home runs for an average of 41 a season and has established a .321 lifetime batting average and earned multiple MVP awards.

Albert is an intensely competitive and disciplined player who typically arrives at the ballpark around 7:00 a.m. during spring training and five hours before every regular season game. He takes nothing for granted and is as focused a player as you will find.

There is perhaps no other batter so feared today by opposing pitchers than Albert Pujols. At 6 feet 3 inches tall and weighing 230 pounds, Albert is one intimidating athlete.

When I began to research Albert's background and eventually gained an agreement through his foundation to capture his story of faith for our nationwide broadcast, I began to learn more about what actually makes him tick.

Albert grew up in the Dominican Republic (one of the poorest countries in our hemisphere) but attended high school in the United States. When he and his future wife, Deidre, met, she was a single mom of a special needs child. Many of the men she had dated had discontinued their interest in a relationship once they learned of her child, but not Albert.

Albert not only embraced Deidre's daughter as his own, but he and his wife now minister to hundreds of people with Down syndrome and other disabilities each year through the Pujols Family Foundation (www.pujolsfamilyfoundation.org).

Those closest to Albert will tell you that he is fond of saying, "If you spend five minutes with me, there are two things that you will hear about for sure. You might hear about baseball, but you will definitely hear about my family and about my Lord and Savior, Jesus Christ."

Which leads me to the locker room at spring training in March of 2010, when I and members of the BGEA film crew met with Albert to conduct our interview. The typically "tough-faced" Pujols entered the room with five bottles of water in his left hand, an outstretched right hand, a warm, humble smile, and the words, "Sorry you had to wait. I brought you some water in case you might be thirsty."

We could sense Albert's nervousness and respect for what was taking place as we prepped him for the filming of his personal testimony and reminded him about how his story would be broadcast on prime-time television to conservatively 680,000 viewers in the Dominican Republic.

Albert took several deep breaths as he reflected on the fact that God might use his words to impact tens of thousands of individual lives, families, and future generations in the Dominican Republic.

As we filmed, Albert reminded those who would view his interview that his life was not about baseball. Baseball for Albert Pujols was simply the platform that God had given him, not for home runs and MVP awards but rather as his opportunity to glorify Him.

He shared with us that the stat that mattered most to him was how many souls would one day be in heaven because of his witness to others and because he was available to be used by God.

As we were gathering our equipment and getting ready to leave, I could hear another interview with Albert just beginning. The first question was asked: "Albert, what do you think about the moral failings of professional athletes?" Without hesitation and in a sensitive voice, Albert responded, "There has only been one man in history who never committed a sin, and his name was Jesus Christ."

The next time you watch Albert Pujols cross home plate and pause to look and point upward with both hands, join him as he gives glory and tribute to the Creator of the universe, acknowledging his full surrender as a servant of the Most High God.

And in case you were wondering if Albert's testimony was a "home run" as part of the Billy Graham broadcast in the Dominican Republic, with 24 percent of reports received, more than twenty thousand people have already indicated that they made a commitment to Jesus Christ in response to the invitation given following the program. That's one stat that will circle the universe for all of eternity.

PAT MURDOCK

3. John Wooden's World War II Miracle

Remember how the LORD your God led you all the way in the wilderness
these forty years, to humble you and test you in order to know what was
in your heart, whether or not you would keep his commands.

DEUTERONOMY 8:2

On November 24, 2005—Thanksgiving Day—John Wooden brought his son, Jim, his daughter, Nancy, and the eleven members of the Wooden family back to Coach's high school hometown of Martinsville, Indiana. With the fierce winds, a 24-degree temperature, and falling snow, conditions were miserable for the Wooden family, so used to the warm days they had left in Southern California a day before.

But Coach Wooden's final trip back to Martinsville, to dedicate a museum and photo gallery in his honor, brought a surprise that would bring back memories. It would also provide his family and a crowd of his hometown friends a flashback to World War II that revealed a Christmastime miracle that saved the life of the beloved Coach Wooden in March of 1945.

Wooden was returning to the town where, as a high school boy, he led the Martinsville Artesians to three consecutive Final Four appearances in Indianapolis (1926–28) and helped bring back the championship to "the City of Mineral Water" in 1927. It was the second of what would eventually be three state championships legendary coach Glenn Curtiss would bring to this hotbed of Hoosier hysteria (the Artesians also won the state title in 1924 and 1933).

However, on this bitter cold and windy Thanksgiving Day, it was not basketball that captured the attention of the assembled Wooden family and his hometown friends.

In 2003, I, along with the capable assistance of some World War II, Korean War, and Vietnam War veterans, had erected the Morgan County Veterans Memorial in downtown Martinsville's O'Neal Park. Standing at the rear of the impressive memorial was a large, 16-by-16-foot black granite monument on which two young New Albany, Indiana, master engravers had etched battle scenes from America's wars of the twentieth century.

As the Wooden family gathered close together to shelter their beloved father, father-in-law, and his grand- and great-grandchildren from the icy Indiana winter winds, what caught John Wooden's eye would remind him of God's divine providence and deliverance from what most likely would have been certain death in the closing months of World War II.

Etched in granite on the large memorial depicting the historic events of World War II (just below the bombing of Pearl Harbor) was the scene of death and destruction brought about by a surprise attack by a Japanese plane that dropped two powerful bombs on the American aircraft carrier the U.S.S. *Franklin*.

John Wooden had joined the United States Navy in 1943, just as he was completing his ninth season as an English teacher and basketball coach at South Bend Central High School in northern Indiana.

In 2005, as John and his family gathered around this World War II Memorial in his boyhood hometown, the events of the days preceding the United States Navy's invasion of the Japanese-held homeland island of Okinawa came flooding back to his memory.

It was another Thanksgiving-Christmas season John Wooden's mind flashed back to. For in 1944 (some sixty-one years earlier) Lieutenant John Wooden received orders to report for duty in San Francisco as a gunner's mate assigned to the *Franklin*.

After a few days' leave he was granted to visit his family in South Bend, Indiana, Lieutenant Wooden departed his home and headed for California. But as he approached Iowa City, Iowa, he was stricken with such incredible pain that driving farther became impossible. In Coach Wooden's own words, "I became quite ill. Stubbornly ignoring the pain in my side, I pushed on to Iowa City and the navy residence area at the University of Iowa. The doctor checked me over and told me that I had a red-hot appendix and that they would have to operate right away."

Coach continued, "Since Navy regulations said that you could not go to sea for a minimum of thirty days after certain types of surgery, my orders to the *Ben Franklin* were rewritten. I was assigned to Iowa preflight, and a friend and fraternity mate from Purdue replaced me on the *Franklin*."

Coach had years earlier explained, "Freddie Stalcup and I were not only fraternity brothers, but he was an outstanding quarterback on our Purdue Boilermakers' football team. . .and we were really look-alikes. His battle station was the gun station originally assigned to me. A few days later, in March 1945, on its way to Okinawa, the carrier *Franklin* was struck by two deadly bombs delivered by Japanese bombers that virtually destroyed our ship. . .and Freddie Stalcup along with the hundreds of our fellow shipmates were killed."

On that Thanksgiving Day in 2005, pointing to the large black granite memorial depicting the bombing of the *Franklin* that took the lives of 832 American sailors and Marines aboard the blazing inferno some 100 miles away from Okinawa off the coast of Japan, Coach Wooden, hardly able to keep back the tears, softly shared his long-felt pain regarding this tragic and second greatest loss of life in United States Naval history.

In words that captured all the gratitude for a full life that has inspired millions of basketball fans and others around the world, John Wooden softly, and with a deep-felt appreciation to his Lord and Savior, reminded his family on that cold Thanksgiving Day, "There but by the grace of God, John Wooden would have died on March 21, 1945, in the South Pacific in World War II."

As the Wooden family and a few of his dearest Indiana friends from his hometown proceeded to walk through the Veterans Memorial Park, a deep sense of genuine thanksgiving to our almighty God and Creator rose up. . .for the Christmas miracle in the form of an acute attack of appendicitis that gave the world more than a half century of blessings that have flowed from the life of one remarkable Christian teacher and coach, whose life shows us the truth of Edgar Lee Masters' immortal words inscribed on Lucinda Matlock's gravestone (near the burial site of President Abraham Lincoln's tomb in Springfield, Illinois): "It takes life to love life."

Truly the life of John Wooden was a nearly hundred-year testimony to that great truth.

ELMER REYNOLDS

4. Jesus Walks Out of the Stadium

"Do not be afraid, you who are highly esteemed," he said.
"Peace! Be strong now; be strong."
DANIEL 10:19

In 1996, on the day before my Florida Gators's game against the Tennessee Volunteers in Knoxville, I was reading Oswald Chambers's spiritual devotional, *My Utmost for His Highest*. I came across this passage: "The secret of a Christian's life is that the supernatural becomes natural to him as a result of the grace of God, and the experience of this becomes evident in the practical everyday details of life, not in times with intimate fellowship with God."

Then the following sentence absolutely blew me away—and would also prove to be prophetic: "And when we come in contact with things that create confusion and a flurry of activity, we find to our own amazement that we have the power to stay wonderfully poised even in the center of it all."

The next day, we played Peyton Manning and the Tennessee Volunteers in what was billed the "Game of the Century" (we played in about three or four of these so-called games of the century in one year). It was raining, and I often had trouble throwing a wet ball.

On the opening series of the game, we faced a fourth-and-11 from Tennessee's 35-yard line. We called a timeout and decided to go for it. The 107,000 fans there that day—the largest crowd gathered for a football game in NCAA history—were collectively going berserk. Coach Steve Spurrier's mind was racing and his eyes were jumping back and forth as he tried to figure out what play to call. As I stood there in the midst of the chaos, Oswald Chambers's line came to me: "We find to our own amazement that we have the power to stay wonderfully poised in the center of it all."

I don't know if I've ever had a pure vision or a clear epiphany, but what happened next is as close as I've come: while everything and everyone around me was consumed with the magnitude and the chaos of the moment, I looked over, and in my mind I saw Jesus standing by the tunnel that went out of the stadium. He simply looked at me with soft and loving eyes. While this was happening—the crowd was screaming.

As Coach Spurrier was pacing and the rain was falling, in my mind I saw Jesus turn, go into the tunnel, and walk out of the stadium while Coach Spurrier was calling the play. In the midst of the tumult and shouting, I imagined that I turned, walked across the field, and followed Jesus out of the stadium. I didn't run; I didn't trot; I just walked after Him and left the madness behind.

It was such a freeing and amazing feeling to know that in the midst of one of the most pressurized situations in college football, I was absolutely content to be a part of it—or not be a part of it. I didn't *have* to have it; I didn't *need* it; it wasn't my obsession. Football was. . .well, it was just football. Now that is a liberating thought.

Then Coach Spurrier called a post pattern. I threw a long touchdown pass to Reidel Anthony, and we went on to win the game, the national championship, the Heisman Trophy, everything.

When we are not paralyzed with the fear of failure or the criticism of others, when we realize we're playing for an audience of One (who happens to be the God of the universe), when we learn to focus on eternal things, things that will last longer than a thirty-minute *SportsCenter* episode (even with five straight reruns), that's when we have the ability to live with a true sense of freedom and security. I have no doubt that my faith not only provided a foundation for life, but it actually helped me to be the best football player I could be.

DANNY WUERFFEL

5. The Comeback Kid

"Do not fear, for I am with you; do not be dismayed,
for I am your God. I will strengthen you and help you;
I will uphold you with my righteous right hand."
ISAIAH 41:10

Call me "the comeback kid." There I was in San Francisco's Candlestick Park on August 10, 1989, and we had just beaten the Cincinnati Reds 4–3, and I had allowed only one hit through seven innings.

Flash back to ten months earlier, when I underwent an eight-hour operation to remove a cancerous tumor in the upper part of my pitching arm, surgery that took away 50 percent of my left deltoid muscle. My doctors informed me that I would never pitch again, but after an intense rehab and three starts in the minors, I returned to Candlestick Park that night to face Cincinnati.

My next start, five days later, was memorable not because of thunderous applause but for the harmful snap I felt in the humerus bone in my left arm. At the time, the Giants were leading 3–1 in the bottom of the sixth, and my sixty-ninth pitch of the evening turned out to be the last one of my career. I heard my bone break in mid-delivery. Then I crumbled on the mound in severe pain.

My arm was put in a cast, but two months later, when I rejoined the Giants in a marvelous celebration after we had won the National League pennant, my arm broke once again. My doctors informed me that the cancer had returned. I took radiation treatments then underwent two operations that failed to eliminate it. On June 18, 1991, my left arm and shoulder were amputated.

From that point on, simple tasks such as dressing myself became torturous. Admittedly, I felt frustrated and angry at these newfound challenges. It was at the same time, however, that I discovered that the problems that ended my career and my celebrity as a baseball player gave me an opportunity to help others.

In August of 1991, two months after the amputation of my arm and shoulder, my wife, Jan, and I started Outreach of Hope, an organization based in Denver. Our mission is to help people deal with emotional and spiritual aspects of living with cancer, amputation, or serious illness. We seek to provide faith-based guidance and encouragement and send baskets of print, audio, and video materials. During the past two decades–plus, we have brought hope and help to more than fifty thousand people.

Happily, I have resumed an active lifestyle that includes fishing, skiing, hunting, and riding my beloved three-wheeler Harley-Davidson. I've learned to write with my right hand so that I'm able to inscribe each book we distribute through our ministry. I get to sign four thousand autographs a year. People even tell me that my handwriting is beautiful.

Jan and I have moved to Highlands Ranch, south of Denver, to be closer to our children, Jonathan and Tiffany, and their spouses and our grandson Jude. I enjoy giving motivational speeches. I tell audiences, "It's not what you do that matters most, but who you are. And who you are is about relationships."

After more than three decades, I am still in love with Jan. She's the wind beneath my wing—*singular*.

DAVE DRAVECKY

6. Coy's Joy

In everything that he undertook in the service of God's temple and in obedience to the law and the commands, he sought his God and worked wholeheartedly. And so he prospered.
2 CHRONICLES 31:21

Having played in the major leagues and having been in and around professional baseball at all levels of the game for a long time, I have been privileged to witness many great achievements on the field. I have seen unbelievable athletes playing and competing at the highest level of sports. I have observed events that astonish and beg to be reviewed over and over on instant replay. I have marveled at how such talented men—many of whom will one day be in the Hall of Fame—could play the game of baseball with such grace and poise and motivation and inspiration.

I was a small, overachieving pitcher who made it to the major leagues in spite of overwhelming odds, so these kinds of spectacles and performances exceed my personal achievement. The most inspiring and motivating event I have been a part of concerns my autistic son Coy, who inspires not only me but all who see him and are around him. His love for life and zeal for the game of baseball truly motivate us all to believe that no matter what we face in life, there is hope.

Though Coy cannot speak clearly, his actions and the resounding joy that flows out of him shouts to heaven that when you have faith, you can make mountains move. The obstacles and challenges he faces every day just to survive are enough to weigh down even the strongest-minded positive thinker. But to Coy, life is no match. With a faith reserved only for the most blessed of saints, he faces life with the audacity and tenacity of Moses standing before the Red Sea with the Egyptians hot on the Israelites' tails. No disability or "Red Sea" will stand in the way of Coy getting to the promised life God has intended for him.

Coy's life is baseball. He loves being at the field and running around dreaming of playing in the major leagues. He dreams of being just like those players he sees out on the field and on television. But he just doesn't *dream* about it; he *believes* he is one of them. He will walk out on the field and step on the mound, look in to the catcher to get the sign, and throw the pitch like it is strike three in the clinching game seven of the World Series.

Or he will imagine stepping up to the plate, digging in the batter's box, and swatting the pitcher's fastball out of the park for a World Series–clinching home run, followed by a victory trot around the bases that ends with him diving into the pile of celebrating teammates at home plate. I have seen this scene portrayed over and over. There is nothing more motivating and heartwarming than to see my little boy live out his dream and do it with such passion. Equally inspiring is the response of those players and spectators who participate in this special event time after time.

I have seen grown men, players, scouts, and fans come to tears as they watch this astonishing scene take place. I feel that no one can leave the field unmoved after watching Coy. No one can watch him without feeling that a passionate life is to be lived with joy and faith.

Believe that you are somebody and that the passionate way you live your life greatly motivates and impacts the lives of those you are around. My son Coy is proof of that. Though autism is a limiting condition, those who know Coy feel it is more of an enabling strength used to inspire others to live with joy and passion, with a sense of letting nothing prevent our dreams from coming true.

No matter what besets us, each of us is capable of doing something special and achieving great success. A successful life that pleases God goes way beyond determination, courage, and hard work. Hebrews 11:1 says, "Now faith is confidence in what we hope for and assurance about what we do not see." God the Creator empowers us to overcome life's difficulties and turns our weaknesses into strengths for His glory.

RANDY TOMLIN

7. What's in a Name?

A good name is more desirable than great riches;
to be esteemed is better than silver or gold.
PROVERBS 22:1

NFL Hall of Famer Frank Gifford has a son named Kyle. Super Bowl broadcaster Pat Summerall also has a son named Kyle. In fact, at least a dozen of my father's (Kyle Rote) New York Giants teammates named sons after him. But why?

What was it about my dad's career. . .or life. . .or personality that compelled his friends to grant him such a high privilege?

As a youngster growing up in the 1950s around the New York Giants team, I was already aware that something unusual had occurred when so many of my friends shared "my" name. In my child's mind, I thought that maybe my dad was such a good card player that he won "children's naming rights" from his teammates in the team's nightly games. I assumed my father must've won a lot of naming rights.

It really wasn't until years later that I began to get some clue as to the real *why*.

The first possibility was that Dad's teammates admired his persistence, and hard work in recovering from two knee injuries so devastating that he ultimately had to change positions from running back to wide receiver. Amazingly, he still set several Giants receiving records and went to several pro bowls. Maybe they admired his endurance.

The second possibility was that he helped organize the NFL Players' Association, which standardized the benefits the players would receive. As an example, some clubs washed your socks and jocks between two-a-day practices while other teams had you wear the same wet stuff for the second practice. Some teams traveled by planes—other teams used overnight trains. Thankfully, my father played for a team that treated its players well, but there were significant differences in treatment on other teams. Of course, at that time there wasn't any free agency either—so you had no choice but to spend your entire career playing only for the team that drafted you. My dad, at significant personal risk, was one of those who stood up for equal treatment of all players. Maybe they admired his courage.

The third possibility was that my dad's teammates watched him go through a personal financial crisis one year when his offseason business partners cashed in all the assets of their joint venture and abandoned the partnership. They left my father alone to handle all the debt by himself. The amount was well over three times his annual gross income—and several attorneys kindly offered to help him with the bankruptcy papers. However, my father refused to walk away from the innocent creditors and take the easy way out—so he began a "payback" journey that took about ten years before the last dollar was paid. Maybe they admired his integrity.

Oh, I could go on—but I think you get the idea that I still can't tell you for sure exactly why there were so many kids named Kyle in the New York Giants locker room.

Was he a leader? Absolutely, but it wasn't his high-performance football skills that made him a leader. It was his character in dealing with disappointments, disaster, and dramatic change. It's funny how what you and I have in common with my dad isn't the NFL or world championships—it is the daily challenge in dealing with the same kinds of personal issues he faced. Sports historians consider my dad a champion of football—but you and I know better. At his core, he really was a champion of endurance, a champion of courage, and a champion of integrity.

What did God create you to be a champion of?

The bottom line is that my dad gave me what every parent can give a child: a good name that comes from how we handle the struggles and failures of life and not so much how we handle the successes.

Here is the paradox: a good name comes from how we deal with bad things in life.

Here is the truth: God wants to use our "failures" to glorify Him. . .if we'll just let Him. A good name rarely comes from the exciting glory of business achievements or athletic mountaintops. It often comes from the daily, faithful grind in the valley of defeat as you confront discouragement and failure in clear view of your peers, your friends, and your family.

I encourage you to fight your battles righteously. And I encourage you to also embrace those battles joyously and see them as an opportunity to demonstrate what your name can mean to your children's children.

What a legacy—to have been a champion of Christ!

If we will just ask Him, God will empower us to "bring back the harvest that the locust has taken away" in our failures. So may you and I, as transparent "teammates in Christ," help each other offer up to God our humble, imperfect selves, and then watch in amazement as He redeems our times of regret to the benefit of our families, to the clarity of our legacy, and, most importantly, for His glory.

As a "Kyle," I am attached to a name above *many* names.

As a "champion of Christ," I am attached to a "Name above *all* names."

May this be an experience we share together. . .forever.

KYLE ROTE JR.

8. Remember, God Is in Control

You will keep in perfect peace those whose minds are steadfast, because they trust in you. Trust in the LORD forever, for the LORD, the LORD himself, is the Rock eternal.
ISAIAH 26:3–4

When I have a good day, it is great. When I have a bad day, I know a good day is coming. I have had a lot more good days than bad ones. I love the verse in the book of Psalms that says, "The Lord is the one who sustains me" (54:4). Another of my favorite verses is, "You armed me with strength for battle" (2 Samuel 22:40).

My favorite book in the Bible is Philippians, which the apostle Paul wrote while he was in a Roman prison. I like it because it is about joy. Christian joy differs from happiness, which I have certainly had throughout my life, with my family, my players, and my team. It is about having a joyful heart, no matter what the circumstances. It is God-given.

I thought about this many times after I was first diagnosed with cancer. Joy comes from inner conditions, not outer conditions. If our spiritual attitude is centered on Christ's principles, power, and promises, then our spiritual condition will always be healthy and enjoyable, not permitting circumstances to rob us of our joy.

I feel that the secret of Christian joy is found in the way we think, in our attitude. Proverbs 23:7 tells us that we are what we think in our hearts. I think our mind-set is everything. If we have that kind of attitude and mind-set that Christ gives us, we have the chance to really influence the outcome of our lives.

I have never been worried about the outcome of my illness. When you believe in God, as I do, you know that worshiping Him and worrying cannot coexist. When God is your focus, there can be no worry. I also have found that gratefulness and faithfulness can replace worry and depression. I cannot even count all the blessings I have had in my life. There are far too many. Gratefulness is the opposite of discontentment, worry, discouragement, or depression. If you just focus on gratefulness and putting God first, there is no room for any of the others.

I have always believed that attitude is the key to success. It impacts your relationship with people, your determination, and your willingness to make sacrifices. If you look for the positive and the good in everything, then you see everything differently than if you are always looking for the negative in everything. It is a daily battle.

Many times we have little or no control over the circumstances we face. That has certainly been true with my cancer. But we always have 100 percent control over our attitudes and our reactions to our circumstances. We have to make the choice to find the positive. My way of doing this is focusing on God, rather than on the circumstance. I am looking for ways that God is helping me grow through this or how I might help others get through. Focusing on Him helps me with that.

When I focus on God, rather than the problem, God becomes great and the problem becomes smaller. But if I focus on the circumstances, then that becomes great and God becomes smaller.

I give my mom, Lib Yow, credit for teaching me that there is a silver lining in every dark cloud. She used to tell me, "The man without shoes felt bad until he met a man without feet."

It's a matter of getting your perspective right and understanding that your ability to deal with obstacles and adversity has everything to do with whether you will really have a chance to be successful.

I thank God for allowing me to see early in life that attitude is the key to success. It affects every facet of our lives. You have to make adversity work for you, rather than against you. Is this easy? No. But as you practice looking for the positive, it becomes easier to find.

When I am gone, I don't want you to fret over the fact that I'm not here or to question why I'm not here, because God knows what He is doing. God doesn't make mistakes. He knows what is best for each of us. He is in total control.

KAY YOW (1942–2009)

Editor's note: The late Kay Yow accomplished most everything a woman's basketball coach could dream of. Over a thirty-seven-year career that included thirty-four seasons with North Carolina State, she compiled 737 victories, leading the Wolfpack to twenty NCAA tournament bids, eleven Sweet 16 appearances, and the Final Four in 1998. Outside the college ranks, she coached the 1988 US Olympic team to a gold medal in Seoul, South Korea.

9. The Perfect 10

Jesus said, ". . .whoever wants to become great among you must be your servant, and whosoever wants to be first must be slave of all."

Pamela Dylag is a social worker for the state of Ohio. Almost every day she has the challenging duty of investigating families to make certain that children are being properly cared for. Her job requires working many hours, hearing endless heartbreaking stories, and showing lots of love. In her fifteen-year career, she has assisted literally hundreds of children.

One child holds a special place in Pamela's heart. His name is Chad. He is a teenager who was born with severe learning disabilities and mental retardation. His mother was a drug user who lost custody of him when he was about ten years old. Her drug use evidently contributed to his mental condition. Chad's father was never really around. The rest of his family wasn't interested in taking in Chad, so he is now in custody of the state. Pamela is his assigned caretaker. As of this writing, they have been together for about six years.

Physically, Chad looks like a typical teenager, but he has the mind of a six-year-old. He speaks slowly, has a slight lisp, and suffers from a low self-image, having been bounced around from home to home and facility to facility. Finding a permanent home for Chad has been difficult. Because of his challenges, no one has been willing to take him in. Sadly, he is a child without a home.

Being all boy, Chad loves to fish. He also loves to get dressed up in a suit and sport around being "cool." When Pamela visits him on special occasions, he always asks to go to his favorite restaurant, Red Lobster, where he always orders his favorite meal of fried shrimp.

On cold, wintry days, Chad longs to be on the sunny beaches

of Florida. Florida holds a special place in his heart. You see, when Chad was five years old, he underwent multiple cancer treatments. The Make-A-Wish Foundation heard of his plight and sent him and his biological mother to Disney World. This visit to see Mickey is the most precious memory he has of his mother and maybe of his life. He often speaks about it and tells how he one day is going to live on the beach in Florida with his own family. Maybe one day he will fulfill his dream, but for now he still lives in an institution, far from any beach, with no one to call "family"—except his social worker and a few other facility workers.

One thing that always brings a broad grin to Chad's face is his love for the Cleveland Browns. His favorite player is Ohio native and former Browns quarterback Brady Quinn. Though the media and others have often given Brady a difficult time, no one has stood up for the one who wears number 10 quite like Chad. He thinks Brady is the best quarterback in the NFL, and he will fight with anyone who doesn't agree.

Knowing this fact, Pamela, decided to do something special for Chad one Christmas. She approached my brother Phil Savage, who at the time was the senior vice president and general manager of the Browns. She knew Phil had helped hundreds of people throughout his career. She also knew that Phil had arranged for dozens of individuals and groups—including orphans, inner-city kids, and children with special needs—to visit the Browns's facility. To no one's surprise, Phil immediately agreed to assist in getting Quinn's autograph for Chad.

With snow on the ground and Christmas only a few days away, Phil told Pamela to come by the Browns's training facility to pick up a few autographed items. When she arrived, she was overjoyed to learn that Phil had a box waiting for her. Inside the box was a football signed by the entire team, some T-shirts, hats, books, and the ultimate gift, a number 10 Browns jersey signed by Brady Quinn himself.

The next day, Pam took Chad to Red Lobster to give him

his Christmas gifts. He first opened the T-shirts with the words Cleveland Browns emblazoned across the chests. A big smile came across his face. He then opened the books, then the hats, and then a few other authentic Browns items. Excitement grew with each new item. When he opened the football bearing the autographs of the entire Browns team, he couldn't believe it. At no time had he received gifts like these.

With great anticipation, Pamela finally handed Chad his final gift. As he pulled it out of the package, the white jersey with brown and orange trim bearing the number 10 and the name "Quinn" on the back unfolded. Written largely across the numbers was the handwritten signature of Brady Quinn.

Chad leaped with joy, as it was almost too much to take.

After lunch, Pam and Chad went back to his housing facility. He asked if he could wear his new "Brady Quinn" jersey so the whole world could see. For the first time in his life, he now had something that was his own. . .something that was the envy of every person he saw. He had Brady Quinn's autograph.

When asked why the gift meant so much to Chad, Pamela explained, "That one jersey is the most meaningful and most valuable thing Chad owns. He absolutely cherishes it more than anything else in life. It is his greatest possession."

To this day, Chad keeps the prized jersey under lock and key and brings it out only on special occasions to show it off. He still cheers on the Browns and is still convinced that Brady Quinn is the best quarterback in the NFL—even though Quinn is playing elsewhere.

What Chad doesn't know is that on December 27, only five days after providing the gifts, Phil Savage was released from the Browns after a disappointing season. His getting Chad this most meaningful possession would prove to be his final, and quite possibly his greatest, benevolent act as general manager of the Browns.

In the Bible, the book of James says that "real religion is taking care of. . .orphans in their distress." If this is true, then

Pamela Dylag, Phil Savage, and Brady Quinn are each living out a "real religion." Not only did they serve God by caring for an orphan, but they also gave him the greatest and most meaningful Christmas of his life.

If you are ever in Florida and you see a young man walking the beaches of Florida wearing an orange and brown number 10 jersey, don't be surprised if it is Chad. I am convinced that he holds a special place in God's heart, and I know that there will be many others who will practice "real religion" by taking care of him.

JOE SAVAGE

10. "You Need What I Have"

You desired faithfulness even in the womb; you taught
me wisdom in that secret place.
PSALM 51:6

The quality of character Christians are to demonstrate was forcefully brought home to me one Sunday in September of 1981. Bud Palmer of Sandy Cove Bible Conference in Maryland arranged for a young man named Cordell Brown to speak at the Philadelphia Phillies pregame chapel at Veterans Stadium.

Cordell is a victim of cerebral palsy and carries the evidence with him everywhere he goes. His gait is awkward and his speech is slow and difficult to understand. Feeding himself is a long and arduous task. It would appear that he was shortchanged in life, that God wasn't fair to him. But if you expect to hear that from Cordell Brown, you're mistaken.

As Cordell and I slowly made our way through a brief tour of the stadium and then into the Phillies' clubhouse, the players who knew me and were aware that I had brought the chapel speaker looked up and greeted me and quickly looked away again.

No one wants to appear to be staring at an unfortunate handicapped person, and the ballplayers had to wonder what in the world I was doing with this poor young man. I imagine Cordell felt a bit inadequate for his task that day as he got an up-close look at the players who had become the world champions of Major League Baseball that previous October.

These were men like Mike Schmidt, Garry Maddox, and Bob Boone, all of whom made their livings and earned their fame and fortunes with their bodies. They were cheered, applauded, praised, and written and read about because they were fine physical specimens. Not only were they in shape and at the peaks of their careers, but they had honed their physical skills to perfection and used their bodies to support themselves and win ball games, all to delight the fans.

Cordell Brown's body was his cross to bear. It was in his way. It slowed him down. People didn't like to look at him. They turned away, pretending not to see. And those who did stare often laughed, made fun, or rejected him.

I introduced him to the players, and he began by putting the Phillies at ease. "I know I'm different," he explained laboriously. And then he quoted 1 Corinthians 15:10: "But by the grace of God I am what I am."

Cordell spoke for about twenty minutes on the power and goodness of God in his life. He concluded in a loving and simple way. He said, "You may have a .350 lifetime batting average and be paid $1 million a year, but when the day comes that they close the lid on a box, you won't be any different than I am. That's one time when we'll all be the same. I don't need what you have in life, but one thing's for sure: you need what I have, and that is Jesus Christ."

People less handicapped than Cordell Brown have retreated to wheelchairs and let others wait on them for the rest of their lives, but he believes God has a purpose for him just the way he is. He gave his life back to God and today directs a huge complex for the handicapped in Ohio.

The secret to Cordell's work among his peers is not the clean rooms and the wondrous facilities he provides. Rather, it's in the fact that he treats his "clients" as the precious people they are in the sight of God and convinces them that they have a purpose for living.

Cordell Brown is an inspiration to me to get on with the business of living for Christ. He makes me want to remain cured of the pride that marked my life previous to my relationship with Christ, yet to always remember that I am special enough in the sight of God that I can accomplish great things through Him.

PAT WILLIAMS

11. From Bags to Riches

And my God will meet all your needs
according to the riches of his glory in Christ Jesus.
PHILIPPIANS 4:19

On January 29, 2010, I announced my retirement from the Arizona Cardinals and the National Football League. What a ride it had been for me! The media has chronicled my journey well, and perhaps by now you are familiar with my story.

After I graduated from Northern Iowa University, I was invited to the Green Bay Packers' training camp. The Packers were loaded with quarterback talent, so I was cut from the team.

I worked as an assistant football coach at NIU and supplemented my income ($5.50 an hour) stocking shelves at the Hy-Vee grocery store in Cedar Rapids, Iowa. I met and fell in love with my future wife, Brenda, who was a cashier at Hy-Vee. I was immediately attracted to Brenda and asked the store manager to let me bag groceries so I could work near her. We married on October 11, 1997, and God has blessed us with seven children.

My desire to play professional football continued to drive me, and I seized the opportunity to play for and have three good seasons with the Iowa Barnstormers of the Arena Football League. We twice played for the league championship in the Arena Bowl. I also played one season in NFL Europe.

My chance to start at quarterback for a Super Bowl–bound NFL team took place after I signed with the St. Louis Rams. In 1999, Trent Green, our starting quarterback, suffered a season-ending injury, and I was named the starter.

It seemed as if the Rams came from nowhere to get to two Super Bowls under Coach Dick Vermeil. We went 13–3 in 1999, made the playoffs, and topped the Tennessee Titans in Super Bowl XXXIV. I was blessed to receive one Super Bowl

MVP (1999) and two league MVPs (1999 and 2001) during my years with the Rams.

My next stop was with the New York Giants, and then I journeyed to Arizona to play for the Cardinals. When starting quarterback Matt Leinart was sidelined with an injury, Coach Ken Whisenhunt gave me the starting nod. I started in forty-eight of the remaining forty-nine games of my career, including Super Bowl XLIII following the 2008 season.

I could not have scripted things better. I could never have dreamed that my life would have played out like it has. I have been humbled every day that I have awakened and have been amazed that God would choose me to do what He has given me the opportunity to do. As a result, I have a platform to share with you what is most important in my life.

Success didn't just happen for me. It wasn't like everything has always been great. There have been times when I struggled, and I think the Lord used those times to keep me humble. I know I'm here to do the Lord's work. He has given me many great blessings, and I know I'm here to make a difference for Him.

God has given me an unbelievable platform that reaches an enormous number of people. The platform God gave me through the Super Bowl allowed people to see through my life that all things are possible. It also set me up to say, "I'm a Christian," from a national platform. The impact has been huge. I've seem God use this to catapult me to another level as a warrior for Him.

The greatest day of my life had nothing to do with winning the Super Bowl or with throwing more than forty touchdown passes in a season or with being named the NFL's Most Valuable Player. It was the day that I asked Jesus into my heart. Now my life is dedicated to living out God's will and telling others about Him.

I look for any and every opportunity to share Jesus with people. I don't worry about what anybody is going to say or think—I just try to take the platform I have, expand it, and touch as many lives as I can.

In Luke 12:48, Jesus said, "from the one who has been entrusted with much, much more will be asked." With everything I've been given, that really speaks to me at this point in my life. I know that God has given me a greater responsibility to share Jesus with others.

Each of us is called to do different things—sometimes several different things. I was called to be a football player, but I'm also called to be in the ministry and to share Jesus with people. My goal is to be exactly what God wants me to be and do what He wants me to do. More than anything, I want people to see my life as an open book with Jesus smack down in the middle of it.

KURT WARNER

12. It Does *Matter*

For we are taking pains to do what is right, not only in the eyes of the Lord but also in the eyes of man.
2 CORINTHIANS 8:21

On December 11, 1992, the San Antonio Spurs had just beaten the Minnesota Timberwolves 98–85 at the Target Center in Minneapolis. I was completing my internship for graduate school, and part of my game-night responsibilities was to check on the visiting team's medical staff after the completion of the game. After my initial check on the Spurs, I decided to take a second walk through the locker room to ensure that the Spurs players and coaches had everything they needed.

As I was walking through the locker room, I saw that one

of our newer ball kids was asking the Spurs All-Star and future Hall of Fame center David Robinson for his autograph on a basketball card. After David autographed the card, he handed it back to the young man, who looked at the autograph, pointed to it, and asked, "What's this?" Along with the signature, David had written a reference for a Bible verse on the card.

What happened next is one of those life moments that affects you for as long as you live. You never forget the experience and how you felt at the moment it happened. David looked the young man in the eyes and quoted the Bible verse that he had written on the card along with his autograph. In his deep baritone voice, he then told the young man (and me) these words—words that will never leave me—"Because it *does* matter what people think of you."

David reached down, picked up his bag, and headed for the Spurs' team bus.

Just as quickly as he said those unforgettable words, Mr. Robinson was gone. Gone to play another basketball game, and gone to help change the world.

I will never forget the words he spoke to that young ball kid. Throughout our lives, we are told to be ourselves, told, "Don't worry what others think of you." As a Christian and a believer that Christ died and rose from the grave to forgive us of our sins, I believe it is vital that we *do* care what people think of us. Caring about what others think of us is vital to being a witness for Christ.

In my research I found the Bible verse that Mr. Robinson quoted that December night in 1992: "For we are taking pains to do what is right, not only in the eyes of the Lord but also in the eyes of man" (2 Corinthians 8:21).

Because it *does* matter what people think of you.

Tom Smith

13. Exemplary Coaching

Nobody should seek their own good, but the good of others.
1 CORINTHIANS 10:24

Coaches can have a profound impact on their players—not only in helping to craft their game, but in molding their lives. Coaches cannot control what their players do out on the field or court, but they can offer the skills for making the best decisions in each game situation and can model the foundation for a solid life by living with integrity.

Consider these three coaches whose legacy is marked as much by their examples as by their win-loss records:

Tony Dungy

Tony Dungy holds the distinction of being the first National Football League head coach to defeat all thirty-two NFL teams, as well as being the first African-American head coach to win a Super Bowl.

Despite his impressive numbers, at one point Dungy considered leaving coaching to work as a prison minister. After his retirement from coaching, he penned a bestselling book on living one's beliefs, as well as a devotional series to accompany it. His goal has always been to be a Christian first and a coach second. The practice of his faith has always come before his professional concerns. "Faith, family, football" is the order of priorities on which he bases all his decisions.

Dungy has sought to make an impact by working with several mentoring programs, community programs, public health initiatives, and family-building initiatives. He has continued his interest in working in prisons, and also by reaching out through organizations and to specific individuals in order to impact their lives for the better. These efforts, like everything else he does, are rooted in his unshakable belief in God and his determination to serve others.

When his son died in 2006, Dungy was very public about both his grief and the way he was coping with it. "My faith in Christ is what's gotten me through this," he said. Only six weeks after losing his son, Dungy explained his outlook in a speech: "If God had talked to me before James's death and said his death would have helped all these people, it would have saved them and healed their sins, but I would have to take your son, I would have said, 'No, I can't do that.' But God had the same choice two thousand years ago with His Son, Jesus Christ, and it paved the way for you and me to have eternal life. That's the benefit I got, that's the benefit James got, and that's the benefit you can get if you accept Jesus into your heart today as your Savior."

Bobby Bowden

One of the winningest coaches in college football history, Bobby Bowden made a special effort to help his student athletes stay grounded in their faith. Each year, his team would take a trip to two different local churches—one that was predominantly white and one that was predominantly African-American. Church attendance is the first thing many college students drop from their routine when they move away from home, and Bowden's goal was to prevent that from happening. He hoped that by introducing his players to several congregations, they would feel comfortable and be willing to return on their own.

He never pushed them to practice one faith or another, but he encouraged each of his players to pray before any decision, be it asking out a girl, switching a major, or entering the NFL draft. As a testament to his faith, in 2004 the Fellowship of

Christian Athletes named an award in his honor that celebrates the character, scholarship, and talent of one outstanding college athlete.

As successful as his program was, Bowden understood that the most important thing was not producing top-level athletes but in developing young men to become community leaders, husbands, and fathers of character. The same has always been true of his goals. When asked about whether the possibility of setting the record for most wins by a college football head coach might affect his retirement decision, Bowden replied, "My religion and faith won't let it matter to me. Sure, winning matters in this job. But some record? You're not going to take it with you when you go, are you?"

John Wooden

There is no more respected name in college basketball than the legendary John Wooden, whose ten national championships in twelve years is a record likely to go unmatched. But Wooden is probably just as famous for his calm demeanor and kind ways as he is for his dominant teams.

He was determined to coach quietly, without screaming or cursing at the referees, as many coaches often do. He chose not to drink or carouse, but instead was very open about the love, respect, and fidelity he had for his wife, Nellie. Wooden realized that, as a coach and a public figure, he was an example to not only the players on his team, but to men and women across the nation who followed basketball, who cheered for UCLA, or who simply admired his leadership.

He lived with integrity and encouraged his players to do the same, because he felt he was pursuing something far more significant than championships. Wooden required that his teams leave orderly locker rooms, whether they were playing at home or away. The common courtesy that such a small gesture would show to the janitorial staff was a life lesson on how to treat others. He is famous for saying, "You can't live a perfect day without doing something for someone who will never be able to repay you."

Wooden also found great comfort in seeing his students practice their beliefs. During one team trip, when the players were all piled onto a bus for a Saturday-night-to-Sunday-morning drive to their next game, he listened in awe as each student began his own private devotions. Years later he would recall that trip as one of the most memorable and touching moments in his long career of coaching.

He famously sought not only to teach his players how to be better basketball players, but also how to be better people. Their abilities on the court were only a small part of who they were; their faith, character, and attitude were far more important. Wooden would often remind his teams of a few simple truths to keep in mind: "Talent is God-given. Be humble. Fame is man-given. Be grateful. Conceit is self-given. Be careful."

DON YAEGER

14. The Man Who Invented Basketball

To God belong wisdom and power; counsel and understanding are his.
JOB 12:13

Dr. James Naismith, my grandfather, invented the game of basketball. He was born in Almonte, Ontario, Canada, in 1861. Like most people, he was shaped by the conditions of his childhood. He was able to profit from the challenges he faced and the lessons he learned as a boy and young man in that they served as building blocks for the remarkable person he became.

His parents died three weeks apart from typhoid fever. His older sister, Annie, younger brother, Rob, and he went to live with their grandparents. Papa Jim was an orphan at nine and a lumberjack at sixteen, and he was expected to do a man's work from the age of twelve.

From this humble and rugged beginning there came a man who was able to make responsible decisions concerning his life's objectives. His life was devoted to leaving the world a better place than he found it. His sister, Annie, kept reminding him how disappointed his mother would have been to learn that he had chosen to suspend his education. Jim quickly realized that Annie was right and that he would need an education to turn his dreams into realities.

He returned to finish high school and then matriculated to McGill University in Montreal. It was at McGill where athletics became a major part of his life—and where his devotion to God and his Christian faith blossomed. His growing faith led him to enroll in McGill's seminary, where his objective was to prepare for a career that would help as many young people as possible through athletics.

This desire motivated him to seek a college that had a similar vision of wedding his love for athletics with his Christian beliefs so that he could prepare himself to help young people. Springfield College in Springfield, Massachusetts, met those prerequisites. His decision to attend Springfield impacted every major aspect of his life thereafter. The college's aim, then and now, is to educate a student's mind, body, and spirit.

The college offered a training course for potential YMCA directors. After finishing this course, he was asked to join Springfield's faculty. His supervisor, Dr. Luther Halsey Gulick, commissioned James to create a game that would meet the needs of restless and hard-to-handle directors-in-training. The game must be played indoors, require as little equipment as possible, involve a number of people, and be just as strenuous as football. With these parameters in mind, my grandfather created the game of basketball. The first basketball game ever played was in Springfield, Massachusetts (now the home of the Basketball Hall of Fame).

Papa Jim believed that one could be a good athlete and fine Christian simultaneously. He instructed his students to have fun and to show sportsmanship and character on and off the court. Exemplary conduct was his rule, and for many it was a new way of viewing athletic competition. The game caught on in the United States and spread, due in part to his former students who became ambassadors for basketball at various YMCA locations.

Papa Jim left Springfield for Denver, Colorado, where he became a YMCA director. While in Denver, he decided to pursue a medical degree so that he could develop an understanding as to how athletics affected the body. He would apply his learning to best help young men and women. He earned his MD and then decided to move his family to the University of Kansas in Lawrence. The university had asked Amos Alonzo Stagg to recommend an individual for the athletic director's job, which had several facets. One responsibility was for the athletic director to also act as chapel director, a task my grandfather enthusiastically embraced.

Stagg sent a telegram: "Recommend James Naismith, inventor of basketball, medical doctor, Presbyterian minister, teetotaler, all-around athlete, non-smoker, and owner of vocabulary without cuss words. Address: YMCA Denver, Colorado."

The University of Kansas years were busy and fulfilling for Dr. Naismith. Grandfather helped students, regardless of race, with studies, prayers, other professors, medical problems, and even money to go home, stay in school, or buy food. He was not wealthy, but he generously shared with students whatever he could.

At this juncture of his career, many young people were being sent to France to fight in World War I. So, at the age of fifty-six, he went to France with the YMCA to serve as a chaplain. He met ships at various ports to counsel young men and to keep them safe, thereby helping them to adjust to a new environment and to deal with temptations they faced away from their homeland. He profited from the life lessons he learned as a boy, which, combined with his education and self-reliance, made him a very effective servant-leader. He spent nineteen months in France because, as he put it, "My boys need me."

When he returned home, he was surprised and happy to note how popular his game of basketball had become, both in schools and professionally. He still thought of the sport as a nice little game he had invented to fill a need. But when basketball was first played in the 1936 Olympics in Berlin, Germany, he became the guest of honor at the games. He then understood that he had accomplished one of his life's major goals. He would leave the world a better place because of his work.

Grandfather Naismith was a prolific writer, and hundreds of his letters to family and friends reveal that in spite of his notoriety for inventing the game of basketball, he thought of himself primarily as a man who loved God, his family, his adopted country, and the thousands of people he was able to help. He was truly a renaissance man.

HELLEN CARPENTER

15. "Me, I Give"

"For God so loved the world that he gave his one and only Son,
that whoever believes in him shall not perish but have eternal life."
JOHN 3:16

As a youngster, my life was built around football. After high school, I was granted an appointment to attend the United States Naval Academy at Annapolis, Maryland. I was a quarterback, and I looked forward to a great career playing for the Midshipmen.

When I arrived for fall practice in 1962, I discovered there was a pretty fair quarterback one class ahead of me. His name was Roger Staubach.

I'm often asked if I saw greatness in Roger as a player, person, and leader. My answer always is an emphatic yes. There were two indicators—Roger had the remarkable ability to focus on whatever task was before him, and he was trustworthy and would stick with the task until it was completed.

I didn't play much football at Navy until Roger was injured his senior year, and then after he graduated. I played my senior year, 1965, and still have great memories of being a member of those Navy teams.

I graduated from Navy in June 1966. The Vietnam War was in full engagement and it was just a matter of time until I was assigned to the field of combat.

I arrived in Vietnam just before the Tet offensive in 1968. After the enemy slaughtered nine thousand civilians at Hue, American forces recaptured the city. I got involved with a local Vietnamese church and helped construct an orphanage. One day the facility housing thirty-two children—ages four to thirteen—was hit by an enemy mortar attack. An eight-year-old boy was severely wounded and was rushed to the hospital, where it was determined that he needed a blood transfusion.

I wanted to give blood, but my type did not have the immunity that a Vietnamese person's does. So I went back to the orphanage to explain to those children that their friend was going to die unless one of them gave blood. A nine-year-old named Hai raised his hand and said, "Me. I give."

He was rushed by Jeep to the hospital, laid on a stretcher near his friend, and prepared for the transfusion. A little while after the needle was inserted into his arm, Hai started to whimper. I walked over and asked, "Son, what's wrong. Does it hurt?"

Hai gave no reply. A little while later, he began to cry severely. I asked again, "Hai, what's wrong? Are you scared? Does the needle hurt your arm?"

The little nine-year-old boy, giving blood to save his friend's life, looked up at me and asked, "How long will it take me to die?"

Hai had never heard of a transfusion. He didn't know he was giving just a little of his blood; he thought he was giving it all. But he was willing to give all of his blood so that his friend might live.

A greater sacrifice was made at Calvary when Jesus Christ gave His blood to redeem lost mankind. He gave His life that we might experience an abundant life on earth and an eternal life in heaven.

I think of that every time I think of Hai.

BRUCE BICKEL

16. A Bus Ride to Sports History

*Finally, brothers and sisters, whatever is true, whatever is noble, whatever
is right, whatever is pure, whatever is lovely, whatever is admirable—
if anything is excellent or praiseworthy—think about such things.*
PHILIPPIANS 4:8

I've had the privilege of serving many years as the volunteer
chaplain for the Denver Nuggets. In 1994, the Denver Nuggets
entered the first round of the NBA playoffs as the number eight
seed in the Western Conference. Their opponent in the five-
game playoff series was the Seattle SuperSonics, who had the
best record in the league and, thereby, the number one seed.
At that point in NBA history, no number eight seed had ever
beaten the number one seed, so the Nuggets went into the series
as big underdogs.

Game one in Seattle saw the Nuggets fall behind 62–27 by
halftime. Seattle's talent looked to be much, much better than
Denver's. We went on to lose games one and two in Seattle,
but then we miraculously won games three and four in Denver
on our home court. As I boarded the team plane to fly back to
Seattle for the final deciding game five, I noticed that spirits
were high among the players.

The enthusiasm continued the following afternoon as we
boarded the team bus to head for the game. I was one of the
first to board the bus, and as the coaches, trainers, and players
followed, I noticed it was not going to be a normal pregame bus
ride. Everyone was talking and smiling, which is not the norm.
Usually it is quiet as everyone anticipates the task at hand—
especially the difficult task of winning a deciding game five
on the road. I interpreted the relaxed atmosphere as a feeling
of accomplishment and relief that we had pushed the heavily
favored SuperSonics this far.

The last player to enter the bus was our star forward,

LaPhonso Ellis, one of the finest men I have ever met and a truly strong Christian example. He also had one of the most intense "game faces" I have ever seen and an ability to focus like few men I have ever known. As he climbed the stairs onto the bus, he caught my eye immediately, and I stayed fixed on him as he began to slowly walk down the bus aisle and touch the shoulders of each of his teammates and ask them the question, "Do you believe that we're going to make history tonight?" It took a few minutes for the players to understand what Phonz was up to. Eventually, each man looked him in the eyes, sensed the seriousness of the question, and then responded by saying, "Yes, I do."

By the time he had talked to all eleven of his teammates, the bus was very quiet. *Everything* had changed. Because of that one player, LaPhonso Ellis, our attitude was no longer one of elation to be back in Seattle for game five, but one of determination to make history by winning the game.

Over and over that night, our team faced adversity. Our coach would rally his players, lift their attitudes above the roar of the home crowd, and get them refocused on the task at hand. Phonz continued to push his team to believe they would do it. The SuperSonics rallied near the end of regulation time and tied the score. In overtime, however, the Nuggets won 98–94 to make NBA history.

Oftentimes, it only takes one individual to lift an entire group of people. One person's attitude can make all the difference. The Bible teaches, "Your attitude should be the same as that of Christ Jesus" (Philippians 2:5). We can *think* like Jesus. We can have His attitude—toward situations, people, problems, and opportunities.

I learned many years ago that thoughts lead to actions, and actions become habits. The habits we live out in our daily lives help to shape our character, and our character ultimately determines our destiny. Our thought-life becomes all-important as to who we are and who we become as God's people. The protective shield of a positive attitude can lead us to fulfilling lives as God's people. We are to be salt and light to this world (see Matthew 5:13–14). We are to be encouragers and lifters of people who are hurting. How can we do that if our attitudes are not right? The answer is, we can't.

The Seattle Supersonics probably never knew it, but the minute Phonz stepped on that bus, the Nuggets as a team changed their attitudes and had taken the first step toward victory. I'll never forget LaPhonso's impact on that team as he individually helped his teammates to mentally prepare themselves for the game with positive attitudes. One man and simple words of encouragement can make all the difference in the world.

You can have that same kind of impact in your sphere of influence. Just be humble, have the mind of Christ, and take your first step toward victory.

Bo Mitchell

17. The Coach of the Worst Team in Florida

But thanks be to God! He gives us the victory through our Lord Jesus Christ.
1 Corinthians 15:57

Dwight Thomas is a recruiting specialist at Levi, Ray & Shoup, Inc. who provides recruiting information to football programs across the United States. But for three decades, he was Coach Dwight Thomas, one of the most renowned high school football coaches in the state of Florida. Coach Thomas won two state titles at Escambia High School in Pensacola and sent thirty-five young men on to play college football.

Before coming to Escambia, Thomas coached football at

Choctawatchee High in Fort Walton Beach. In his four sea-sons at Choctawatchee, he had coached the team to a 30–12 record and was about to embark on his fifth season with fifteen returning starters plus a kicker ranked number one in the state. But before the start of the season, the Choctawatchee principal called Thomas in and told him that since he had not won a state championship during his first four years at the school, he was out of a job.

Thomas replied that he was going to get a job coaching the worst team in Florida—then he'd bring that team to Choctawatchee High and make the principal eat his words. A few days later, Thomas signed on as coach of the Escambia High Gators—a team that had not had a winning season in twenty-one years. In fact, the Gators' combined record for the previous three years was a dismal three wins and twenty-seven losses.

When Coach Thomas took over the team, he began by laying down three simple rules: "Be where you're supposed to be, doing what you're supposed to be doing, when you're supposed to be doing it." He set forth a penalty that was every bit as simple as the rules. "If they break a rule," he said, "I don't run 'em and I don't whip 'em. I just toss 'em [off the team]—that day. And they know that they're gone so I can save the other kids. I love 'em enough to chase 'em off."

The theme of that first season was discipline—tough, hard-nosed discipline. He began the season with thirty-eight seniors and ended with four. His critics called him "Gestapo" or "Dwight the Barbarian." But the Gators went 7–3 that season—and even his critics couldn't argue with that kind of turnaround.

That first season was also when Dwight Thomas discovered that he had a freshman running back with amazing potential—a guy named Emmitt Smith. The following year, the Escambia Gators won a state title. And they repeated that feat the year after that.

Coach Thomas sees the coach's role as one of building young

people's bodies, minds, and souls. "We lose so many kids over the summer that run with the wrong crowd," he says. "How we raise these kids affects how they'll raise their kids. It's where discipline and character are taught. Christ strove to teach those qualities, and when His people got them, He stepped back and watched them work. That's what coaches do. We step back on Friday night and watch them work."

Discipline enabled Dwight Thomas to take charge of the worst high school football program in the state and transform it into the best. But Coach Thomas doesn't teach discipline to his players merely to win games. He disciplines them so they will win the biggest game of all—the game of life.

JIM DENNEY

UNDERSTANDING

....

1. Tale of the Tapes

[Jesus said,] "Store up for yourselves treasures in heaven, where moths and vermin do not destroy, and where thieves do not break in and steal. For where your treasure is, there your heart will be also."

MATTHEW 6:20–21

During spring training in 1992, I was released by the Philadelphia Phillies organization as a player but was offered a coaching job in the minor leagues. They flew me home to discuss this with my wife. With no other offers to continue playing, I accepted the coaching position. Frustrated about not being able to play anymore, I was empty, wondering where my life would end up in professional sports.

Mike Lamitola, a college teammate of mine, had been talking to me about the Lord and how important He had become in his life. I thought he was nuts, because this was the same guy who in the past had gotten drunk with me as we hung out in bars and other questionable environments. Little did I know that Mike had begun to plant spiritual seeds in my life. That spring and summer, Happ Hudsons, a rehab trainer for the Phillies organization, began watering the seeds my college teammate had sown. Happ gave me cassette tapes from Pastor Bob Russell of Southeast Christian Church in Louisville, Kentucky. I threw the tapes in the trunk of my car with no intention of listening to them.

On November 2, 1992, I began listening to the series of tapes from the "What We Believe" class Pastor Russell taught new believers. That fall, the seeds Mike had sown and the water that was sprinkled by Happ gave birth to my Christian walk, and I became a born-again believer. Today I believe with all my heart that God took playing the game away from me and put the right people in my life. He called me out of darkness to His marvelous light.

I never made anywhere near the money that my close friends and teammates made, but I am spiritually rich and know that earthly riches would have ruined my life because I had no self-control. I was dead in my sins and spiritually lost. Today I am a sinner saved by grace, and God has taught me how to be a godly husband and father. He has also given me multiple opportunities to share His love.

During my travels, God has used me as an instrument to take His gospel to many. Sin still lingers and pulls at me, so when I fail at pleasing God, His abiding presence convicts my soul to repent daily in order to keep in close fellowship with my Lord. I do not have *religion*. I have a healthy relationship with the Lord, and He gives me access to come before His throne because of the substitutional death of Jesus, my Messiah, who has given me eternal life. It was nothing that I did but was totally orchestrated by God.

DANA BROWN

2. Give 'Em Heaven

"The LORD does not look at the things people look at. People look at the outward appearance, but the LORD looks at the heart."
1 SAMUEL 16:7

One of the best third basemen in baseball sat quietly sipping a cup of coffee in the cozy, home team locker room at Orlando's venerable Tinker Field, then the spring training base for the Minnesota Twins.

This was Easter morning 1989, a sunny and very special day in the life of Gary Gaetti. Knowing the significance of the day, a newspaper columnist pulled up a stool next to Gaetti's locker and launched what turned out to be a touching and insightful interview hours before his Twins would play an exhibition game against the Boston Red Sox.

This was Gary's "first" Easter—first since he became a born-again Christian a few months earlier. Normally a brash and jocular type, Gaetti's mood was serene and reflective as he discussed the impact of this special day in his life. During the half-hour exchange, Gaetti became dewy-eyed and had to pause a few times to gather his emotions.

He acknowledged both the inner peace he felt and the concerns of his teammates and coaches about how his baseball production might be affected by his ramped-up faith. Some of those in Twins uniforms rejoiced; some were penning his baseball obituary. When a star athlete finds Christ, too often teammates and coaches act as though he had a car wreck, not a spiritual uplifting. Gnarly, veteran baseball men often shift their chaw to the other cheek, shake their heads sadly, and more or less allow that God has gelded another one, plucked the spirit right out of another stallion athlete. Such were the mumbled laments of the Twins' manager, Tom Kelly, and a couple of the team's coaches. A couple of high-profile team-mates said they could only hope this wasn't the death of Gary's fiery, aggressive play.

"That's foolishness," Gaetti scoffed. "I'll still have my ups and downs and some days may seem like that. But, believe me, I still enjoy playing, and I get just as frustrated if things don't go like I want them to go. I want to win more than I ever did."

The concerns that surrounded him included that elusive and invaluable commodity known as clubhouse chemistry. As an All-Star, an eight-year major league veteran, and one of the true leaders for the Twins, Gary was a vital cog in team chemistry, which has been known to vanish almost overnight under the strain of "reborns" who become too evangelical with heathen teammates.

"It's tempting to tell some of these guys about Jesus," Gary said, "but I know it's a delicate situation. You have to be sensitive to others' needs. A lot of times, that straightforward approach is counterproductive—knowing inside that you'd like to shout and tell everybody about it. You have to let people approach you about it in a situation like baseball.

"Hey, I'm not ashamed of my Christian beliefs, and I'm not afraid to talk to anyone about it. I'd love for all of these guys to experience the inner peace I now feel."

He paused, misty-eyed, cleared his throat, and continued: "I'm not going to cram it down anyone's throat. But if the situation arises to share about Jesus, I'm not going to refrain from speaking about it—at the other guy's pace."

Gaetti insisted his new faith would be more of an asset than a detriment. In the first place, his abstinence from alcohol and tobacco—a byproduct of his Christian rebirth—would only help him physically. "Obviously, I did okay before," nodded the guy who had belted ninety-one homers over the previous three seasons. "But I don't feel what I was doing with my body was enhancing my performance. Who knows? Maybe this won't improve my performance. But it certainly isn't going to hinder it. My natural ability is still there. Why would that all of a sudden leave my body?"

Obviously, it didn't. Gaetti's major league career would stretch for another dozen years, and his numbers remained strong right into his late thirties. He would win his fourth Golden Glove award that summer as a newborn. Seven times in the years after he became a believer, Gary hit better than his career .255 batting average, and his personal season high of thirty-five homers would come six years later, when he played for the Kansas City Royals.

Clearly, God didn't geld this stallion.

Still important, he said, was the continued, positive interaction with teammates when in uniform. Out of uniform, he admitted there would be some differences. For one, for the first time in five years, he would no longer room with fellow Twins star Ken Hrbek on road trips. "I'm going to need Bible time," Gary explained. "And that has no reflection on Ken or our relationship. It has only to do with my own personal feelings."

Hrbek had been kidding Gaetti about his new spirituality—a good sign. An absence of needling in a baseball locker room is the first sure sign of a player gulf. Gaetti had worn a turtleneck shirt to Tinker Field a couple of days earlier, and Hrbek added a piece of tape to make it look like a priest's collar. Gary wore it and laughed. Hrbek and other players laughed with him.

Gary laughed again as he told the story that morning. Easter morning.

"Today is a very, very special day," he said. "I don't know if it's symbolic with today and what I feel inside. It's just like a new start and new victory. The thing that happened on this day that we're celebrating is the basis of the entire belief. I just have a good feeling of victory and peace and love. Today is just special."

The newspaper columnist stood and explained that he typically concluded interviews with athletes by adding a well-wishing, "Give 'em hell!" But he amended that practice for Gary by urging him to "Give 'em heaven!"

Gary Gaetti nodded approval and parted his face in a wide smile. A glowing smile.

LARRY GUEST

3. A Left-Handed Compliment

> *"Blessed is the one who trusts in the*
> *LORD, whose confidence is in him."*
> JEREMIAH 17:7

In 1957, my Dad transferred with IBM from a very small town in New York to Lexington, Kentucky. I was fifteen at the time and my sports experience in that small town consisted of Little League baseball and Catholic Youth Organization basketball. Mostly we did Huck Finn adventures along the Hudson River.

Moving to Lexington was like moving to a "big city," and my new school of sixteen hundred students was quite a change. But the real surprise came when the first day of basketball tryouts arrived and 120 young men showed up to make the team. Fortunately for me, the school (Lafayette) had one of the best coaches in the state, Ralph Carlisle, and he was the kind of coach who was feared and worshiped at the same time.

On this first day of practice, Coach Carlisle gathered the 120 prospects around him and proceeded to show us the proper way to make a layup. He explained that he wanted us to approach the basket at a 45-degree angle, to use the backboard, to jump straight up, and to use the right hand on the right side and left hand on the left side. At that point, I got very nervous because I had never shot a left-hand layup in my life. He asked for volunteers to demonstrate the right-hand layup and chose a young man who demonstrated it very well.

On the left-hand layup, he decided not to ask for volunteers and instead pointed at me and said, "You, son, show us how." Of course I totally botched the demonstration and thoroughly embarrassed myself, but what was more frightening was that I thought I had ruined my chances to make the team. I was crushed, but I continued with the tryout.

The final hour of practice was devoted to tryout scrimmaging.

Coach Carlisle took his seat high up in the bleachers and settled in to evaluate the prospects. Very early in my first scrimmage game, I stole a wing pass entry on the left side of the court. As I dribbled down the left side, all I thought about was a left-hand layup on the left side, and that's what I tried. And try I did, but the missed layup hit the backboard so hard it almost went to half court.

Coach Carlisle came flying out of the bleachers, and I thought for sure he was going to throw me out right there. Instead, he shouted to the whole group, "That guy is going to be a player. He's going to be a basketball player, and you know why?"

Of course, no one could answer because I just blew an easy layup. He said, "He is going to be a basketball player because he listens and follows instructions." I went from feeling six inches tall to feeling ten feet tall.

I will always remember that day as one of my many basketball highlights and a great life lesson.

The spiritual application to my story is this: sometimes God requires us to do things that we perceive to be impossible, or, at the very least, challenging. Our divine Coach will empower us to do all that He asks as we daily submit ourselves to His desires for our lives. God's approval is so much better than any left-handed compliment.

JEFF MULLINS

4. Knowing How the Game Ends

*{Jesus said,} "I tell you very truly,
the one who believes has eternal life."*
JOHN 6:47

I believe that Christianity is relevant for the world of professional sports. Perhaps the church or religion or the code of ethics, or whatever a person might think Christianity is all about, does not directly relate to many problems of today. But to me, Christianity is Christ. And He is relevant. In many ways, He is meek and mild and sweet because He loves me. But He is also a friend I can count on in my world of ups and downs. Whether the Magic are winning or losing, whether the fans are happy or irate, my Christ remains constant. It moves me to think that Christ would have suffered and died for me even if I were the only person who ever lived. He loves me.

Many people think that the criminal or the addict would be the toughest type of person to reach with the love of God. But I tend to think otherwise. People like me, people who think they're all right and that they are doing God a favor by just being around, are the ones who just can't see God for who He is. The derelicts know what they are. They often see God. God had to come looking for me, because I sure didn't think I needed Him.

I was sure that becoming a Christian would mean giving up everything I enjoyed for a life of sacrifice and dullness. I fought and fought against letting go, giving up, and releasing the reins of my life to God. But when I finally trusted enough to take a step in His direction, I found that He cared more for me than I did. And I've never been the same.

I remember one night when I was still with the Bulls. The Chicago radio station was carrying the Bulls game live from Phoenix, but the local television station was to show a delayed telecast. I've never been able to listen to my own teams on the radio. It's too nerve-racking. For some reason, I feel less helpless if I can't see what's happening rather than just listening to the game on the radio.

So I left the radio off and then turned on the television until the news was off. I wanted to watch the delayed telecast of the game without knowing the outcome. Early in the second half, the game was very close and I was enjoying the tension. I found myself shouting and carrying on as I do with the home games, though I knew the game was already over and nothing I did was going to change the outcome. Then my secretary called. She was shouting and cheering, "Pat, we won! We won! The Bulls won!"

I would've rather seen it myself, but a strange thing happened to me as I watched the rest of that delayed telecast. The Bulls would take a five-point lead, and I would think, *Here's where they blow it wide open and walk away with it.* Then they would have some problems, and Phoenix (then coached by Cotton Fitzsimmons) would rally and go ahead by four or five. I would wonder, *How will the Bulls overtake them again?* But I sat there calmly. I wasn't worried. I knew the outcome. It was a sure thing. It was more like watching an opera than a noisy professional basketball game.

With a minute and a half to play in the last quarter, the Bulls blew a nine-point lead. The Phoenix crowd was in hysterics, stomping and shouting. With three seconds on the clock, the Suns trailed by one point and had the ball. They called a timeout and set up a play. Normally I would have been bouncing around on the edge of my seat, going crazy and screaming for the Bulls to stop the play—*Don't let them score!* But I knew the Suns weren't going to score. I sat chuckling. "Go ahead and shoot it up there," I shouted at the television. "I know it's not going in." The shot went up and bounced out. What a glorious feeling it was to know what was going to happen in that ball game.

I have that same feeling about the return of Christ.

Nothing compares with knowing, despite the personality clashes, the economy, the bigotry, and the shortages that the people who love Christ and have received God's gift of eternal life will be the ultimate winners. We can't lose. We trust in the power of the resurrected Christ. We go through life battling mortal problems and facing hardships and difficulties, yet we know that it will all be insignificant someday. If we have Christ, we know how the game ends—we win!

PAT WILLIAMS

5. God Knows the Score

"Be careful, and watch yourselves closely so that you do not forget the things your eyes have seen or let them fade from your heart as long as you live. Teach them to your children and to their children after them."
DEUTERONOMY 4:9

As a twenty-six-year-young head basketball coach at Iowa, I had a lot of confidence in myself—maybe too much. At the end of the first semester of the 1960–61 season, our team was ranked fifth in the country. We had the makings of a really good team. I was on top of the world. But then I found out at the semester break that four of my starting players were ineligible due to low academic performance.

My stomach dropped when I heard the news, as if I had been strapped in to one of those old roller coasters. I tried to put on a brave face for my team, saying, "We've just got to play our best, guys." But inside, I was frustrated, disappointed, and scared. Our first game of the semester, against Indiana, was one week away, and I was basically playing with a new team. We weren't that deep before, and now we were in serious trouble.

I'd like to think I was worried for my players, but I was young and worried mostly for myself. How humiliating would it be to get blown out? How would I recover from this? I was looking at the possibility of losing to Indiana by thirty points (my estimate).

I finally had to admit that I just couldn't handle this situation myself. I started to look inside myself that week as I prepared the team for Indiana. I told God I wasn't able to do this on my own. I said, "I need help." I wasn't asking Him for a win. I needed strength and—if He saw fit—to be spared a career-changing blowout.

That week I realized that my four replacements listened better than just about any players I had coached. My other players stepped up, too, as we centered our offensive strategy around Don Nelson (later a Hall of Fame coach and the winningest coach in NBA regular season history) and braced ourselves for whatever waited for us in Indiana. I just kept asking for help and admitted that I didn't have all of the answers. It was hard to admit, and harder to let go.

We showed up. We played. My players worked hard and exceeded all expectations. I tried to stay calm. With four minutes left in the game, I distinctly remember turning to Dick Schultz (my assistant, who later became executive director of the NCAA and subsequently the head of the United States Olympic Committee) and saying, "Don't tell me we have a chance to win this." We were up by eight. I can't describe my amazement and gratitude. When we won the game, I was completely stunned.

The rest of the semester went well for Iowa. The players all worked hard and played beyond their abilities. I learned that letting go and admitting, "I need help—I need God to help me handle this," is a powerful strategy for life. If we had lost that day in Indiana, my developing faith in God would have helped me through it. And when we won, by some kind of miracle, I realized that the real miracle here was how a young coach's spiritual journey can unfold while he's busy watching the score.

SHARM SCHEUERMAN

6. Crazy Jack Pitches Perseverance

Since the promise of entering his rest still stands, let us be careful that none of you be found to have fallen short of it.
HEBREWS 4:1

As a professional softball player, I have had to stand on many ball fields, unsure of what was going to happen next but prepared nonetheless to receive whatever came my way. How did I do that? By paying attention and simply keeping my glove open. I prepare for life in much the same way. I pay attention and keep my heart open, ready and able to receive God's gifts.

In 1985, I was just eighteen years old and beginning my second season with the Linden Majors, a women's semi-professional fast-pitch softball team out of Linden, New Jersey. My first year had been a tough one. As the youngest player in the league, I spent much of that first season trying to settle my nerves, contending with being on the road without my family, and proving to a very loyal fan base that I deserved to be there. As much fun as it had been, I was ready to put the "rookie" label behind me and get busy playing some serious ball.

It started almost immediately. I had remembered from the previous season that there was one particular fan who was more robust with his cheering than the others. He was loud, oftentimes inappropriate, and regularly got on a lot of people's nerves. He was annoying, impossible to ignore, and—according to most—crazy. In fact, that is what everyone called him: *Crazy Jack*. Unfamiliar with me my first year, he had pretty much left me alone. It was not a luxury he would afford me again. It started almost immediately.

After the first game of that second season—one in which he heckled me nonstop—Crazy Jack called out to me as I was walking toward the dugout: "Michele, Michele, come here. Michele come here. I need to tell you something. It's important!

Michele, here, here, I have something for you." I hesitated, uncertain of what to do. Finally, I decided to just get it over with and meandered over to Crazy Jack as my teammates laughed and implored me to "just ignore him." Why I didn't, I would not fully understand until some eleven years later.

As I tentatively approached Crazy Jack, he reached over the fence and thrust a small piece of paper toward me. "Michele, here I have something for you. I want you to take this word home with you and look up its meaning. I want you to remember that word, remember what it means and apply that word to everything you do in life. Michele, if you will do that, you will not only be a very successful pitcher, but you will be successful in everything you do in life. I promise."

I stood speechless, uncertain what to say. To my knowledge, those were the only sane, and certainly the only serious, words Jack had ever spoken. I just nodded, took the paper from his hand, and jogged back to the dugout.

Later that night, I remembered my strange encounter with Crazy Jack and wondered what he had actually given me. I dug around in my ball bag and came up with a small piece of paper torn from the back flap of a white envelope. On it, he had penciled the word *perseverance*. I just stared at it for the longest time, and then I decided to do what Jack had asked me to do. I looked it up. *Perseverance: to persevere; to keep trying, especially through difficult times; to never give up, no matter what.*

It was late. I needed to get to bed. So without giving it too much thought, I slipped the little symbol of inspiration into my right cleat. That is where it remained for the rest of the season. Before each game, just before I put on my cleats, I would pull the little paper out and read the word and repeat its meaning in my head much like a mantra. Eventually, by the end of the season, the word itself had faded, but I continued to keep the slip of paper in my cleat anyway. In fact, it was a ritual that I maintained throughout my long career as a professional softball player.

The following year, when I was the starting pitcher at Oklahoma State University, I was involved in a car accident that left my tricep torn from the bone and the end of my left elbow basically chopped off. The verdict from the doctors: I would most likely never pitch again. I was devastated. Eventually, as the shock began to wear off, I decided that I had two choices: give up or take the advice of an old acquaintance. . .and persevere. I chose the latter, and with the help of a very dedicated and talented rehabilitation department at OSU, I worked for almost a year to be able to at first just move my arm and, in time, to pitch again.

The day of my accident was July 21, 1986. The day I stepped out onto the field in Atlanta, Georgia, to play in the first-ever softball game in the Olympic Games was July 21, 1996—ten years to the day. I will never forget what went through my mind as I stood there on the mound, listening to the roaring cheers of thousands of fans and proudly wearing my USA jersey: Crazy Jack!

I have no doubt that Crazy Jack was my gift from God. God knew I would need help in the near future, and He sent it to me through a very unlikely source. You have heard it said time and again: God's greatest gifts sometimes come in the strangest packages. Be prepared. Pay attention. Keep your mind and your heart open and ready to receive whatever comes your way. Otherwise, you risk losing something much more important than a ball game. You risk losing the opportunity to catch the gifts and blessings that God is tossing your way.

WANDA ROWLAND
(As told by Michele Smith,
two-time US Olympic softball gold medalist)

7. I Know Who Holds My Future

*Because of the LORD's great love we are not
consumed, for his compassions never fail.*
LAMENTATIONS 3:22

I was cut from the National Football League three times. The first time I was sad, the second time I was mad, and the third time I was glad.

In September of 1982, I was a rookie with the Los Angeles Rams, sitting in a hotel room in Anaheim, California, on the day of the last cuts in the NFL. It was the day that every team in the league had to cut, release, or let go of about ten guys to get down to rosters of fifty-three players. I was one of nine defensive backs at the time, but the Rams would only keep eight.

I walked over to the team's facility. The strength coach looked at me and nodded for me to go see the general manager. I got cut. When you get cut, they tear up your contract. Since the contracts are not guaranteed, you do not get paid any more money after you are cut.

I remember lying in my hotel bed later that day and crying. I had worked for years for this opportunity, and just like that, it was gone. My situation seemed hopeless. Every other team in the league had just made their last cuts, so no one needed a defensive back. Even if they did need someone to play my position, they probably had a guy like me sitting in a nearby hotel—a guy who knew their playbook and could step right in and contribute. I called my agent, and he told me that no one was interested.

The only chance I had was for someone on the Rams to get hurt, someone specifically in my position. You never want to see someone get hurt, but that was the only way I would get an opportunity. Then, just when I didn't think things could get worse, they did. The entire league went on strike. No one was playing football.

During the seven-week strike, I worked out two or three times per day—and worried myself to death. I practically lived with a knot in my stomach for two months. I did not have God in my life at the time and felt like I was standing in sinking sand.

It was a sad and uncertain time in my life.

The strike ended and a player got hurt in the second week—not on the Rams but on the San Diego Chargers. I drove down to San Diego, tried out, and was signed to a contract to play.

God had come through.

Three years later, I was cut again. This time it was little different; it was due to the politics typical on every team. The cut came three weeks into the season, one day before I qualified for my NFL retirement benefits. My wife was seven months pregnant, and we had just bought a house. As you might expect, I was mad.

I felt like the general manager had a vendetta against me. I was the only guy backing up both defensive safeties on the team, and he timed it so I would not get my retirement. I sat home for five weeks watching them play without a backup for my position. Again, I did not get paid during that time.

Five weeks later, I was re-signed to the team and finished the season. God had come through once again, but I was still mad at what the general manager had done to me. The third cut came after my fourth year in the league, during the off-season. They called me into the office and told me that they were "moving in a different direction."

This situation was very different from the first two cuts, though. I was not sad or mad, but glad. I wasn't glad to be leaving the team. I was glad because I knew that God had my back, and I was glad to be in a position to be reassured of that.

I handed in my playbook. As I was walking out of the stadium, I saw the Chargers' head coach, Don Coryell. Coach Coryell is one of my favorite people in the world. He was always kind to all of his players, including me.

Even though I had just gotten fired and was the only one on the team to be losing my job, God had given me so much comfort that I was able to put my arm around Coach and pray for him. Under normal circumstances, this would have been a very low time for someone like me. I was losing my job, my dream job, and for the third time. But there wasn't anything normal about this situation. God had brought me from the University of New Haven, a Division III school that had never had a player reach the NFL. In the spring after my second season, He saved me from a cocaine addiction in one day and made it crystal clear that He had bigger plans for my life.

Because of such faithfulness on His part, I was not thinking about me when I saw Coach Coryell. God directed my heart toward blessing him for the opportunity he had given me. The only reason I was able to do that was because I had Jesus in my life and knew my future was secure.

Trust me, I had no idea what the future held, but I was glad I knew who held the future. I needed to get cut from the NFL three times to learn to trust God through thick and thin.

Today I pastor the Rock Church in San Diego, California, and I believe that God laid part of the foundation for that church through my experiences in the NFL.

You might be going through something now that you think is way too big for you to handle. It probably is, but it is not too big for God. Tell Jesus that you need His help. Cast your burden on Him and allow Him to guide you through your trial. It took me three times to learn that lesson. My prayer for you is that you get it right the first time.

MILES McPHERSON

8. Learning like a Child

Be on your guard; stand firm in the faith;
be courageous; be strong. Do everything in love.
1 CORINTHIANS 16:13–14

My father was a self-made man who was strong, proud, and boisterous—a typical alcoholic. He was a stern disciplinarian, and though I longed to be close to him, he continued to push me away.

When I gave my life to Christ, the chasm between Dad and me grew even deeper and wider. Shortly after my decision, Mom gave her heart to Christ, and Dad became more defiant and angrier than ever, calling us both weak and gullible. He couldn't accept our newfound faith in God. Mom and I tried to share our faith with him, but he had no interest in listening.

Several years before Dad died, he was in the hospital preparing for serious surgery. The doctors said we had a fifty-fifty chance of losing him. The thought that I might never see my father alive again weighed on my heart and spirit, and though I knew it was going to be tough, I had to talk to him about the Lord. I bent down beside his bed, and for the first time in our lives, we had a heart-to-heart talk. I tried to explain God's grace and forgiveness to him, to tell him what it means to be forgiven. I shared the essence of Ephesians 2:8–9 with him: "For it is by grace you have been saved, through faith—and this not from yourselves, it is the gift of God—not by works, so that no one can boast." Still, he couldn't seem to comprehend it.

"Wally, I'm not a bad person," he told me. "I've always tried to do my best to take care of Mom and the family." My heart sank. I knew he still didn't understand. As always, Dad was trusting in his own performance instead of God's forgiveness. Dad refused to let go of his preconceived ideas about God. He was convinced that if heaven did exist, the way to get there was to do the right things, to live a good life, to try to be honest—and then maybe God would accept you.

Thankfully, God gave us several more years with Dad. During his recovery, he was forced to stop drinking and chain-smoking, and I could tell he was becoming more receptive. He began to read some of the Christian books I had given him, and for the first time in his life he read from the Bible. Dad began to change, and I saw a new man starting to emerge. We knew he might not have long to live, and we prayed daily that before he died Dad would accept Christ and His forgiveness.

Then one night, just a few months before his death, Dad called me into his room to talk. He told me that Mom and he had attended a Billy Graham Crusade. Dad said to me humbly, "Billy said that when Christ enters your life, He takes the slate where He has been keeping a record of your sins and erases it. But not only that, He throws the slate away. Son, that's the kind of forgiveness I've needed."

I couldn't believe my ears. Dad had just explained the gospel to me. He went on to say that he had taken Mother's hand and had gone forward that night, giving his life to Christ by making a public confession of his faith. "Son," he said, "you don't have to worry about me anymore. I know where I'm going." It was one of the happiest days of my life.

Over the next few months, we watched Dad's health deteriorate—but his spirit soar. Every day brought a fresh discussion about his new faith. He was like a child again, learning and experiencing new and exciting things every day. The Bible tells us in 2 Corinthians 5:17, "Therefore, if anyone is in Christ, the new creation has come: The old has gone, the new is here!" That's exactly what I saw happening with my dad. He began treating Mom and others with a kind of love and respect I'd never seen from him before.

During Dad's last few months, he and I developed a closer relationship than we'd had during my entire childhood. My only wish was that he could live longer, giving us more time to share in his newfound faith.

As Dad's health worsened, the doctors were forced to admit him to the intensive care unit of the hospital. Even though he was weak, he continued to share Christ with every person he came into contact with—from the doctors to the nurses to the fellow patients on his ward. He never tired of talking about Jesus.

One evening, just a few weeks before Dad went to be with the Lord, I could tell he was in a lot of pain, so I asked if he wanted me to pray for him. He shook his head and said, "I'd like to sing a song." I was a bit taken aback, since I couldn't remember the last time I'd heard Dad sing. Then, in a small, almost childlike voice, he began singing "Jesus Loves Me." I wondered if this might be a song Dad once sang as a little child in Sunday school. I'll have to ask him the next time I see him—in heaven.

WALLY ARMSTRONG

9. Building on a Solid Foundation

It is God who works in you to will and to act in order to fulfill to his good purpose.
PHILIPPIANS 2:13

I first broke into the big leagues in 1993 with the Houston Astros. After that, I was with several teams, most notably the Detroit Tigers. In my sixteen years with eight different clubs, I was good and I was bad, I was an All-Star and was released—twice.

Up until 2003, my career had been chugging along. I had a lot of good times and some bad, but basically I was just a guy passing through the game of baseball. My life, my career, and, most of all, my relationship with my Savior, Jesus Christ, changed forever for the better in 2003.

I did well enough in 2002 for the Colorado Rockies for them to pick up my pretty big option for the 2003 season. The season began like many others—"just keep it in the middle of the road" until the weather warms up. During that season, that "middle of the road" never came.

Early in the campaign, I was asked a question about a moral issue in the big leagues. Since I hail from the "Bible Belt" in Georgia, I responded with a biblical perspective. I took a stand and was subsequently crushed by the fans and by the Rockies. It messed me up mentally.

I was never ashamed of what I said, but my statement was out and I owned it. I tried to put the matter behind me, but I found that I now had an eight-hundred-pound gorilla on my back. Even today there are still stories circulating on the Internet about how much of a bigot and narrow-minded redneck I was. People questioned how, in this day and age, I could be such a Neanderthal and morally intolerant of alternate lifestyles.

By the end of May that year, I was packing a "solid" 8.50 earned-run average. I had gone the entire month of May giving up runs in seventeen out of eighteen outings. I was demoted to being the long man in the bullpen. I had started out the season as the number one setup man, making $3 million to throw the eighth inning. I was now a team liability. I was more mentally fatigued than I had ever been in my career—and, believe me, it showed. I was released June 28 and was signed by the Boston Red Sox. I surrendered a heartbreaking game-winning home run to Aaron Boone in the 2003 American League Championship Series that put the Yankees in the World Series.

After suffering the playoff loss, I was convinced I was done. I had my ten years in, God had provided me a sufficient income to provide for my family, and I couldn't bear the thought of going through another emotionally draining experience like the

Aaron Boone disappointment. Apparently, the time had come for me to move on.

God, however, had other plans. When I got home, I learned of a child in my hometown of Pell City, Alabama, who was a freshman on the football team and had suffered a spinal cord injury. John Paul Montgomery was fifteen and paralyzed from the middle of his neck down. After learning of the boy's family situation and getting to know John Paul personally, something started to beat in my heart. I prayed about it all winter. God had laid a huge burden on my heart and on the heart of my wife, Michelle. I will forever be convinced that God instructed us to build a home for John Paul.

After God confirmed that He wanted Michelle and me to take action, I told the Montgomery family what was brewing. The home they were renting was a three-story house with no wheelchair access to anything but the bottom floor. The family living room was now John Paul's bedroom, and it was a real challenge to get him in and out of the bathroom.

So I decided we would start a fund to pay for a brand-new wheelchair-accessible house for the Montgomerys. The response of Pell City residents to our dream was nothing short of thrilling. People from Pell City donated the land and about half the funds we needed for the house. People from around the nation send donations, too. We even received letters from inmates in prison who had heard about what we were doing and sent several dollars. A check for $5,000 came from a man I had never met. It was truly supernatural how God had worked and used His "helpers" to make the home a reality. God led me to play in the 2004 season and to use a portion of my salary to pay for the rest of the John Paul Montgomery house. God blessed His project and, in turn, brought great blessings to Michelle and me.

My career lasted another four years, and I got to pitch in the 2006 World Series with the Detroit Tigers. Over my career, I notched 319 saves. God proved to me that I should stand up for what I believe, even if I get knocked down for it, and that it's not okay to sit and stew and not get back up. God wants us as Christians to take up His cross daily and fight on. Be certain that there are going to be tough times, but also be certain that in those times God can reveal Himself in supernatural ways. God wants us to depend on Him every day. We can do that by getting to know Jesus and then making Him known.

After enduring the issues of 2003, I wouldn't change one thing about how it all shook out. I was tested so much during my trials, but I'm way better for it. The New Testament book of James instructs us that we are to count it all joy as we endure trials. Glorify God in your daily life and He will never leave you or forsake you.

TODD JONES

10. A Busted Game Plan and God's Plan

Wait for the LORD; be strong and take heart and wait for the LORD.
PSALM 27:14

As a Division 1 football player and student athlete at Clemson University, I had a life that was as good as it gets. Up to this point, life had been easy. I was born into an All-American Christian family with two loving parents (Barry and Barbara Streeter), one older brother (Jason), and two younger sisters (Kelly and Lindsey). With my father as a head college football coach and mother a former member of the USA field hockey reserve team, athletics were always part of our family. My siblings and I were involved in a variety of sports, but I always dreamed of being a college quarterback.

Now my dream had come true. It was spring of 1998, and

after three years of waiting, I had officially been named Clemson's starting quarterback. I gave my all at every practice to prove I was the right guy for the job, but it was in one of those practices that I faced my first major setback. Getting hit by two defensive players at once resulted in a dislocated ankle and broken leg. I pushed myself through the grueling rehab sessions that spring and summer to make sure I got back for the season. Through this setback, I found myself praying constantly for God to heal me and assist me in making my dream come true.

Fortunately, I started that fall season healthy and was able to remain injury-free for the rest of the year. Looking forward to my senior season as a player was an exciting time for me. I had prepared for many years to get to this point in my football career. Not only was this my final year of playing at the college level, but my team also honored me, naming me team captain. It seemed everything was starting to fall into place. I was on cloud nine, to say the least.

We were four games into the 1999 season when setback number two took place. Once again, injury halted my progress and success. We were playing the University of North Carolina, and on one play I scrambled out of the pocket and was hit by a linebacker. I heard a loud crack in my right shoulder. I knew something was wrong. The hit broke the collar bone of my throwing shoulder, and I was told I would be out for the rest of the season. I was frustrated but determined not to let my senior year come to an end so soon. I pushed through treatments and rehab and found myself back on the playing field in four weeks. The trainers and coaches were amazed at the quick recovery.

I soon got back into the routine of being a starting quarterback again. My third game back, we were in Atlanta playing Georgia Tech. Things were going well. Clemson was leading, and I was feeling more and more comfortable with each throw with my recovered shoulder. But the injury bug bit me again. This time I was hit, and as I fell to the ground to brace myself, another defensive player landed on me. I suffered a dislocated hip, which turned out to be the most painful of all the injuries.

Trainers and doctors were not able to get it back into place on the field, so one long ambulance ride and one epidural later, my hip was back into place. Severe damage was done to my hip joint. The doctors told me my senior year was over and to move on with my life. I was devastated. We still had one more regular season game and a bowl game to play. I could not go out of my senior year on the sidelines.

Once again, I began the hard road of rehab and praying that God would heal me quickly. And once again, the medical personnel were shocked by my recovery. Within three weeks, I was able to come back and start in our bowl game, the Chick-fil-A Bowl. This opportunity was well worth the frustrating year I had as a player. It helped write the final chapter of my college playing career by allowing me to experience this bowl opportunity.

Throughout my career as a football player at Clemson, I went through several adverse times that really tested my faith. I would often ask the questions, "Why me? What did I do to deserve these setbacks?"

But I learned so much from going through it all. I learned how to be patient. Being patient with God's plan for my life was difficult for me at that time. I wanted it to be *my* plan and *my* timing. I also learned how to persevere. No matter what the setback, I had to keep my focus on getting back on track. I was forced to work hard and do whatever it took to get back on the playing field.

These trying times forced me to be dependent on my prayer life. I learned that prayer is very powerful and comforting. I found myself dealing with injuries way too often, but I often stunned the medical staff by how fast I could come back. I firmly believe that the power of prayer was an integral part of my speedy recoveries.

Finally, I believe that God allowed these things to happen

so I would be prepared for the toughest test of my life. In the summer of 2004 my mother, Barbara Hall Streeter, was diagnosed with pancreatic cancer. The chances of beating this type of cancer are very slim. My mother fought this horrible disease for a year and a half before she died in February 2006. This was the toughest experience I had ever gone through.

Again, I found myself asking, "Why?" Why would God allow this to happen to such a great Christian woman? Why would He choose to hurt such a strong, closely knit family like ours? I really believe that the adversity I went through in college helped prepare me for this challenge. I had to stay strong and trust God. I had to trust that He was doing this to somehow glorify His kingdom.

When we attended the funeral, I realized how many people loved my mother. She had impacted so many people in her life, and her influence continued at her funeral. That day our family was able to witness to thousands of people to the glory of God. I thank God every day for the mom I had and for the family I am a part of.

Throughout these experiences, I found myself trusting God more and more in my life. I trusted that He would take care of my everyday needs, and I learned that He has the perfect plan for my life. Through all the patience, perseverance, and prayer, God has molded me to trust in His plan for my life. Through these experiences, I have been able to keep my life in perspective and prioritize the important things. God's plan, not my plan, is the best plan for my life.

BRANDON STREETER

11. God Is with Us in the "Ifs" of Life

*No temptation has overtaken you except what is common
to mankind. And God is faithful; he will not let you be
tempted beyond what you can bear. But when you are tempted,
he will also provide a way out so that you can endure it.*

1 CORINTHIANS 10:13

I often wonder how coaches maintain a positive outlook when their team has more losses than victories in a season. When I was in high school, our football team rarely lost a game. We were part of a winning tradition. History was made recently when my old high school football team lost its first conference after a winning streak that dated back to the early 1980s. My old high school football team had won more than 150 conference games in a row—until the 2009 season. My experience in playing for Penn High School (Indiana) was always positive. So today when I work with teams that are struggling to win, I sometimes feel helpless and wish I could hand them the secret to having more wins than losses. But the reality of life is that we must all endure losses and disappointment, on and off the field.

In times of question, discouragement, and defeat, how do you maintain a positive outlook? When nothing seems to go right for you, even when you are doing all the right things, do you still have confidence to keep going? If you knew beyond a shadow of a doubt that God is with you today, walking by your side every step, hearing every word, directing every conversation, and seeing what you see. . .how would that change you?

If you were going to work today and you knew God was standing next to you in every circumstance, would you be more confident? If you lost your job today and you knew God was standing next to you in this moment, would you still have peace? If you were to be injured today at practice and would have to miss the rest of the season and you knew God is standing next to you, how would that change your outlook on your injury and the rest of the season?

While reading in Genesis 37 one time, I was reminded of all the disappointment, pain, unfair treatment, and discouragement Joseph faced in his life. Here we find a seventeen-year-old boy who seemed pretty special, according to his father. His brothers, however, hated him. They abused him, tossed him into a deep pit, and later sold him into slavery. Later, in Genesis 39, we read that Joseph served as a slave for Potiphar. While serving as a slave, Joseph was put in a position of high temptation by Potiphar's wife. He was then falsely accused of rape and tossed in prison. In prison, he thought he found a way out but was forgotten when the cupbearer was released.

Yet, as we read further, the scriptures relate, "The LORD was with Joseph." Yes! In those moments, God never left his side. In those anxious times of pain, slavery, temptation, imprisonment, and loneliness, Joseph maintained his integrity. He did not waver or take these miserable circumstances and use them as an excuse to abandon God. Why? Because the Lord was with him.

What does that mean for us? Even when there are no signs of blessings on the horizon, we must learn to trust in God's promises and not focus on our pain and problems. Because God is faithful, we can make great choices, remain confident, find hope, and remain faithful in the midst of our circumstances. We may doubt that truth because it doesn't always feel like God is here. But the truth is clear—God is with us!

How will you live today, knowing that God is with you?

REX STUMP

12. Winning on Empty

Consequently, faith comes from hearing the message,
and the message is heard through the word about Christ.
ROMANS 10:17

My first introduction to the Lord Jesus Christ was an interesting one. It was back in 1976, when I was in Montreal with Team USA, preparing for the Olympics. My team's coach, Billie Moore, was the Hall of Fame coach from UCLA. I can remember her sitting in the locker room with us and telling us that this moment, when we got to play for the silver medal, was going to change our lives.

Here I was, this little, poor Jewish kid from a one-parent family in New York City, and I really didn't have a lot of direction—except the direction the basketball was bouncing. That was my confidence, my self-esteem, and my identity. I was a high school senior and the youngest player on the team (or in Olympic basketball history, for that matter), and my coach was telling me that my life was about to be changed—by a basketball game.

The USA went out and beat Czechoslovakia to win the Olympic silver medal. After we received our medals, we went back to the Olympic Village. I remember sitting in my room feeling completely numb. I was waiting for that feeling my coach told me I was going to feel, but it wouldn't come. I started to cry because I was feeling empty, because the experience didn't meet my expectation. One of my older Christian teammates, Nancy Dunkle, asked me what was wrong.

I looked at her and said, "Nancy, I thought winning was going to change our lives, that it was going to be a different feeling, and it's not."

Nancy left the room and came back with her Bible. At first I didn't know it was a Bible, and I asked her if it was like a playbook. Nancy explained, "This is about the Lord." I read some chapters and asked Nancy who Jesus was. She told me He is Jesus Christ, our Lord and our Savior. I asked her more questions about Jesus and what He could do for me, and my teammate walked me through it all. I was nervous about these new revelations and didn't know if I could accept the Bible's teachings.

Nancy planted that seed in me. I knew I needed some authority and direction, which I wasn't getting in my home life. I was achieving a lot of success at a young age, but it was when I went to Old Dominion University in my freshman year that Athletes in Action (AIA) paid a visit to the campus. I remember going to the ODU field house and sitting in the stands and seeing the AIA team practicing. Ralph Drollinger, who is most famous for being Bill Walton's backup at UCLA, was with AIA, and when he saw me watching him, he motioned for me to come over. We started talking, and I told about him my situation, explaining how Nancy Dunkle had shown me scriptures and introduced me to Jesus but that I never accepted Jesus as my Savior. I also told him I was Jewish.

Ralph walked me through the plan of salvation, and he offered to pray with me. "You can accept Jesus to be your Lord and Savior," he explained, "and He offers eternal life to those who trust in Him." He told me how God gave His only Son, Jesus, to die on the cross for our sins and how He rose from the dead on the third day.

From age eighteen to where I am today, receiving Christ as my Savior is the single most important thing that has ever happened to me. As a follower of Jesus, I have learned to love and have passion, to surrender and to put people first while living a life of integrity and character.

As an athlete who has been touched by God, I am really thankful for that moment when Nancy Dunkle introduced me to Christ and when Ralph Drollinger "filled in the blanks" and answered my questions about receiving Christ as my Savior. I am continually thankful for that moment in Montreal when I was feeling empty, because winning a silver medal did not meet my expectations. I'm grateful because it allowed me to turn to someone who could exceed my expectations—and that someone is Jesus Christ.

NANCY LIEBERMAN

13. Ah, the Gift of Pain

Now I want you to know, brothers and sisters, that what has happened to me has actually served to advance the gospel.
PHILIPPIANS 1:12

During my last years of high school and first year of college, I was a runner. No, not a marathoner, but a prodigal. I was mad at God. I could not fight Him, so I fought my parents. All the while, I knew I was wrong and stupid, but I couldn't change. But while I was playing an intramural basketball game at my university, everything changed. The game was between the top two teams on campus, so the winner would win the championship that year.

Before the game, a friend invited me to go to a Bible study with him. I reluctantly went, but I didn't hear a thing the preacher said. However, a thought flashed across my mind: *What if I get hurt tonight?* I dismissed it immediately, thinking, *I've played sports since I was young and I've never been hurt, so why would it happen tonight?*

Less than two minutes into the game, I went up for a rebound and came down on the side of another player's foot. My ankle rolled out with the full weight of my body coming down on top of it. I will never forget the sound—it was like something popping and tearing at the same time.

What followed was the most incredible pain I have ever felt. I was lying on the court under the basket with players all around me, but I couldn't do a thing. Finally, I gathered myself enough to crawl off the court underneath the basket. A couple of trainers who were there came and carried me out. When they saw the size of my swollen ankle, they took me straight to the emergency room of our local hospital. When the ER doctor saw me, he told me it was too serious for him to treat and I would need to go to a specialist in Little Rock, Arkansas, the next day. He scheduled the appointment and sent me to my dorm with pain medications and a simple, "Good luck, son! You are going to need it!"

That night was a defining moment in my life. I spent the night in agonizing pain, staring at the ceiling and asking God, "What do You want with me? Why did You do this to me?"

At some point, my roommate turned on some music to try to help me relax. All I remember is this line in a song: "Sometimes we have to be knocked down to make us look up. I was looking up when His light shined on me!" I know now that was God speaking. Not only did He speak through the song, but He answered my question later in the night.

When I asked, "What do You want with me?" I heard Him say, "I just want to love you! When are you going to stop running?"

The next few weeks found me back at my parents' house because I couldn't do the rehab and stay at school. But home was different this time. I didn't fight my parents; I couldn't. I was broken. I attended a worship service one night with my mom, and the preacher told the crowd to turn to the one next to them and tell them, "I love you!" I hadn't told my mom that in years. But I knew I had to do it. Something in me would not let me avoid it, as awkward as it was. When I turned and began to speak, nothing came out but the sound of me sobbing and the rush of tears. It was as if all the anger and bitterness from the past few years came pouring out of me. I couldn't stop crying and really didn't want to because I felt such release. I wanted it all out.

My life was never the same after that. Apart from my salvation as a child, I have never had a more life-changing season in my life—and it came through pain. Dr. Paul Brand calls pain, "The gift nobody wants." That night it really was a gift. It saved my life.

DAVID UTH

14. How to Practice Not Quitting

> *I have fought a good fight, I have*
> *finished the race, I have kept the faith.*
> 2 TIMOTHY 4:7

"I quit!" I announced to my family. It was just weeks after our high school cheerleading squad had placed second in a city-wide competition we had worked so hard to win. We had practiced for months, putting in plenty of overtime—jumping, getting our stunts down pat, perfecting our dance moves. When the big day arrived, our routine went flawlessly. That is, until the final stunt—when one of the girls lost her footing and we faltered. So I decided cheerleading wasn't the life for me. I threw in my pom-poms.

It wasn't the first time I'd quit—nor would it be the last. It's not that there's any disgrace in winning a silver medal. It's just that I was impatient. If I couldn't be number one, it must not be what I was supposed to be doing, I reasoned.

Like the time I was sure I'd be the next Mary Lou Retton, winning gold in the 1992 Olympics. From the first time I put on my brand-new purple and gray leotard, the one with long sleeves for competition, it was all I could think of. But in competition after competition when the judges' scores were revealed, I found myself on the second tier of the medal stand holding a silver medal—second place. At the age of twelve, I'd decided gymnastics must not be for me. I quit.

Four years after the cheerleading debacle, I was a junior in college. On a whim, I decided to enter the Miss University of Florida pageant. To my great surprise—I won. It qualified me to compete in the Miss Florida pageant later that summer. Look out world, Karyn Williams was coming through: two-a-day workouts, a strict diet, and daily singing practice with a professional vocal coach. Nothing was going to stop me now.

By the final night of competition, I was considered the favorite to win. That is, until the last round of questions, when a totally unexpected curveball was thrown my way. When the winners were announced, I heard my name called as first runner-up. Second place, again.

"Karyn, you came so close," my dad said. "Don't give up! Try again next year." But my mind was made up. No more pageants for me. I quit.

Just one year later, I found myself sitting on the bleachers at the Chicago Marathon, grinning as my then fifty-eight-year-old dad came trotting across the finish line. He was limping and exhausted, but the exhilaration on his face said, "This is for me!" I knew I wanted it, too. So I registered for my first marathon.

In the spring of 2003, Dad asked if I'd join him in running the Boston Marathon. "Sure, Dad!" I said. But I had no idea what I had just signed up for. When the big day came, I was a ball of energy, at least for the first half of the race. When I saw that Dad was dragging a bit, I did my best to stay energetic and keep his spirits up. Halfway through the race, at mile 13, we stopped for a bathroom break. I cramped up. . .bad.

The rest of the race became the longest two hours of my life. As we trekked up the aptly named "Heartbreak Hill," I looked over at my Dad. Fighting back tears, I cried, "Why are we doing this? Have we lost our minds?" I was sure it would be the last marathon for me. In that moment, I could hardly wait to say it again: "I quit!"

And then Dad said something that afternoon that literally changed my life. "You know why I do marathons, Karyn?" he said. "I do them because it's the best way I know how to practice 'not quitting.'"

Wow! What a lightbulb moment! Have you ever thought about practicing your "not quitting" skills? I certainly never had.

What I had failed to see until that day was that life is all about preparation. How can we possibly win if we quit before we've even gotten started? We need to see that every experience we have—all the practice and training—is part of the process. It's what we've been put here to do.

We were created by a great God to do great things. It is in times of crisis or disappointment that we most want to quit. It's human instinct to walk away when things get hard. But the Bible says, "at the proper time, we will reap a harvest if we do not give up" (Galatians 6:9).

Running with perseverance is what's most important. What is perseverance? It's not giving up. It's what my dad was talking about. It's the fine art of "not quitting."

It took me awhile to get this lesson. But nine marathons later, whenever that medal is placed around my neck at the finish line, I don't care whether it's silver, gold, or cheap plastic. It is a symbol of not giving up—of finishing what I started.

Now, as I am building a career in the music industry, my dad's advice has become my life motto: It may take me awhile to get to the top, but I will work the hardest and persevere the longest. And for those waiting in line to take my place— wear comfortable shoes, because it's going to be a long wait. I won't quit!

KARYN WILLIAMS

MEDITATING

....

1. These Two Will Bowl You Over

Be on your guard; stand firm in the faith;
be courageous; be strong.
1 CORINTHIANS 16:13

Clips from the 2009 Super Bowl between the Arizona Cardinals and the Pittsburgh Steelers will be replayed for years to come. One play in particular is a classic: Steelers wide receiver Santonio Holmes's touchdown reception with thirty-five seconds remaining in the game.

Watching that play, I observed two things with great spiritual application:

First, in the play preceding the famous catch, Santonio dropped a pass. He failed on one play, yet Steelers quarterback Ben Roethlisberger called his number again.

Most of us on God's team have dropped the ball and failed to live up to His standards. Yet God in His grace calls our name again, giving us a new opportunity to score for His kingdom.

Second, the winning catch involved two simultaneous realities. While the quarterback threw the ball high so the opposing team couldn't get it, Santonio reached high above the defenders to make the catch. Of equal importance is that he kept his feet planted on the ground. If both feet had not been inbounds when he made the catch, the Steelers would not have won the game—no matter how spectacular the catch.

Christians also must simultaneously live in two realities. God calls us to look to heaven for direction while keeping our feet firmly planted in history. If we reach for heaven without our feet on the ground, we risk turning people off rather than turning them on to God. But if we are grounded on earth but drop the ball spiritually, we face losing our effectiveness for God's kingdom.

Speaking of bowls, I was raised in Maryland, one of the few Eastern states that still offered duckpin bowling during that time. Duckpin bowling is similar to regular bowling, except that the balls are only about five inches in diameter and the pins are only nine to ten inches tall. The alley itself is basically the same as the typical bowling alley.

In those days, the automatic pin-setting machines were not as reliable as they are today and would often miss a pin or two when they reset the pins. So there was always a guy in the background, sitting on a high bench built into the wall behind the lane, and he would hop down and reset any pins the machine missed.

No one ever got to see his face. If your own brother worked there, you couldn't prove it from what you could observe…unless he wore neon shoes no one else could match. All anyone ever got to see from the front were legs, feet, and sometimes hands.

Many times God is like that. When the pins in your life are getting knocked down all over the landscape, you can't always see Him in the background. But He is still there, setting them back up so that you can roll again.

TONY EVANS

2. Huddle Up

Two are better than one, because they have a good return for
their labor: If either of them falls down, one can help the other
up. But pity anyone who falls and has no one to help them up.
ECCLESIASTES 4:9–10

I must admit, I am not a big pro football fan, but I do like to watch college football. The tailgating, the bands, the traditions, and the school spirit all add to an electrifying event.

Whether I am in the stands or sitting on my couch, after the players break from their huddle and head to their positions on the line, my stomach is tight with anticipation to see what they will accomplish on the next play.

Most football fans like the big plays, but have you ever thought much about the huddle and how important it is to the game of football? Where did the huddle come from? Well, it seems that it started with the Gallaudet University, a school for the deaf in Washington, D.C. The Gallaudet teams were not able to get off their plays because the other teams could see their signals. So to resolve that issue, the players made a tight circle so they could sign to each other in privacy.

The huddle is all about the players coming together for unity and for communicating their plans so that they can effectively run the next play. They do this in hopes of putting points on the board. But who are you huddling with in your own "game of life"?

Since 2004, I have been part of a group of six or seven guys who get together every Thursday at 6:30 a.m. for a time of prayer and accountability. It would be impossible for me to adequately share with you what an encouragement these men have been in my life. Even if I am on the road traveling for work, I can always count on at least one of them to call to check on me and to pray with me.

The apostle Paul had men in his life who were a great help

to him and the ministry God had called him to. He mentions a couple of them in this verse: "Only Luke is with me. Get Mark and bring him with you, because he is helpful to me in my ministry" (2 Timothy 4:11). What about you? Do you have someone in your life who is helpful to you?

The Bible talks about how the early believers had their own huddle going on: "They devoted themselves to the apostles' teaching and to fellowship, to the breaking of bread and to prayer" (Acts 2:42).

Meeting with other Christ-followers for teaching, fellowship, worship, and prayer is crucial. Some say they can worship God without attending a fellowship with other believers. Not so, I say. Could you have a football game without the huddle? You may run a few plays with your "hurry up" offense, but after the two plays are over, it's time to huddle up again so the team can progress.

It would be hard to compete in a football game without the huddle. This is true also with your life. So huddle up, and then put some points on the board. It all starts with joining God's team and then huddling with other "teammates" who will work with you and encourage you to run victoriously.

TODD SHAW

3. Managing the Clock

Be very careful, then, how you live—not as unwise but as wise, making the most of every opportunity, because the days are evil.
EPHESIANS 5:15–16

In football there are sequences. The quarterback relies on his offensive line to protect him. On the defensive side, the linemen must do their jobs in order for the linebackers to do theirs. A race car driver, likewise, depends on his crew chief, mechanics, and pit crew.

Life, I have come to realize, is a team sport here, too.

I remember how one morning during the early years of my success with the Redskins, I was sitting at the breakfast table the day after a big win, reading the sports page and feeling "very content" with myself. We were prepping for the divisional championship game in Dallas the next Sunday, and, of course, the papers were giving my ego a nice boost by reporting how smart I was. Who was I to argue against my own press clippings?

I was bouncing around the house, peacock proud, getting ready to go to the office, when my wife, Pat, said, "Would you mind picking up your bathrobe and socks?" (Isn't it great how God gives us the perfect wife to bring us back to earth?)

I picked up after myself as requested, but in the back of my mind I was thinking, *The nerve of her, coaxing and coaching a professional coach!*

Next, she started in on our sons and how I needed to get them to toe the line on some matters of discipline.

She obviously was not aware of all the *important things* I needed to do to get the team ready to face Dallas.

That's all I needed. I headed out the door, giving it an emphatic slam. (Listen, if you're a married guy, you know what I'm saying!)

I pray during my drive to work, and that morning was no exception. About halfway to the office, I awakened to what had just occurred. I reflected, "Is life just about winning football games, or is it about my kids and family?"

When I arrived at Redskins Park, I called home and told my wife, "What you're taking care of at home, with our two boys, is more important than what I'm taking care of at work." From that day forward, I began to focus on maintaining a healthy balance between my work and my family.

I've come to realize that, despite all the benefits that have come with my career—the championships, privileges, and honors—the most important thing that I am going to leave behind is the influence, good or bad, I've had on others— particularly on our two sons, their wives, and our grandkids.

Face it, friend. No matter what your job is, some days you get cheered, and the next day the same crowd is booing. An individual can be so focused on career success that before he knows it, years have flown by. He discovers that he has missed out on the most important things in life.

I can foresee a day when I'll be sitting in an old folks' home with a bunch of other chronologically gifted guys, and I'll be telling them, "I coached the Washington Redskins!" That's when they'll call the nurse and tell her, "Get this bozo a reality check. He thinks he coached the Washington Redskins."

Philippians 2:3–5 says, "Do nothing out of selfish ambition or vain conceit. Rather, in humility value others above yourselves, not looking to your own interests but each of you to the interests of others. In your relationships with one another, have the same mind-set as Christ Jesus."

For the Christian, life isn't all about our individual accomplishments and accolades. As the apostle Paul pointed out in the above passage, it's about what we do for others, about being like Jesus, who came to earth for one reason: to give.

JOE GIBBS

4. Double-Duty Dungy

*{Jesus said,}" "I have set you an example that you should do as I have done
for you. Very truly I tell you, no servant is greater than his master, nor is a
messenger greater than the one who sent him."*

JOHN 13:15–16

In the summer of 1996, the Tampa Bay Buccaneers were going
through a difficult stretch. This was an NFL team I had been
privileged to speak to on numerous occasions through the years,
and the invitation to speak before their first home game of the
year was exciting. This was a chance for me to meet the new
coach, Tony Dungy, who I had heard was a unique and respected
leader. It would also allow me to have a part in inspiring one of
my favorite teams to revive their spirits.

One of the first changes Coach Dungy made was to require
the team to stay at a team hotel rather than in their homes for
a home game and to move the chapel service to the same hotel
rather than the training facility. Since I had never been to that
hotel or met the coach, I made my way to the facility an hour
early and found the room I would be speaking in. Entering the
room, I greeted a casually dressed man arranging the chairs
and asked, "Is this the room where the Tampa Bay Bucs will
be meeting this morning?"

He nodded and answered, "I believe so." I didn't recognize
the man, nor was there anything noteworthy in his appearance
or speech to indicate that I should. As I left, I felt compelled
to go back and speak to him and thank him for the job he was
doing. He was such a kind guy, so I invited him to come back
later and meet a few of the players. I put out my hand and said,
"By the way, I'm Jay."

He shook my hand and replied, "I'm Tony." Pleasantries
ensued, and I was about to leave again when it hit me: "Excuse
me, are you Tony Dungy?"

"Yes, I am," he replied. Immediately, I started helping

with chairs and offered to take over the job, thinking such an important man shouldn't be setting up chairs. I will never forget that moment when he looked at me with a smile and said, "I appreciate that, Jay. I don't always get to do it, but when I can, I set up and pray over each chair where my players will be sitting. These young men, gifted as they are, are young and face great pressures and temptations. I try and take the time to pray for them, and coming in here to set up chairs affords me that opportunity."

That was my first encounter with the man who would turn out to be one of the most beloved and successful coaches in modern history. This very humble and gracious man allowed me an insight into his true character and to learn one of his life secrets: genuine concern for his players means leading through serving.

JAY STRACK

5. Does He Feel Our Pain?

> *"The LORD brings death and makes alive; he brings down to the grave and raises up."*
> 1 SAMUEL 2:6

It is hard to admit, but I struggled tremendously with my religious beliefs after my wife, Nellie, died. It was difficult to grasp how a benevolent God could have allowed her to suffer so much at the end, or how He could expect me to go on living without her. I have often found myself (and sometimes still find myself) questioning God when some kind of unspeakable tragedy occurs—an earthquake striking an impoverished area in Haiti or a hurricane destroying an orphanage in Central America.

How can God allow such things? The tragedy does not even have to be on such a large scale. I wrestle with the idea of how a loving God could let a teenager lose a limb in a car accident or a child to suffer from leukemia. The question of pain has always weighed heavily on my soul.

But losing Nellie was the worst for me, because it wasn't just that she was taken from me, it was that I had to watch her suffer first. I cried out to God again and again, asking how He could permit her to endure so much pain. What good could possibly come from that? How was it fair that a woman who had dedicated her life so fully to Him should have to meet such a difficult end? And, of course, what would I ever do without her in my life when he did finally take her home?

I never did receive direct answers to those questions. Sometimes they still beleaguer me. I feel that perhaps God means for me not to share my perfectly contented worldview, but rather to admit to my struggles so that others, too, can know that they are not alone with such questions. This is why the book of Job is contained within the Bible: so we can all learn from a righteous man who suffered the loss of his family, belongings, and health—and, though in his struggles he questioned God, he never cursed Him.

JOHN WOODEN

6. The Ring's the Thing?

> *Praise be to the God and Father of our Lord Jesus Christ!*
> *In his great mercy he has given us a new birth into a living*
> *hope through the resurrection of Jesus Christ from the dead.*
>
> 1 PETER 1:3

Every professional athlete begins the season hoping it culminates in a championship ring. Some know they don't have much of a chance, but when the games begin, all teams have the same record—no wins and no losses.

Winning the Super Bowl, a World Series, or an NBA championship is a daunting task. There are so many variables that go into garnering a ring. Team chemistry, injuries, illnesses, parity, and playoff pairings are but a few. The result: many of the greatest who ever played never won the coveted ultimate prize.

In baseball the list includes Ted Williams, Barry Bonds, Ken Griffey, Jr., Ty Cobb, and Ernie Banks. In football the notables include Dan Marino, Barry Sanders, Y.A. Tittle, Fran Tarkenton, Jim Kelly, Eric Dickerson, O.J. Simpson, and Gayle Sayers. In basketball the bigger names are Elgin Baylor, Karl Malone, John Stockton, Charles Barkley, Patrick Ewing, Dominique Wilkins, Reggie Miller, and Pete Maravich. These athletes are proof of how elusive championships really are.

Winning a ring means a team was the best, but it doesn't say much about the individual that owns it. A ring says the owner is a champion, but it's not really a statement of how great he or she is as a player. Actually, anyone can luck into one. If not for a basket by Boston's Don Nelson in the final seconds of game seven in the 1968–69 NBA finals, I would have won one. Had Nelson missed, the Lakers would have beaten the Celtics, and even though I never got off the pine and into any of the playoff games, I would have had a ring. But having one would not have made me a great player—just fortunate.

Becoming a champion and getting a ring is a big deal, but a

select few can look forward to something better. Given enough ability, desire and time without injury, the best might be selected to their respective sports Hall of Fame.

In terms of significance and importance, enshrinement in "The Hall" far exceeds a ring. "The Hall" is the ultimate statement of a player's lifework as an athlete. To be chosen by your peers, committee members, and sportswriters as one of the best to have ever played is the ultimate achievement in sports. Still, most players would rather have a ring.

People tend to live life the way the pros play ball. They seem to be more interested in rings than being enshrined in God's Hall of Fame. The importance of the here-and-now has replaced the importance of eternity.

That is one of the reasons I like the following so much:

God's Hall of Fame
ANONYMOUS
Your name may not appear down here in this world's Hall of Fame.

In fact, you may be so unknown that no one knows your name.

The All-Stars here may pass you by on neon lights of blue,

But if you love and serve the Lord, then I have good news for you.

This Hall of Fame is only good as long as time shall be,

But keep in mind God's Hall of Fame is for eternity.

To have your name inscribed up there is greater yet, by far,

Than all the halls of fame down here and every man-made star.

This crowd on earth may soon forget the heroes of the past.

They cheer like mad, until you fall and that's how long you last.

But, God... he never does forget, and in his Hall of
Fame,
By just believing in his Son, inscribed, you'll find
your name.
I tell you, friend, I wouldn't trade my name, however
small
Written there, beyond the stars in that celestial hall.
For any famous name on Earth or glory that they
share,
I'd rather be an unknown here and have my name up
there.

JAY CARTY

7. The Plan

I can do all this through him who gives me strength.
PHILIPPIANS 4:13

"I'm sorry to tell you this, Mrs. Manning, but your little girl has
spinal meningitis, and we have done all we know to do, but she
is not going to live."

My mother sat by my hospital bed at Charity Hospital in
Cleveland, Ohio, heartbroken and in shock. She did the only
thing she knew to do—pray. She made a bargain with God that
if He let me live, she would raise me up in the ways of the Lord
the best she knew how.

By morning, the doctors were astonished with their mis-
diagnosis and with my significant improvement and said that
I was doing 50 percent better. They told mom if I survived, I
would be "mentally retarded, and never capable of physically
doing what the normal child does." By this time, mother knew
God had another *plan* in store for my life. Just what the plan was

she did not know, but she knew it must be pretty special.

That is how my life started out in inner-city Cleveland. The attitudes of the people in the projects were quite depressing. The mind-set was, "You ain't nothin'...you ain't gonna ever be nothin' ...so don't even try!" That is literally how people lived. We were culturally diverse but with one thing in common: we were all poor. Some people were more hopeless than others—like my dad, who had given up and become a hopeless street drunk. My mother's hope was secured in her faith in Christ Jesus. She found her strength to survive in this environment by reaching out to her church family when things got tough.

I was a sickly little child who was a slow learner. I missed many days of school because of my anemia, which caused nausea, weakness, and loss of weight. Some students would make fun of me because I was so scrawny looking. I became introverted and extremely shy, even though I liked people. I did not know how to reach out to others. I struggled to keep up with the other students during our play at recess. Many times I would need to run away and hide to vomit, only to return as if nothing had happened so that the nurse would not send me home. Inadvertently, this was helping me to become an *overcomer*, which was part of the *plan*.

It was not until my freshman year in high school that I was discovered as an athlete, through the Physical Fitness Program in America. I scored as the highest physically fit female student in the school and began to set national standards. My gym teacher, Miss Maralyn West, requested that I go out for girls' sports.

My response was "Okay! Whatcha got?" She told me that our school had girls' volleyball, basketball, and track. I went out for all three, and *the plan* began to unfold. By the next year, we played for the state championship in basketball, were unbeatable in volleyball, and won the state championship for girls track and field (I think I had a lot to do with that outcome).

It was at the Track and Field State Championship that I

met Alex Ferenczy, the Hungarian-born coach for the women's track team in Cleveland. He spoke with Mom about working with me to try for a college track scholarship. That was all she needed to know. She was excited about the idea that I would have a chance to go to college. No one in our family had ever attained a college degree. God had kept His side of the bargain and saved my life. Mom had kept her side of the bargain by raising me up in the church and teaching me biblical principles.

Now the plan God had for my life was unfolding. I had accepted Jesus Christ as my Savior and Lord at the tender age of six, fully aware of what I was doing, and now my purpose for existing on this earth was being revealed. Little did I know that the plan included me becoming a four-time gold and silver Olympic medalist in track. By the time I was in my senior year of high school, I had become the first girl in the world to run the 440-yard dash in 55 seconds, and I also set a new world indoor record in the 880. I went on to receive a scholarship from Tennessee State University, where I joined the Tigerbelles, the legendary world record setters in women's track. I became the first and at present only American woman to win a gold medal in the women's 800-meter run, setting a world, Olympic, and American record. I also was the first American woman to break two minutes in the 800 meters, my best time being 1 minute 57.87 seconds, which is still considered world-class time.

My athletic platform has opened doors of opportunity for me worldwide to share my faith in Christ. As an ordained Christian minister, I have been a sports chaplain at the last six summer Olympic Games. I am a contemporary gospel recording artist and founder and president of two not-for-profit organizations: Ambassadorship, Inc., and the United States Council for Sports Chaplaincy (USCSC). I am fulfilling the plan through a master of divinity and doctoral degree at Oral Roberts University in Tulsa, Oklahoma. I am developing an educational program to prepare sports ministers for service in the sports community as professionally credentialed chaplains.

When this work is fulfilled, the purpose for the plan will have come to fruition. I thank God for His faithfulness in helping me carry out the plan He chose for my life.

MADELINE MANNING MIMS

8. The Coach's Playbook

Do your best to present yourself to God as one approved, a worker who does not need to be ashamed and who correctly handles the word of truth.
2 TIMOTHY 2:15

During my days as a college football coach, I would tell my athletes, "Men, believe me, when things seem the darkest, have faith in Jesus. No matter how impossible things look, don't ever give up."

To me, the number one thing is that all people are born with an innate hunger for God, and their lives are spent trying to fill this hunger. Some search for it all their lives. Some don't know how to find it.

In forty-plus years of coaching, I' learned one big fact of life: God doesn't want your *ability*, He wants your *availability*. He wants people who will say, "God, here I am. I'm making myself available to You. What do You want me to do?"

I never believed God was going to make us win, and I never prayed for that. We knew better than to pray for a win. We knew every coach in the country wanted to win. We knew that everybody wants to win, so we just asked God to give us wisdom in decisions we had to make.

All that has happened in my life has reaffirmed what I have always believed. . .and believe more than ever today: that God has a purpose for everyone. I believe that things that happen in a person's life are just rest stops along the highway as he or she travels to get where God wants him or her to be.

There are many scripture verses I wrote down in days of trouble. Every one of them is based on fear—*my* fear, fear of failure, which is the big thing that causes people not to try. I've always gotten strength from scriptures and prayer. I have a deep belief that God hears prayer.

I see miracles happen every day that a person without faith would never see. God is still performing miracles, and the thing that has had the greatest impact on me is watching a young man change from being out of the reach of God to being in His arms.

Jesus made the invisible visible. I've never seen God, but I know He is there. He's like the wind. I've never seen it, but I feel it and I've heard it.

The greatest story is this: God didn't just stick out His hand from heaven; He came down here in the person of Jesus Christ. Jesus says, "I am the way, I am the truth, I am the life. You're not going to get to the Father but through Me."

If you will put your faith in God through Jesus Christ and ask Him to lead you, He will bring you to the Father and make you right with Him. That's what He did in my life. People think God's not alive, that He can't work miracles. Well, He worked one with me.

I'm a sinner. I haven't shot anybody lately, and I haven't stolen anything. But I still think things I shouldn't think and say things I shouldn't say. But I've been saved by God's grace—and to me that's the greatest miracle of all.

One day I will die. I ain't scared, by the way. When I die, I will live again.

BOBBY BOWDEN

9. A Strong Weakness

This is what the LORD says: "Let not the wise boast of their wisdom or the strong boast of their strength or the rich boast of their riches, but let the one who boasts boast about this: that they have the understanding to know me, that I am the LORD, who exercises kindness, justice and righteousness on earth, for in these I delight," declares the LORD.
JEREMIAH 9:23–24

I am truly humbled whenever I am invited to speak from a platform in the name of my Lord and Savior Jesus Christ. I never want anyone to look up to me as the example of one to follow in their walk with the Lord. The only true example of living the ultimate Christian life is that of Christ, and He is the only one we should be striving to emulate. Therefore, I always make this clear when I do share my faith by quoting my favorite disclaimer, Philippians 3:12–14: "No, dear brothers, I am still not all that I should be, but I am bringing all my energies to bear on this one thing: Forgetting the past and looking forward to what lies ahead. I strain to reach the end of the race and receive the prize for which God is calling us up to heaven because of what Christ Jesus did for us" (TLB).

As a young man, I had the opportunity to hear many Christian athletes share their testimonies. I must admit, I began to develop a desire to become famous enough that someday people might ask me to speak. At times, I would even ask God to give me the kind of platform that would make me worthy of such an opportunity.

I always thought that platform would be one of great accolades and honors from a career as a major leaguer. But sometimes you have to be very careful what you ask God for. You see, He did give me the platform and a story that has given me the opportunity to speak to corporations and associations all over the country. The message He gave me, though, was quite a bit more than just that of a professional athlete who is also a Christian.

In recent years, my life has been like one big, incredibly wild roller coaster ride. I was at the top of life's mountain, enjoying the fruits of all those years of hard work on the athletic field, when all of a sudden, down I went. For six years I held on for dear life as I went speeding through one hard, nasty curve after another. I was mentally and physically out of control. I sometimes wondered if I would survive.

This certainly was not the testimony I had in mind. Yet, through it all, God gave me the strength to persevere.

In the spring of 1991, it became obvious there would be no more opportunities for me in baseball. It was a crushing blow to have such a promising career end so prematurely because of an injury, but I tried not to dwell on my misfortune. Instead, I chose to take the same values and principles that had helped me to be a success on the athletic field and apply them to making a strong transition into the "real world."

Just three months after starting my new career in the business world, I was diagnosed with three very serious and potentially life-threatening illnesses that made my baseball career-ending shoulder injury pale by comparison. I had gone from being a big, strong professional athlete to a man who was too weak to get out of bed without assistance.

Today, after three kidney transplants, a successful battle with cancer, the aid of a breathing machine each night, a $2,500 IV treatment each month, and $40,000 of medication per year, my prayers have been answered. I now have the opportunity to travel around the country speaking on the platform God has provided through the peaks and valleys of my life.

It took me quite a while to realize what God had planned for me. Quite honestly, there were times over the past several years when I wondered if He really *had* a plan for my life. About two years after the heart transplant, I read the following scripture from 2 Corinthians 12:7–10:

*I was given a thorn in my flesh, a messenger of Satan,
to torment me. Three times I pleaded with the Lord to take it
away from me. But he said to me, "My grace is sufficient for
you, for my power is made perfect in weakness." Therefore I will
boast all the more gladly about my weaknesses, so that Christ's
power may rest on me. That is why, for Christ's sake, I delight in
weaknesses, in insults, in hardships, in persecutions, in
difficulties. For when I am weak, then I am strong.*

From that night on, I slowly began to see what God had in mind for me. Through a series of events, I finally realized that He had a purpose in allowing me to go through all of those challenges. He gave me a story that is far greater than just being a former major league player.

Today, because of my *weakness,* I have the opportunity to share this story and the lessons of life God has taught me. I have had the chance to touch more lives than I could have if I had played twenty years in the big leagues. When I speak, if just one person grows closer to the Lord as a result of the "seeds of hope" I try to share, then every challenge I have faced will be well worth the "thorns" He has allowed in my life.

I believe God has designed all of us for greatness. But His plan may not be exactly what we have in mind for our lives. His plan certainly was not my plan. I speak from experience, though; if you let Him, He will work wonders in your life.

Yes, He did work wonders in my life as a member of that 1986 World championship New York Mets team. I have the prestigious honor to proudly wear a beautiful World Series ring as a symbol of what I once thought was the greatest thrill a man could have. Yet now I have learned and thus speak the truth—the World Series and my days as a major league player are nothing compared with the thrill of having a personal relationship with God through Jesus Christ.

ED HEARN

10. Taking Scripture for a Ride

Surely your goodness and love will follow me all the days of my life,
and I will dwell in the house of the LORD forever.

PSALM 23:6

As a race car driver, it was my privilege to win NASCAR's Winston Cup championship in 1981, 1982, and 1985. I've been retired from racing for quite a few years now. During my career, my wife, Stevie, would write verses of scripture on note cards and give them to me before a race. She would sit down on a Sunday morning and go through the Bible. Then, at some point during the race, I would look at the card.

In 1994, just after Dale Earnhardt's really close friend, Neil Bonnett, was killed at Daytona, Dale asked Stevie, "Will you do that [prepare a scripture card] for me, too?"

From that day on, Stevie made one card for me and one for Dale. The three of us would meet at the racetrack, and she would have two scripture cards ready: mine and his. Dale would read both of them and then say to me, "You take that one; this one's mine." He would wink at me and say, "I got the good one, didn't I?"

That's what happened on the day of Dale's final—and, as it turned out, fatal—race. Since I wasn't racing that day, he wasn't sure if Stevie was even going to be at the track to see him before the green flag. But, just as she had for seven years to the day, Stevie had gone to the scriptures and picked out an appropriate message for Dale to take with him on the road.

When Dale saw her with a note card, he was really pleased. Since race day was February 18, Stevie chose the eighteenth chapter of Proverbs and settled on verse 10: "The name of the LORD is a strong tower: a righteous man runneth into it and is safe." I have a note in the margin of my Bible by Proverbs 18:10 that says, "Precious truth: the Lord is the only place of safe retreat from the judgment upon sin and from the perplexities of life."

Stevie handed him the note. He read it, kissed her on the cheek, then looked at her and said, "I got the good one now, don't I?" and he headed to his car.

That was February 18, 2001—a day all NASCAR fans remember with sadness. That day, on the last lap of the Daytona 500, my friend Dale Earnhardt died in a crash. Hardly a day goes by when I don't think about how much I miss Dale.

One of the lessons I take from what happened to Dale is this: never pass up an opportunity to bless a friend with the love of God—just like Stevie did for Dale that day. You never know when that friend will pass from this life and into eternity.

DARRELL WALTRIP

11. Pistol Straightens His Aim

By the grace given me I say to every one of you: Do not think of yourself more highly than you ought, but rather think of yourself with sober judgment, in accordance with the faith God has distributed to each of you.
ROMANS 12:3

Pete Maravich was a gym rat at an early age. He always had a basketball in his hands. By the time he was twelve, he was spending eight hours a day during the summer months and four hours a day the rest of the year working on his game. Few athletes have ever been as proficient with the object of their sport as the "Pistol." Pete was intimate with "the rock" and handled it like none before him and few since.

Freshmen couldn't play varsity ball at the time Pete entered Louisiana State, nor had the three-point line been instituted. In spite of those hindrances, Maravich scored 3,667 points and averaged 44.2 points per game for his college career. He still holds the all-time NCAA record in both categories. Almost forty years later, and with four years to do what Pete did in three, the second place all-time scorer is still more than 400 points behind.

Maravich played in the NBA for ten seasons. During his tenure, he was voted to the All-Star team five times and led the league in scoring during the 1976–77 season, averaging 31.1 points per game. With his trademark baggy socks and floppy hair, the "Pistol" knew what to do with the ball. Basketball was his god, the ball was his idol—but ultimately both let him down. Alcohol began to consume him, depression took its toll, his body broke down, and he retired from the NBA to life as a reclusive alcoholic with bad knees.

After two more years of wandering, searching, and trying a variety of lifestyles and New Age belief systems, Pete Maravich turned the excitement he'd had for basketball to Jesus Christ. A fleeting few years later, Pete died of heart failure while shooting hoops in a church gym with Dr. James Dobson before a scheduled taping for Focus on the Family. Pete was only forty years old.

In those few years, Pete started a fabulously effective ministry to kids through basketball camps and for the first time became an effective role model. He gave his testimony wherever anyone would let him talk. He was as outspoken about how his life had changed as anyone who has ever preached God's Word. Alcohol lost its hold, depression disappeared, and Pete came alive. Pete credited his intimate prayer life with Jesus as the reason.

God created you to have a profoundly in-depth relationship with Him. He wants to be the most important part of your life, and He wants to be intimate with you. He wants you to share your secrets, and that will only happen when you are alone with Him—one-on-one. Walk with Jesus throughout your day, but make sure a portion of it is spent only with Him.

JAY CARTY

12. Strawberry's Planted on Solid Ground

*The kingdom of God is not a matter of eating and drinking,
but of righteousness, peace and joy in the Holy Spirit.*
ROMANS 14:17

If you are a baseball fan, you're probably aware of my exploits when I played for the New York Mets in the 1980s. Managers, scouts, and baseball writers agreed that I was destined for greatness. Those forecasts gave me a really high opinion of myself, causing me to think that I was omnipotent and indestructible. The temptations away from the game of baseball were innumerable. Alcohol, drugs, and womanizing took an indestructible hold on my life. My career was plunged into a downward spiral.

At the depths of my degradation, I asked God, "What is it? What is it You want from me?"

I was stunned by God's response. He said, "Walk away from everything."

Wow! That wasn't exactly the answer I was hoping for. I came to realize that you have to be very careful when you ask God a question, because He doesn't joke when He responds.

"I have to give it all up?" I asked God.

God confirmed, "Yes, you have to let it all go." I sensed that He wanted me to strip away everything from my life—my habits and my ways of thinking and acting—so that I could discover who He was and what purpose He had for my life on earth.

I flew out to San Dimas, California, to stay with my sister Regina in her one-bedroom apartment. She, too, was going through a transitional time in her personal life and had just moved into a new apartment with her children. While she was at work, I helped her out by looking after her children. I love my nieces and nephews, so it was a real treat for me to be around them.

I spent six months at Regina's apartment, working consistently to better myself. You might say I lived like a monk in a

monastery during that time. Regina and her children were practically the only people I saw. I rarely left my room except to go
to church. During this time of isolation, I read and studied the
Bible with the same sort of focus that I used to devote to playing
baseball. I would read into the wee hours of the morning and
then lay back with my Bible on my chest, asking God to let His
words breathe inside of me.

It was during this time that I completely surrendered to
God. Surrendering required me to do some things I was not
inclined to do and to avoid the things my natural desires told me
to do. It meant taking responsibility for my spiritual and physical
life, even when I was feeling so down that I could barely drag
myself out of bed. It meant avoiding people, places, and habits
I knew would lead me astray, no matter how badly I wanted
to pursue these "pleasures." I was disciplining myself, and that
meant telling God, "I'm listening to You, Lord. Please give me
the strength and desire not to do these things anymore."

A transformation was taking place in my life as I avoided
liquor, drugs, and sex. It is hard for me to tell which was the
toughest of the three to give up. Believe me, none of it was easy.
Prior to this change in my life, there were very few days that I
went without drinking alcohol, taking a drug, or engaging in
sex. I felt as if I needed those things to make me happy, to fill
the emptiness inside of me.

Now, however, after completing six months of complete
abstinence, I discovered that I didn't *need* any of those former
pleasures. Once they were stripped away, I found that I didn't'
miss them. I had discovered that they did not produce lasting
joy. God took all these things away so that I could realize this.

I had to relearn how to pray. Loving God and living a dirty
life don't mix. I had to return to my knees and humble myself
in front of God, asking for His help. I begged and pleaded with
Him as I prayed on the floor.

"God, today please help me to do what is right in Your eyes,"
I prayed. "Please help me not to hurt anyone or myself today.

I ask You to give me the courage and the strength to do right. You can have it all, God. Take anything. Money, fame, parties, success, and women have kept me away from You. What I care about most is my kids and loved ones and You helping me to become the best person I can be for them."

Yes, God was listening. It seemed as if He had been waiting for me to surrender.

I have learned that God has extreme patience with us. I was not aware at the time that God was with me, even when I was engaged in my wicked ways. He knew the personal damage I was doing to myself, but He also knew that my evil behavior would eventually be so extreme that I would turn away from it and return to Him.

God healed me and gave me the strength I needed to bring about a dramatic change in my life, and He also gave me a new vision to seek His face and follow Him.

DARRYL STRAWBERRY

13. Getting to Know God's Playbook

Do you see someone skilled in their work? They will serve before kings; they will not serve before officials of low rank.
PROVERBS 22:29

Every young athlete would probably admit that playing professionally would be the ultimate dream fulfilled. When the Detroit Pistons drafted me with the eleventh pick in the 1993 National Basketball Association Draft, emotions flew through my body. I knew I was prepared, but no new player to the NBA can anticipate what it's like to compete against the best in the world every day. There were times I had to sit back and reflect, while asking, "How did I get here? Am I really in the NBA?"

My first three years in Detroit flew by. My first year was tough because I didn't get a lot of playing time. I would call my father and other NBA players he had coached in college. They would encourage me to just keep working. "You'll get your time," they would tell me. My years in Detroit taught me that God honors humility, and that hard work eventually pays off.

After my third year, I became a free agent. I was never planning on leaving Detroit. But over a very short period, I also learned that we have to be prepared for the unexpected. The New York Knicks offered me a more-than-favorable contract. I felt they really saw me as a significant part of their future. What I never anticipated is how my future was much more than a relationship with the Knicks or Pistons—it was a relationship with God Himself.

In my kitchen, my cousin George Hughes would often have conversations with me about the game, strategies, players, and other parts of NBA life. One day, he asked me a question that changed my life forever. "Do you talk to yourself on the court?" he asked.

I thought hard. I tried to think of guys who did—like Kevin Garnett, or Karl Malone when he was at the free throw line.

"No, not really. Why?" I responded.

"I believe that some people do it to build themselves up, give themselves confidence," he said. "Even the Bible says in Proverbs, 'As a man thinks in his heart, so shall he be.' Do you think Michael Jordan talks to himself?"

By this time, my head was spinning. For some reason, all I could think about was Michael Jordan playing for the Knicks.

At that point, it was as though someone had walked inside my head and turned on a light. And this light started to flicker, as if it was waiting for more power from its source. I immediately felt God say to me, "You are here because I brought you here to share with people who I am, and what I can do for them." I realized that everything I had been working for was not just for me to be glorified. It was so I would have a platform where

God's grace and power could be seen.

So many of us are in a search of our purpose. We ask ourselves questions like, "Why am I here?" or "What am I ultimately supposed to be doing besides going to work or school every day?" In Ephesians 2:10, God tell us that we are His "handiwork, created in Christ Jesus to do good works, which God prepared us in advance to do." God created us for a specific purpose. He knew before we were born what He saw us becoming as persons and doing as workers—the same way the Pistons drafted me for the specific purpose of following in the footsteps of Joe Dumars, or the Knicks signed me to learn from John Starks how to be an off-guard. God has drafted each one of us for a role in His kingdom, and that is to glorify Him and show others how masterful, good, and powerful He is.

We are His handiwork. We are tools He uses to do good works. I also believe these *works* He has called us to do are not to be confused with just being a good person. There are a lot of good people who may not do what God has prepared them in advance to do. This takes a personal relationship with God.

Shortly after my conversation with my cousin, I began to search for this relationship with God—a relationship outside of religion and traditions, a real relationship with Him. Some of my teammates began showing me how this relationship is available through Jesus Christ. As I began to search for truth and meaning through a relationship with Jesus, my life began to have meaning, peace, and power. Jesus showed me how to execute God's plays in His playbook, the Bible.

I am very aware of all this because I know how a team's playbook works. I have insight. Jesus can do the same for anyone. He has divine insight on how God desires our lives to be, how we can have peace of mind through chaos, how we can receive blessings because of how we live our lives. Jesus can pass on to us these nuances of God's playbook for life.

ALLAN HOUSTON

PRAISING

....

1. A Father's Blessing

[Jesus said,] "Look at the birds of the air; they do not sow or reap
or store away in barns, and yet your heavenly Father feeds them.
Are you not much more valuable than they?"

MATTHEW 6:26

My earliest memories were of a father who sat on the edge of
my bed at night before I slept and rubbed my back—or at least
ran his fingers through my hair and hugged and kissed me. He
loved to dream with me about my future in sports and college.
He never went to college, but he insisted on all his children
graduating from a good university (all three of us fulfilled that
dream).

I have only one complaint about my dad—he died too quickly
at age forty-five. I was only fourteen at the time, and I really
thought I would die too. I had no father to rub my back or to hug
or to dream with me. His death left a huge hole in my heart.

My brother was an all-state quarterback in high school. He
was a preseason All-American pick the year our Dad died. I
was slow, small, and clumsy, and seemed to have no potential
in sports. I floundered with insecurity; everyone expected a lot
from me because my brother was so great.

A year after my father's death, I went to high school and
met a coach who would become a great help to me. I went out
for football. I had to; I was a Glass (a big deal because of my
brother). Every day after our workout, my coach would stay
out with me for extra work. I remember wondering why he
wasted his time working with a loser like me—clumsy, slow,
and small me.

I later learned that he had heard how badly I was hurting because I'd lost my dad. He understood, since he was reared in an orphanage (the Masonic Home in Forth Worth). His parents had both been killed in an auto crash when he was an infant, so he knew what it was like to have no dad. I somehow felt my situation was even worse than his because I had a Superdad who had been ripped away from me when I needed him most.

The coach taught me great technique, which I needed to learn, because I would have otherwise been killed. He placed two big blocking dummies about six feet apart with a big tackle between them, facing me. He worked on my stance: back flat, head up, eyes wide open, and butt low. Fire into the tackle with an extended forearm and shoulder, and never let him touch you on any part of your lower body. He yelled instructions from behind me. I still remember the exact wording of what he was drilling into me: "Keep 'em off of your body, never go around the block, fight pressure, stay in front of the block, keep your head up so you can go to the ball, shed the block, and don't let 'em get lower or higher than you!" He always had a back carrying the ball, running between the dummies. He yelled, "Shed the block and make the tackle!"

I played football for twenty-two years. I played in junior high, high school, college, and the pros. I was coached by some of the greatest coaches in college and the pros. My first coach in the pros at Detroit was Don Shula, and the second was Paul Brown of the Cleveland Browns. (Both are in the Professional Football Hall of Fame.) But I learned more from my high school coach than from those Hall of Fame pro coaches.

Why was he so pivotal in my life? Why did I blossom under his coaching? He lifted weights with me every day at noon, rode next to me on the bus going to games, and walked in with his arm around me after workouts. To be honest, I didn't even like football. But I did like the feeling of a father's blessing. When he sat beside me on the bus or when he put his arm or hand on my shoulder after a workout, it made me feel like it did when my father sat at my bedside. It gave me a feeling of his blessing.

My mother had always called me "William" and insisted that everyone else did also. But Coach Bill Staggs renamed me after himself. "Your name is Bill!" he shouted. "William is a sissy name! You are Bill."

He was my substitute dad. He filled a huge hole in my soul. My great Dad and my substitute dads, Bill Stages and Fred Smith, filled the vacancy left by my dad well. It is harder to love God the heavenly Father when you have no earthly father. But Bill Stages and Fred Smith filled that role, as only a father can.

BILL GLASS

2. Learning from the Squirrels

Consider it pure joy, my brothers and sisters, whenever you face trials of many kinds, because you know that the testing of your faith produces perseverance.
JAMES 1:2–3

Steve Moultrie, a car salesman from Alabama, told me an interesting story about the trials we face in this life.

"Paul, did I ever tell you the story about the older lady in my congregation who fed squirrels?" he asked, with his thick southern accent.

"No, I haven't heard that one," I replied, thinking, *What can a person possibly learn spiritually from squirrels?*

Steve went on. "This woman began to feed the squirrels in her backyard. She would sit out on a picnic table and crack the nuts on the wood and lay them on the bench. A couple months went by and the squirrels began to trust the lady and depend on her for their food.

"She opened the screen door while they were eating on the

porch because she didn't want the squirrels to face any danger from the outside world, like dogs or kids with BB guns. The lady developed such affection for the little creatures that she began to feed them shelled pecans and cashews from a can of nuts. The squirrels were in squirrel heaven as they lounged around all day getting fat and becoming slow of foot, free from struggles. They trusted the lady so much that they even began to let her pet them. Do you know what happened soon after that?"

I said, "No, I don't, Steve, but how can I get one of those squirrels for my kids? They would be great for show and tell."

"You can't," Steve replied, "because they're all dead. She killed them."

"Killed them? Like in a horror film?"

"No," Steve continued. "They all died because their teeth grew too long. When they didn't have to crack the nuts, their teeth never got filed down, and the next thing you know, they had grown so far out of their mouths that the ends of them began to curl below their bottom jaws. They were grotesque looking and couldn't chew anything, and soon after they were skinny, then dead."

I have read in parenting books that studies show over-protecting or sheltering your children has the same damaging effects on a child's development as constant physical or verbal abuse. Some therapists even believe that overprotecting your children can be worse than abusing them.

By the looks of this world, I am quite sure God is not into overprotection. I guess I should take heart that His Son has overcome the world. I give thanks that He is shaping me for His eternal purposes through the trials I continue to face. I am grateful that my teeth haven't grown so long that I can no longer crack open the nuts He has provided.

PAUL BYRD

Editor's note: Paul Byrd pitched in the major leagues from 1995 to 2009 for the Mets, Braves, Phillies, Royals, Braves, Angels, Indians, and Red Sox.

3. God Serves the Net Results

LORD, hear my prayer, listen to my cry for mercy;
in your faithfulness and righteousness come to my relief.
PSALM 143:1

One of the wonderfully innocent things about being a kid is your total lack of perspective. When you're young, every accomplishment is the greatest thing that's ever been; every discovery is a "first" for all of humankind; every adolescent crush is a love unlike anything that's come before; and every problem is a world-ending drama. I look back on my youth with a smile and a shake of the head. At age seventeen, I was the number one junior tennis player in the world. And I didn't have a clue.

Everything was so cool back then. I played a game I loved, and I was good enough that people wanted to be around me and get to know me. We traveled to tournaments. Organizers and sponsors introduced themselves and made sure I had everything I needed. My parents and I were invited to dinners and social functions where we met CEOs, senators, lords, ladies, athletes, and rock stars. In hindsight, it seems like a surreal existence for a teenager. The fact that it was all a gift from God never occurred to me, until the moment it almost went away for good.

It happened during a practice session with my new friend Martina Navratilova. I had just turned eighteen and had already made a splash, beating two players ranked in the top ten in the world in my professional debut and then playing a good losing match against Billie Jean King in the U.S. Open on Center Court at Forest Hills. In Florida, I was hitting with Martina and, as kids are prone to do, I jumped over the net during a changeover. Only my high-jumping skills were lacking. My foot caught on the net cord and down I went.

The next day at a tournament in Orlando, my bad knee rebelled against me. The pain was excruciating. I tried to gut it out, but it was no use. Barely two months into my professional career, I had to retire from a match.

Things got no better in the weeks that followed. The pain didn't let up, and I was in and out of doctors' offices for almost seven months. I tried everything: massage therapy, stretches, cortisone injections, anti-inflammatory drugs, and nothing worked. A majority of doctors told me I needed surgery—and then I would only have a sixty–forty chance of ever playing top-level tennis again.

Like most kids (and a lot of adults), I said, "Why me?" I guess I was asking God the question, although at the time I was what a lot of ministers call a "ten-minute Christian." I had accepted the Lord at age sixteen, but I was new and not fully immersed in the Word. I certainly hadn't thanked God for all the talents He had given me. Now, it looked as though those talents might be taken away, and all I could do was ask, "Why?"

With no tennis to play, I went with my mom to church, where we both prayed for some divine guidance. Was I meant to play tennis? If so, when and how? Would I be healed? Would I come back? Or was this God's way of telling me that He had other plans for my life?

At Sunday morning services with Mom, I picked up a flier from the bulletin about a healing ministry. Mom and I decided to go to the service. What could it hurt? My back was in a brace, and I wasn't getting any better.

The night of the healing service, which was held in a massive Florida auditorium filled to capacity, I finally woke up to God's message for me. It was in that moment, as I stood in a sea of suffering people, that God filled me with another blessing: the gift of perspective. These were people who might not see another weekend. I was there because I was injured and I couldn't play tennis. They were asking God for another day. I was asking for another Wimbledon.

At first I felt ashamed. Then I felt insignificant. Finally, I felt at peace. My job was to praise God's will, not question it. At that moment—at a time when I thought I was at my lowest—I realized just how much the Lord had provided for me. And it was then that I knew I had to do whatever I could to use His gifts for His glory.

During the service, the minister waved an arm in my direction and said, "Someone is out there with a back pain that God is healing." I didn't move for fear that there was someone else in the congregation with a greater need. Then she said it again. My mother elbowed me, but I didn't move. When she said it a third time, I stood.

There were no scales that fell from my eyes; no leprosy sores that miraculously healed: no tingles or warm sensations. No drama. There was just God and me, and the knowledge that I could do all things for His glory and through His grace.

My career could have ended before it really began. Instead, I played professionally for twenty-three years, winning three grand slam doubles titles and playing in twenty-three consecutive Wimbledon championships.

Tennis was and always will be an important part of my life. But after my injury-plagued rookie season, I looked at the game with new eyes. There is no greater gift than the wisdom of perspective. I will be forever grateful that the Lord blessed me with that healing gift so early and so dramatically in my life.

BETSY MCCORMACK

4. Wearing His Faith on His Face

All Scripture is God-breathed and is useful for teaching,
rebuking, correcting and training in righteousness, so that the servant of
God may be thoroughly equipped for every good work.
2 TIMOTHY 3:16–17

Former University of Florida all-American quarterback Tim Tebow knows how to put on his game face (or "game faith"). On fourteen occasions during the 2009 season, Tebow taped scripture verses beneath his eyes where players normally wear eye black to reduce the sun's glare. As I followed the fortunes of the Florida Gators from afar in Lancaster, Pennsylvania, I was admittedly more interested in what scripture Tebow would boldly display than I was with the outcome of the Gators' games.

Here are the verses Tim selected that year, followed by the games' results:

Proverbs 3:5–6: "Trust in the LORD with all your heart and lean not on your own understanding; in all your ways submit to him, and he will make your paths straight." (September 5: Florida 62, Charleston Southern 3)

Mark 8:36: "What good is it for someone to gain the whole world, yet forfeit their soul?" (September 12: Florida 56, Troy 6)

Romans 8:28: "And we know that in all things God works for the good of those who love him, who have been called according to his purpose." (September 19: Florida 23, Tennessee 13)

Isaiah 40:31: "But those who hope in the LORD will renew their strength. They will soar on wings like eagles; they will run and not grow weary, they will walk and not be faint." (September 26: Florida 41, Kentucky 7)

1 Thessalonians 5:18: "Give thanks in all circumstances, for this is God's will for you in Christ Jesus." (October 10: Florida 13, LSU 3)

Psalm 23:1: "The LORD is my shepherd, I lack nothing." (October 17: Florida 23, Arkansas 20)

Ephesians 4:32: "Be kind and compassionate to one another, forgiving each other, just as in Christ God forgave you." (October 24: Florida 29, Mississippi State 19)

Philippians 4:6–7: "Do not be anxious about anything, but in every situation, by prayer and petition, with thanksgiving, present your requests to God. And the peace of God, which transcends all understanding, will guard your hearts and your minds in Christ Jesus." (October 31: Florida 41, Georgia 17)

Colossians 3:23: "Whatever you do, work at it with all your heart, as working for the Lord, not for human masters." (November 7: Florida 27, Vanderbilt 3)

Joshua 1:8–9: "Keep this Book of the Law always on your lips; meditate on it day and night, so that you may be careful to do everything written in it. Then you will be prosperous and successful. Have I not commanded you? Be strong and courageous. Do not be afraid; do not be discouraged, for the LORD your God will be with you wherever you go." (November 14: Florida 24, South Carolina 14)

Romans 1:16: "For I am not ashamed of the gospel, because it is the power of God that brings salvation to everyone who believes: first for the Jew, then to the Gentile." (November 21: Florida 62, FIU 3)

Hebrews 12:1–2: "Therefore, since we are surrounded by such a great cloud of witnesses, let us throw off everything that hinders and the sin that so easily entangles. And let us run with perseverance the race marked out for us, fixing our eyes on Jesus, the pioneer and perfecter of faith. For the joy set before him he endured the cross, scorning its shame, and sat down at the right hand of the throne of God." (November 28: Florida 37, Florida State 10)

John 16:33: "I have told you these things, so that in me you may have peace. In this world you will have trouble. But take heart! I have overcome the world." (December 5: Alabama 32, Florida 13)

In his final collegiate game, the Sugar Bowl, Tim displayed Ephesians 2:8–10: "For it is by grace you have been saved, through faith—and this is not from yourselves, it is the gift of God—not by works, so that no one can boast. For we are God's handiwork, created in Christ Jesus to do good works, which God prepared in advance for us to do." (January 1, 2010: Florida 51, Cincinnati 24)

As a footnote to Tim Tebow's scripture-display saga, the NCAA Rules Committee enacted a rule that prohibits college football players from writing anything on their eye black. Not surprisingly, sportswriters have dubbed it "The Tim Tebow Rule."

KEN HUSSAR

5. A Visionary/Missionary

Hear, Israel, and be careful to obey so that it may go well with you and that you may increase greatly in a land flowing with milk and honey, just as the LORD, the God of your ancestors, promised you.
DEUTERONOMY 6:3

Upward Sports started in a small way, but God's vision for the ministry was dramatically larger. Upward began in 1986 with a simple basketball league at First Baptist Church in Spartanburg, South Carolina, where I was serving as recreation minister. We wanted to offer something that would honor Christ, would allow kids to have fun and experience healthy competition, and where we could incorporate biblical principles into the sports experience.

We had 186 kids participating in Upward Sports the first year, but within a couple of years we'd nearly doubled in size. Before long, we couldn't fit any more kids into our gym. I still remember the excitement of discovering that we had twenty-seven kids on a waiting list.

But our excitement turned into conviction when a well-known pastor, Dr. Johnny Hunt, came to visit our church. I'll never forget his words. He said, "If you're so much as turning children away from playing basketball, you might as well put up a flashing sign in front of your gym door that says, 'Go to hell; we're full.'" He wasn't talking specifically about Upward Sports, but I knew God was trying to get my attention. Suddenly the waiting list took on a whole new urgency. We needed more room to play, and we needed it immediately.

I searched within the church for ways to expand. A mentor of mine in the church generously wrote a check for $11,576— exactly the amount we needed to renovate an old youth center and turn it into a gym. This provided room for another 200 kids, but the problem returned when we added 200 in the next year. Determined not to run out of space for the next season, we began the process of trying to expand that gym. However, God's vision was a whole lot bigger than mine. My friend and mentor who so generously wrote the check to fund our first expansion said, "Caz, you don't need another gym. You need a thousand gyms!"

So instead of writing a check, he told *me* to do the writing. He challenged me to write a book to help others with the same passion for sports and ministry to reach children and families for Christ in their communities. I went away with a couple of friends and prayer partners and created what we refer to today as the *Upward Basketball Director's Manual*. We didn't know what to do with it, but we had it. A Christian publisher encouraged us to consider that this manuscript could really have an impact—not just locally or regionally, but worldwide. Things were happening fast.

Throughout this time, I remained on staff at the church, and I knew it was where God had placed me. I remember when I first got the call to serve at this particular church. It was a dream job, but it was a long way from home for my wife, Leslie, and me. So I did what I always do when facing big decisions—I prayed. I asked God to speak to me through my wife. If you want the Greek interpretation of the scripture that led me to that, here it is: "If mama ain't happy, ain't nobody happy!"

So we drove to Spartanburg to meet the pastor and visit the church. As we pulled up to the church, sitting in the shadow of its enormous steeple, I couldn't help but think, *This is way bigger than me*. I looked at Leslie. Tears were streaming down her face, and I assumed this was God's answer to me. This was not the right place. But my wife shook her head and replied gently, "This is it. This is where we're supposed to be. I don't want to move, but we've got to come because this is what the Lord wants for us."

So when we walked in the door of the church, we knew this was where God had called us and where we'd stay until he clearly released us.

Fast forward nine years. The church was under new leadership that felt it was time to get finances in order and to move the recreation ministry into "maintain" mode for two years. When I was encouraged to "maintain" for a few years instead of growing the ministry, I knew it was time. I called Leslie and told her that we'd been released from the church. "What?" she asked. "Did they fire you?" I explained to her that I hadn't been fired, but that I knew this was God's way of telling us it was okay to go.

We considered a few opportunities and were ready to settle on a job as a recreation pastor at a church in Charlotte, North Carolina. It was a wonderful opportunity, but there were a few delays that left us uneasy—could these be red flags? In spite of this, we decided to make the move. But before announcing my resignation, I wanted to meet with the man who had been such a wonderful friend and mentor to me during my years of service in Spartanburg. He deserved to hear the news from me, and I wanted to explain to him why we were leaving.

Something unexpected happened during that meeting. After listening to my story, he asked some very pointed questions about whether I was absolutely sure God had released me from the church. He actually used the word *released*, which was the language Leslie and I had been using. Then he asked if we had encountered any red flags about the move to Charlotte. Yes, he used the phrase "red flags," too! I admitted that we had encountered red flags, but we were also sure God had released us from the church in Spartanburg. What did it all mean?

He nodded. "Let me ask you this. If you could do anything you wanted in the whole world, what would it be?" I didn't even have to think. With tears in my eyes, I told him that I would be starting Upward Sports leagues around the world.

To my surprise, this was exactly what he wanted to hear. He smiled, saying, "Caz, if you want to do Upward Sports all around the world, you will never have to worry about finances. We want to support you." Then I said, "There is nothing I would rather do." So he stood up, shook my hand, and said, "Let's start tomorrow."

Today we have more than a half million children in forty-six states and four countries participating in basketball, flag football, soccer, and cheerleading through Upward Sports leagues and camps. In addition, Upward Cricket is being played in South Africa and Upward Ball Hockey in Canada. Ministering to all of these children through sports involves more than 480,000 coaches, referees, and other volunteers serving as role models and mentors.

God's vision for the ministry was so much bigger than mine—and much bigger than a thousand gyms. This is why a core value of ours at Upward Sports is the "expectation of God moments." We believe that God is constantly at work all around us, and we just want to be part of what He is doing.

Caz McCaslin

6. The Music City Miracle

You heard my cry for mercy when I called to you for help. . . .
Be strong and take heart, all you who hope in the LORD.
PSALM 31:22, 24

In the rich annals of National Football League history, there are a select few truly classic plays. To be a part of something people would recall as one of the greatest moments in NFL football is humbling, but I was there, in the moment, a part of an event that redirected my life forever. It was January 8, 2000, the first round of the playoffs, and I was the offensive coordinator for the Tennessee Titans.

With a 13–3 record, we'd earned the right to host the first wild card playoff game in Nashville. It was an electrifying day as the fans poured into the stadium, keyed to the excitement that was just a kickoff away. As I looked down from the press box, my mind reflected on the journey that had brought us to that day.

Just a few months back, on the morning of July 8, 1999, as I sat at my kitchen table enjoying the last few days of our summer break, I opened the *Tennessean* newspaper and spotted the following headline: PLAYOFFS OR PINK SLIPS! It was only a week before our 1999 training camp was to begin, and the Titans' owner was speaking out in a candid interview about the coaching staff. The message couldn't have been clearer: "Make the playoffs or be run off."

You can imagine how I felt—and why our coaching staff had begun the season with a greater-than-usual sense of urgency. I knew that no matter how hard we worked, there were no guarantees that we would make the postseason. I couldn't control the bounce of the ball, the injury of key players, or the movements of twenty-two men on a given play. All I could do was pray that God would care for us. I had to totally depend on Him and trust Him for the results.

The season began with a flourish. For two previous seasons, as the Houston Oilers franchise transitioned into the Tennessee Titans through a move to Nashville, we were without a home stadium and played our games first in the Memphis Liberty Bowl and then at Vanderbilt University's stadium. Finally, the 1999 opener had come and with it our first-ever home game in Adelphia Coliseum in Nashville.

That day, we faced a talented Cincinnati Bengals team. The fans got their money's worth as the game turned into an offensive shootout. Much to their pleasure, we hung tough and won the game 36–35 on a field goal with only seconds remaining. It was the first in a string of victories on the home field that would help launch us into the NFL elite, and one that would start to mold a group of unselfish men into a team worthy of a championship.

There were so many memorable games that season. We overcame torrential rainstorms, critical injuries, and numerous comebacks through the heroic play of guys who put the team ahead of themselves. Those kinds of sacrifices had brought us to this day, our first step toward a Super Bowl and an opportunity to experience something none of us would ever forget.

Standing over my play-calling sheet as I watched the breathtaking flyover signaling game time, I said a prayer and asked the Lord to take us where He wanted us to go.

From the beginning, two great defenses were dictating the pace as both offenses struggled through a scoreless first quarter. A big play by our great defensive end Jevon Kearse to sack Bills' quarterback Rob Johnson in his own end zone for a safety and two points helped to ignite our team. With a great return on the ensuing free kick by Derrick Mason to give us great field position, our offense came alive and drove for our first touchdown. Later we added an Al DelGreco field goal and ended the half ahead 12–0.

Out of the locker room, though, it was the Bills who came into the third quarter with new momentum. By the time the final seconds of the third quarter ticked off, they had scored once and were threatening again. A 62-yard drive ending in a score by Antowain Smith, Buffalo's powerful running back, put the Bills ahead 13–12. The attempted two-point pass play fell short in the end zone, and now it was our turn to step up.

Our guys didn't disappoint me. Another good return on the kickoff, followed by Eddie George's hard running, put us in position for Al DelGreco to nail a 36-yard field goal that put us ahead 15–13 with just 1:48 remaining. The crowd went wild. With so little time left on the clock, we started to breathe again.

But it wasn't long until we realized this game was far from over. It was devastating to watch the Bills roll down the field—two big pass plays and a 12-yard run later, Steve Christie lined up to kick a 41-yard field goal with 20 seconds on the clock. I saw the snap, the hold, the kick, and the ball sailing through the uprights. Bills on top. Sixteen seconds on the clock. Sixteen seconds to oblivion. That's when my spirits finally reached bottom. Coaching was the only career I'd ever wanted, but this was too much.

Then I had one of those extraordinary moments: I heard the quiet voice of God.

I heard Him ask, "Do you have faith?"

I know what you're thinking. But listen, this isn't something that happens on a regular basis. I can tell you, though, that when it does, the words, the messages, and the Source are unmistakable. I answered the question immediately and instinctively.

"Yes, Lord, I have faith."

And just like that, I had hope. I can't explain it even today, but I was excited even as everyone around me had given up. Sure, I was tense, but I was hopeful, too, that something good was going to happen. And it wasn't just good, it was great.

The Bills kicked off, and to our amazement they lofted the ball into the air to give us a shot for a return. We had practiced "the double-lateral return," all season since week one, and we called for it then. It was one of those desperation plays that look good on paper but is an amazing long shot. The play, which our special teams coach Alan Lowry designed, called for a lateral (backward pass) from whoever received the kick back to our tight end, Frank Wychek, who would make a second lateral to our wide receiver, Kevin Dyson, on the opposite side of the field. Then Kevin would sprint down the sidelines for a touchdown. We hoped.

In a live-game situation, with so much on the line, unexpected things will happen. The first was that the high kick fell into the arms of our fullback, Lorenzo Neal, not famous for great hands. Not trusting himself to make an accurate lateral, he ran over to Frank Wycheck and handed him the ball, drawing the entire Bills coverage team to Frank's side of the field. As they converged on him, Frank turned and threw a perfect spiral back to Dyson, wide open on the opposite sideline, and he galloped 75 yards to the end zone untouched. He scored, and we won—it was a miracle. . .the "Music City Miracle."

The stadium gave way to instant pandemonium as our players sprinted from the bench to the end zone to celebrate. I fell back into my chair, cherishing the moment.

I will never forget that incredible play; the pass that somehow became a handoff—and, of course, Dyson's sprint to glory. But most of all, I will carry with me the memory of that powerful lesson: God is in control. Therefore, no matter what situation arises in life, we should never lose hope. Proverbs 21:31 in the *Living Bible* paraphrase says, "Go ahead and prepare for the conflict, but victory comes from God."

When God asked me, "Do you have faith?" the real question was whether I believed He was in control of everything, good and bad—all of it. Step into tomorrow with that thought firmly in mind. Your miracle may be right around the corner.

LES STECKEL

7. From Hero to Zero

The LORD is good, a refuge in times of trouble.
He cares for those who trust in him.
NAHUM 1:7

I share this story with people because I want them to know that there is hope. There is a way out of the deadly, seductive life of drugs. In fact, not only is there a way out, but there is a way to an exciting, joy-filled life that will not only change you, but will bring that same joy to others.

It was 1975. There had been a two-day rain delay; a lot of people began to wonder if this World Series—between my Boston Red Sox and the Cincinnati Reds—would ever be played. Now here I was, standing at home plate with a 2–2 count after just making the worst swing in baseball history. To tell you the truth, I thought I was out. The ball just barely touched the bat, hit Johnny Bench's glove, and then rolled behind us both.

I was sweating bullets. *It's the World Series, the eighth inning; we are behind by three runs; there are two men on, and I am the tying run. I can't strike out. I am going to strike out. I want to be the hero. I am going to be the goat.* All of these things were going through my mind in the split second before Bench called for the next pitch. Here it comes! A fast ball right in the strike zone. . .swing. There it goes; I hear the beautiful sound of the crack of the bat as the ball finds its way to the sweet spot and soars up into the air. It is up, up over the center field wall. A home run! I am running around the bases. I reach second base and yell at Pete Rose, "Don't you wish you were this strong?"

Pete yells back, "Isn't this fun?"

You would think this would be the defining moment in my life. I mean, a home run in the World Series! Well, I am here to tell you that after that home run, I was miserable. I was addicted to drugs and had used some before the game. I thought my father didn't love me, and yet I couldn't stop seeking his approval. My marriage was shaky at best, and I was constantly at odds with my managers. I spent the next few years going from team to team until I was finally out of baseball. In 1989 my mother committed suicide, and my dad died three months later. Devastated, I moved to Florida to play in the Senior League.

There, at a swimming pool in Winter Haven, I learned about Jesus and what He could do in my life. I prayed that day, and Jesus began a work in me. I would like to tell you that everything was better that very day, but it wasn't. I continued using drugs and finally ended up divorcing a second time. I lost all hope. Sitting in my house in Winter Haven, I was ready to take my life when the phone rang. It was Bill Lee. He called Ferguson Jenkins, who then called Sam McDowell. Before I knew it, I was in rehab. Due to having panic attacks in rehab, I ended up in a hospital next to a retired pastor. This man of God took the next few days to share much of the Bible with me. I learned and grew and began to understand what it meant to live for Christ every day, to allow Him to heal all the hurts.

I returned to Winter Haven and joined with a friend, Carl Schilling, to begin the Diamond Club Ministry, which is dedicated to bringing the good news of Jesus Christ to youth and their families through the game of baseball. Carl has since left the ministry, but the purpose remains strong.

In 1994 I had one final relapse. I was again lost and began to sink into a sea of guilt and despair. Then I met Tammy, the woman who would become my wife. She reminded me about Jesus and the forgiveness that comes from what He did for us on the cross, that no matter what we have done, His blood is sufficient to cover it. All we have to do is to accept His forgiveness and live for Him.

No, we cannot live in the same sin day after day. But we can depend on God to give us the grace we need to overcome the strongholds of addiction or any other habitual sin. Tammy and I have been married for fifteen years, and I have been *clean* for sixteen. We have custody of my three grandchildren and are watching them grow up clean and healthy. Their mother is now clean and is growing stronger every day. My son is working on his doctorate in clinical psychology and is going to use his degree to help children.

God is an awesome God!

BERNIE CARBO

8. Talking the Talk and Walking the Walk

I am not ashamed of the gospel, because it is the power of God that brings salvation to everyone who believes: first to the Jew and then to the Gentile.
ROMANS 1:16

Football has afforded me the platform to influence others. It is my aim in life not to turn the spotlight on myself, but to shift the focus to where it belongs—on our Lord and Savior, Jesus Christ.

The way I figure it, if nothing bad ever happened, there wouldn't be a need for faith. The Bible says we are tested and made stronger through trials and tribulations, but it also says God is with us, helping us out.

God has a plan for everything. Some people might say, "Well, God's plan for me is not as good as his plan for this other person." But in God's eyes, it is. Not everybody is called upon to do the same thing or to be here on earth the same amount of time. It's like the body of Christ. Not everybody is going to be the eye or the mouth. Somebody has to be the foot. I'm not saying that that's anything less. In fact, in God's eyes, it's the same. You have to look at what He has called on you to do and then do it to the best of your ability.

John 3:16 is the essence of Christianity: "For God so loved the world that he gave his one and only Son, that whoever believes in him shall not perish but have eternal life." God calls on us to do one thing, and that is to believe. People try to complicate it, but it is very simple.

There are many temptations. It can be a tough daily struggle, but I just try to trust the Lord with everything and surround myself with good, accountable friends, people who give me godly advice. That helps keep me in line, holds me accountable, and encourages me in day-to-day life.

I've had a lot of ups and downs that most people don't know about, but each year has been a blessing. And whatever happens, good or bad, in the future, it's God's plan. So I'm not going to worry about things. I have no expectations; I try to live that way and just have an influence for Him.

A lot of people know Philippians 4:13—"I can do all this through him who gives me strength"—but a lot of people don't interpret that verse the right way. Most people think it means they can do *anything*. . .like star on the football field or make a lot of money. But that's not what it's talking about. I believe the verse is saying I can be content with anything. When you are a Christian, you can be content because God has put you where you are. That's really a different view. I know that I have Christ in me, so I can do whatever He wants me to do, and that's how I approach everything.

In 2007, I was honored as the seventy-third Heisman Trophy winner, the first sophomore to ever receive the prestigious award. When I grabbed hold of this twenty-five-pound bronze statue, the first thing I said was, "I would just like to first start off by praising my Lord and Savior Jesus Christ, who gave me the ability to play football."

I am here today to report that life, focused as a disciple of Jesus Christ is fantastic. Yes, I truly love playing football, but I want you all to know that serving Jesus Christ is my greatest passion.

TIM TEBOW

9. I Just Told Them about My Jesus

[Jesus said,] "The greatest among you will be your servant."
MATTHEW 23:11

If you have ever been in Mississippi in the summer, then you know what I mean when I say it was hot—*really* hot—in Raymond, Mississippi, in July 1994. I found myself serving on staff at a Fellowship of Christian Athletes leadership camp. What makes a leadership camp different from other FCA camps is that the campers are all people serving as leaders in their respective FCA groups back on their school campuses. They come to this camp to be trained to lead an FCA campus group and to be taught how to share their faith and be godly leaders.

It wasn't that big a camp—only about 150 campers. I'm sure there would have been more, but the heat discouraged many from attending. This was a camp for the committed, or at least the well hydrated.

I had been around only a handful of folks who had Down's syndrome, so when I first met Stevie during camp registration, I was a little taken back. Honestly, my first thoughts centered on this being a camp for athletes. Stevie seemed like a great kid, but why was he here? I mean, he obviously couldn't play sports, and how could he be a leader?

I was surprised how easy it was to get to know Stevie. He quickly became the heart of our camp. He was always smiling and excited about "his Jesus." On day two I made it a point to eat breakfast with Stevie. It was an awesome experience. He put what seemed like a half a pepper shaker of seasoning on his eggs, and the whole time he kept saying to me, "I love pepper on my eggs, Mr. Lance. I love pepper on my eggs." And since there were more black speckles of pepper on his plate than yellow eggs, I had no reason to doubt his love of peppered eggs.

We had been prepping the campers for a big experience on

Thursday afternoon. We had been training them all week in how to share their faith. So on Thursday afternoon, we assigned van drivers, loaded campers up to take them into area communities, and watched them go from door to door to share their faith with whoever would listen. The idea of knocking on a stranger's door and relating your faith in Christ will make grown men breathe in brown bags, so to say we had some nervous teenagers would not adequately describe the scene that day.

I was assigned to drive one of the vans. I sat in my van waiting for my assigned campers to arrive and load up. I was also trying to get the air conditioner to bring the vehicle's interior temperature down to a "comfortable" 108 degrees. Imagine my reaction when my group got to the van and Stevie was with them. All the other campers were in shorts and their camp T-shirt, but not Stevie. Stevie had his *going-to-church* clothes on—black polyester slacks and button-down shirt. And instead of the camp Bible we gave out at registration, Stevie was carrying a huge family Bible that he was using to fan himself. "It's hot, Mr. Lance," he said as he boarded the van. "Really hot!"

As I pulled the van to the side of the road in the subdivision we had been given to cover, my heart raced. . .not for me, but for Stevie. People can be cruel enough to door-to-door solicitors, but what might someone say to a kid like Stevie? I thought about trying to talk him into staying in the van with me, but I knew he needed to do this. So off he and the others went to knock on doors, Stevie in full church attire with his big Bible, fanning himself all the way down the street.

It was a relief to see the group coming back to the van about an hour later. Each of the campers was smiling and laughing, even Stevie. I thought that was a good sign and hoped for the best as they climbed into the overheated van and began to share. Every kid in my group said, "Stevie preached!"

I turned to Stevie and said, "What happened? Was anyone mean to you?"

He said, "The first folks slammed the door in our faces, Mr. Lance. But we just kept going house to house."

"Did you ever get a chance to talk with anyone?" I asked.

"Oh yes, sir," he said with a huge grin. "And they are going to see me in heaven."

I looked around the van at the other campers' faces, and they were all nodding in agreement with Stevie. So I asked, "Stevie, when you got to share with someone, what did you tell them?"

I will never forget how Stevie answered. Fanning his sweat-soaked face with a Bible the size of a small car, he said, "Mr. Lance, I just told them about my Jesus."

It was at that moment I realized why Stevie was at camp. It wasn't because he was a great athlete; he wasn't. It was because he may have been the best young leader I have ever met. You see, Stevie understood one of the greatest principles of being a special leader: leadership has less to do with your capabilities and everything to do with your availability.

LANCE BROWN

10. "Tape an Aspirin on It"

Cast all your anxiety on him because he cares for you.
1 PETER 5:7

Growing up as the oldest of three daughters of a highly respected college football coach has great advantages—and a few not-so-great moments. The neat part was that I grew up around my "football-playing brothers" and they knew me—lots of people knew me. The bad part? Well, lots of people knew me! There were a few father-daughter love chats when the "network" happened to whisper in my dad's ear. Fortunately, he coached at home as well as he coached on the field. He had a special way of letting me know that he was not pleased while still holding me accountable in a loving way.

My dad, Grant Teaff, dreamed at an early age of coaching football in the Southwest Conference. His ability to visualize his path and work hard to reach his goals led him to great accomplishments. He was an underweight, fairly slow (don't tell him I said that) linebacker at Snyder High School with no scholarship offers, who strongly believed that God had a plan for him to play football in college, get a degree, and become a football coach. He had a high pain threshold and unmatched physical and mental toughness, and that helped him reach his goal. His faith, and the way he relied on God to lead his life, set the tone for our family and impacted tens of thousands of individuals who came under his influence.

The time I spent with my dad during his twenty-one years as head coach at Baylor University prepared me for the unexpected journey God had planned for me.

We were raised in a "no wimps allowed" zone." As I was growing up, there were many times when I would get a cut, bruise, or scratch, and my dad would say what he always said: "It's nothing. . .tape an aspirin on it!" Talk about tough love! Good thing that my mom, Donell, was always close by with a Band-Aid and some hydrogen peroxide.

Now don't get me wrong. My dad is the most loving, wisest and godliest man anyone could have as a father and friend. I realize now that he was coaching and preparing me for my journey.

On a clear, cool spring day in Dallas in 1982, I was driving on I-35. Something was wrong. I slowly began to lose my eyesight and saw blackness creep in from my outside viewing area all the way to my nose until I was totally blind. During that short span, I was able to make it to the home of a friend, who took me to the hospital. My parents were on vacation in the Eastern Caribbean, and there I lay in a hospital room without Mom and Dad to lean on. I was scared, and the only thing I knew to do was *pray hard*.

Alone, twenty-four years old, single, and blind, my mind swirled with thoughts about "my dreams—finding a husband, having a family, being there to cheer for my kids—all smashed. "Why me, God?" I asked. As the evening progressed, I talked to God a lot, pleading for mercy, healing, and peace. The vivid picture of my dad saying, "Tape an aspirin on it," entered my thoughts.

It was at that point that I realized that the *aspirins* I needed in this circumstance were God's unconditional love, His healing power, and His Holy Word—"I can do all this through him who gives me strength" (Philippians 4:13). As I prayed, I experienced the peace that comes from knowing God has a purpose and a plan for my life. It was those *aspirins* that I taped to my wounds that night.

The next day, I woke up. . .and I was still blind. My parents hurried back home, and my sisters, Tracy and Layne, were in the room. I heard their voices. I was in the hospital for two weeks without sight, and after lots of medication and care, my sight returned. Doc said it was a "demyelinating episode." A what? Well, as I learned, this was the first occurrence of what would be diagnosed three years later as multiple sclerosis.

God's plan and purpose are perfect. The doctor ordered rest for a month, and when I resumed work, it would have to be in a low-stress position. I started my new job—receptionist for the Dallas Mavericks. I soon found out that being a receptionist was anything but low stress.

Here's the neat part. I met "my special someone" at work. Within three weeks, we were dating, then engaged, and married within a year. My husband, Russ, and I have been married for more than twenty-six years. The doctors were not very encouraging about us having children, but we prayed and believed. Our son, Josh, graduated from Baylor University and is coaching college football (Imagine that!). Our daughter, Jessy, attended college at Baylor. We cheered for our kids, watched them grow physically and spiritually, and thanked God for the blessings He gave us. Russ has stayed by my side as the MS has run its course for the last twenty-seven-plus years.

My life hasn't exactly followed the path that I imagined it would. I pray for miraculous healing every day, and there are some days I wonder if God is listening. I have learned that, even in the midst of difficult situations, my Lord will continue to direct my path. He proves that to me over and over. Through my journey, He has allowed me to encourage others.

Over the years, I have fallen many times and come up bloody, only to hear Russ and the kids tell me to "tape an aspirin on it." Today that saying is still alive in our family, but it has greater depth and meaning to all of us.

God's Word is the right medicine to guide us through the challenges we all face. His supply of aspirins will never run out.

TAMMY BOOKBINDER

11. *Trophy-Worthy Character*

"For I know the plans I have for you," declares the LORD, "plans to prosper you and not to harm you, plans to give you hope and a future."
JEREMIAH 29:11

With apologies to our understandably proud and jubilant Crimson Tide faithful, the University of Alabama, in my opinion, wasn't the biggest winner in the 2010 Bowl Championship Series national championship football game.

That distinction went to a young man from Tuscola, Texas, named Colt McCoy. "Colt McCoy? Are you crazy?" you ask.

Yes, Colt McCoy, the Longhorns's all-American quarterback who suffered an injury on the game's opening drive, knocking him out for the remainder of the contest. The same Colt McCoy who won more games as a starting quarterback than anyone in the history of NCAA Division I football.

Yet, you may ask, how in the world can you argue that Colt McCoy was the game's biggest winner? After all, he hardly even played.

In reply, I would reference the young man's postgame interview before millions of people who watched the nationally televised matchup. The reporter asked McCoy, "How did you feel, watching the game from the sidelines?"

Smarting from a shoulder injury that numbed his cannon-like throwing arm after being hit by Alabama's Marcell Dareus, McCoy gazed up in the night sky, cleared his throat a couple of times trying to fight back emotion, and couldn't really respond for five or six seconds. Finally, the recipient of the prestigious Maxwell Award acknowledged that it was unfortunate that he didn't get to play and that he would have given everything he had to be out there with his teammates. He then congratulated Alabama and later called the Tide a tremendous football team.

But what he said next really hit home and still makes me a little misty-eyed. He told the interviewer, "I always give God the glory. I never question why things happen the way they do. I know God is in control of my life, and I also know, if nothing else, that I'm standing on the Rock."

Let's think about that response. Here's a kid who always seemed destined to play in that national championship game. With a name like Colt McCoy, he was born to be the gun-slinging quarterback of the fabled Burnt Orange. His entire experience playing junior high, high school, and college football had pointed toward Thursday night, January 7, 2010, in Pasadena, California at the Rose Bowl.

And he got to play one ill-fated series. One. The 6-foot 2-inch, 210-pound Heisman finalist who had completed better than 70 percent of his passes and threw for 112 touchdowns and 13,253 yards in his storied college career posted phenomenal statistics. Those accomplishments aside, in his postgame interview, the Longhorn quarterback hurled the most important scoring pass of his life—a real Hail Mary if there ever was one. Despite his obvious deep disappointment, Colt McCoy came through like a true champion for his God, offering praise and thanks even in bitter defeat. His postgame remarks schooled a future generation of gridiron wannabes on class and humility.

As we progress through life, we all experience what some call "defining moments." These are the crossroads episodes that establish, for good or bad, whatever legacy we leave on this earth. When our defining moments come, most of us won't have a national television audience like Colt McCoy did, but I have a feeling that in God's eyes ministering to just one individual on a street corner qualifies as a blessed opportunity.

True, Colt never got to hoist that coveted crystal trophy, but on that Thursday night he made a resounding statement to the youth of America about what it really means to be a winner.

SCOTT ELLIOTT AND CHRISTINE PLONSKY

12. Tomorrow Is Promised to No One

God is able to bless you abundantly, so that in all things at all times,
having all that you need, you will abound in every good work.
2 CORINTHIANS 9:8

"Sweetness" seems an unlikely nickname for one of the most dominant football players ever to take the gridiron. Hall of Famer Walter Payton broke National Football League records for touchdowns, carries, and career rushing yards. He was selected for the Pro-Bowl nine times and was twice named the NFL's Man of the Year. He was also a key part of the Chicago Bears' win in Super Bowl XX. But Walter Payton was so much more than an athlete.

He was a dedicated family man. His wife, Connie, was by his

side for more than twenty years, and their two children, Jarrett and Brittney, were an integral part of his life. He found joy in everything he did, including a performance on *Soul Train* while in college, where he showcased his exceptional dancing skills. He was warm and funny, caring and compassionate.

Upon learning of the personal struggles of one of the Bears organization's phone operators, Payton urged her to go home to her family and then covered her shift for the night, answering calls and handling paperwork without ever letting on to the people on the other end of the line just who it was they were talking to.

Payton invested himself in the city that supported him so much, hosting Thanksgiving dinners and holiday parties for underprivileged children. He established the "Wishes to Santa" program, which enabled neglected and abused children to submit a Christmas wish that Payton would provide. His extreme generosity and genuine concern for others seemed to come naturally. To Payton that was simply the right way to live—as if each day was one's last chance to do good. "Tomorrow is promised to no one," he often reminded his fans.

When he was diagnosed with a rare liver disease and cancer early in 1999, he dedicated himself to raising awareness for organ donation. Even though Payton's disease was too advanced to benefit from a transplant, he felt that it was his responsibility to use his blessings of resources and fame to bring attention to such a cause that would help so many others.

Payton passed away on November 1, 1999. But just a few weeks later, more than fifty thousand gift bags of clothes and toys, worth a hundred dollars each, were donated anonymously to needy children in the Chicago area. Many suspected, but no one was able to confirm, the source of such generosity until much later. Payton himself had, in fact, coordinated the effort prior to his death. The Walter and Connie Payton Foundation continues to sponsor Christmas gifts for children each year, and the Walter Payton Cancer Fund still pays for research and provides family support for patients of the disease.

In tribute to the man who celebrated his beliefs and shared his blessings so generously, in 1999 the NFL renamed its Man of the Year Award in his honor. The Walter Payton Man of the Year Award is given to one player each year whose success on the field is surpassed only by his charitable work in the community.

DON YAEGER

13. "Where Seldom Is Heard an Encouraging Word"

Rejoice always, pray continually, give thanks in all circumstances;
for this is God's will for you in Christ Jesus.
1 THESSALONIANS 5:16–18

In 2004, I was in my fourth season as assistant coach of the Dallas Mavericks. This was after coaching in the NBA for almost thirty years, including being the head coach of the Rockets, Bucks, and Lakers. I had coached international basketball in several world events as a head or assistant coach, including two World Games, the Central American Games, and two World Club Championships—winning a bronze medal, a silver, and a gold. But in 2004, as a result of my NBA and international experience, I was asked to be the first foreigner to coach the People's Republic of China national team in the Athens Olympics.

That's the good part. But there were many obstacles to overcome in order to achieve any success. It started with the fact that the Chinese Basketball Association wanted me to stay with young players so as to prepare them for the 2008 Olympics in Beijing. They wanted to represent themselves well at home. So we had a team with limited experience. But worse was that when I saw DVDs of the players, it was obvious they did not have the physicality or the running techniques it takes to compete on the world stage.

Fortunately, I had an excellent assistant coach and strength man—Jonas Ilgauskas and Alvydas Kaslauskas, who were both from Lithuania. They went to China in March of 2004 and immediately started working with the players on strength, running, and basketball fundamentals. When I arrived in April, they had made great progress in those areas. Then the practices started in earnest, along with exhibition games with various other national teams. Those "friendly games," as International Basketball Federation calls them, went well, but they were not against the caliber of teams we would play in Athens.

We had to be ready to compete in August, and then we learned that our draw in the pool was the tougher one of the two. We were in with the defending world champions, Serbia, and New Zealand, which had finished fourth in the 2002 World Games. Worse yet, the other teams were Spain, which would actually end up with the best record at 7–1 but would not medal, and Italy, which would win the silver, and Argentina, the eventual gold medal winner. To get to the medal round, we had to win two games.

As if that were not enough, when we arrived at the Olympic Village, all sorts of problems arose. Seven of us were crowded into a three-bedroom suite with two showers, one of which did not work properly and flooded the hallway with each shower. Worse was that we did not have scouting DVDs of the other teams or electronic equipment to watch opponents or to edit our own games. So, I went to the city and bought two VCRs and a monitor and set up an edit room in my bedroom and appointed myself "video coordinator."

Still, as video coordinator I had nothing to coordinate. The Chinese delegation had nothing. However, we had friends on the staffs of Lithuania and Australia, and both were in the other pool. The Australians in particular saved me, making some copies of their edits of some of our opponents. We had lost to Argentina and Serbia by twenty-plus points each in a tournament in Belgrade just two weeks earlier, but I had never seen the other opponents.

I felt better once I had an idea of what we were facing, but not a whole lot, because the teams looked really good. This was confirmed when we played Spain, with its collection of NBA players, in our first game and lost by about twenty points. Next was a game we had to win, against New Zealand. We squeaked out a four-point victory, followed by two blowout losses to Argentina and Italy. They ganged up on Yao Ming, and we didn't have enough other firepower to compensate. While we were taking these losses, I could sense that the Chinese delegation was having second thoughts about this foreigner who was coaching them—even though the team had been beaten by as many as seventy points in some previous Olympic games.

I was feeling isolated and had one practice to get ready to play the defending world champions, who had also beaten New Zealand but had lost in tight games to our other common opponents. Thus, it came down to a must game for each of us. The winner would go on to the medal round, while the loser would be eliminated.

The night before the game, I was feeling especially depressed. I was staying in terrible living conditions, had no tools to work with, felt like an unappreciated foreigner (and inhibited greatly by the language barrier), and Yao Ming was playing on feet so sore that his socks were bloody after every game. And now we had to face a team that manhandled us two weeks earlier.

I opened my Bible and began reading in 1 Thessalonians. As I moved through the fifth chapter, verse 11 started to speak to me. When I got to verse 14, I read the words, "encourage the disheartened, help the weak, be patient with everyone." And verses 16–18 said simply, "Rejoice always, pray continually; give thanks in all circumstances; for this is God's will for you in Christ Jesus."

Upon reading these words, it all became clear to me. I had just experienced one of the greatest moments of my life when

I entered the arena at the opening ceremonies. I was making history as the foreign head coach of the largest country in the world. I was in the Olympics. I was head coaching again. These players loved me and I loved them. Blessings were all around me.

I decided at that moment that the next day at the game against Serbia, I was going to be joyful and thankful. It did not matter how the game went; we could play great or not so great. The referees could be good, bad, or neutral. I was going to be thankful and joyful in the moment.

We started the game well and were tied at the end of the first quarter and ahead two at the half. In the closing minutes, we were still leading as the clock was running down. They began to foul and we had to go to the foul line and make the most pressure-filled free throws these young players had ever taken. They made them all, and we won the game. We beat the world champions and made it to the medal round. It was and is regarded as China's greatest victory in its history of international competition.

Then in 2008, the key players of 2004, coached by Ilgauskas, made it to the medal round again. China was happy. I was joyful and thankful.

When I am down, I remember times like this and am thankful. God blesses a thankful heart; a thankful heart is God's will.

DEL HARRIS

14. Punts with a Purpose

"Even to your old age and gray hairs I am he,
I am he who will sustain you. I have made you and
will carry you; I will sustain you and I will rescue you."

ISAIAH 46:4

God provides in wonderful, mysterious, and surprising ways. I was cut by Buddy Ryan and the Philadelphia Eagles just hours before the last preseason game of the 1986 season. My wife, Kim, and I had just purchased a home and had a one-year-old daughter, Meghan. Even though I had a college degree and a job in mechanical engineering to go back to, we knew things would be tight. We were struggling to make our house payment when the Minnesota Vikings called.

Two months into the season, I was brought in for a tryout because the Vikings' punter, Greg Coleman, was hurt and doubtful for the upcoming game against the Redskins. I won the tryout; Greg got healthy and cheered on the Vikings from the sidelines. God answered our prayers with a game check, and I went home wondering where the next house payment was coming from.

One month later, the Denver Broncos called. I hopped on a plane from sunny Southern California to snow flurries in Denver. That was quite a climate shock. Four punters were invited, but I won that tryout. After the tryout, Coach Dan Reeves made two comments to me. He said that he wished his pitching wedge worked as well as my coffin-corner punting ability and that the reason he brought me in for the tryout was that Bill Parcells recommended me. I had played four games against Parcells's Giants and must have made a good impression on him.

Several years later, when I was playing for the Giants and Parcells was coaching the Patriots, he came up to me during pregame warm-ups and said, "Horan, if I had a nickel for every punt you've had since I told Dan to bring you in..."

I said, "Thank you. I'd gladly pay it."

The Broncos had a strong Christian presence on the team.

The team chaplain was a good friend of my pastor in Southern California. I attended the team Bible study during the week. The night before my first game in Denver, it snowed heavily. The morning of my first game, I was determined to fight through the snow and get to church where our chaplain pastored. I remember the worship leader saying at the start of the service that on a snowy day like today, it was better to be a Bronco fan than a Bronco player. That brought a chuckle from the congregation.

I was pretty nervous before the game, but I felt I heard the Lord say, "I brought you here, and I didn't bring you here to fail." I took tremendous comfort in those words. We went on to win our division and made it to the Super Bowl, only to lose to the New York Giants. The Lord blessed me with six more seasons in Denver.

We felt the Lord's leading to begin a ministry we called Punts with a Purpose. We used my coffin-corner punting ability to raise funds to care for working homeless families. The program eventually became the Family Rescue Ministry of the Denver Rescue Mission. We trained a volunteer group of ten to twenty people to mentor working homeless families and subsidize their first month's rent and deposit on affordable housing that fit within the family's budget.

The Denver Rescue Mission and the churches helped them with education, employment, food, clothing, furniture, and other necessities. Almost all of the families became self-sufficient within a few months. We found that many working homeless families were paying thirty dollars a night to stay in hotels, but they just couldn't save up the first month's rent and deposit on an affordable apartment. They really just needed a hand up, not a handout. Many of the families have come to know Jesus as their Savior. When a family asks a ministry team member who is carrying a big sofa sleeper up two flights of stairs why he's doing that, he has a divine appointment to share God's love.

I played seven more seasons in the NFL—with the Giants, Bears, and Rams. My final game was a victory in Super Bowl XXXIV with the St. Louis Rams. God is good.

MIKE HORAN

HONORING

....

1. Perfect Pitching with a Purpose

This is what the LORD says: "Stand at the crossroads and look;
ask for the ancient paths, ask where the good way is,
and walk in it, and you will find rest for your souls."
JEREMIAH 6:16

During the 2008 Major league Baseball season, I was blessed to pitch for the Philadelphia Phillies and to have the kind of season most pitchers dream about. You might say it was perfect, because I had forty-one saves in forty-one opportunities during the regular season and went seven for seven in the postseason in save opportunities. It was the most dominant year I've ever spent in sports.

But baseball was never the most important thing in the world to me, and it never will be. I was a growing Christian when I played, and I still am. Christianity gives me perspective and, more specifically, a purpose beyond pitching.

If someone were to define who I was during my playing days, they might have said, "He's a professional baseball player." Occupationally, that was true; however, there was a large part of me that was not just curious about other things but driven toward them.

Let me clarify what I mean: I repeat, baseball has never been the most important thing in the world to me and never will be. My family and my God—Jesus Christ—are the most important things in the world to me, so important that I have a strong desire for the second part of my life to get started.

I never wanted to be one of those forty-ish baseball players with diminished talent hanging on because playing Major league Baseball defines who they are. Not to speak disrespectfully of those who choose this career path, but other opportunities were calling my name, and I believed I'd be fortunate enough to do what God had preplanned for me.

When I consider the second phase of my life, I have a strong yen to become a religious archaeologist. I feel a close association to Catholicism, but I don't label myself as Catholic. I don't define myself as a member of any particular denomination. I've been to a lot of different churches and heard a lot of preaching. I take as much as I can from each one.

As a professional athlete, I was in a position to do some pretty amazing things. But the two most amazing things a person can do, no matter what platform he is given, are to honor God and let people know that he understands how very blessed he is.

Give thanks to God and show it. When you do those things, people will understand that you are more than what you do for a living.

Why am I more blessed than the guy down the street? Not because I'm better. It's because God gave me a gift for a purpose: to honor Him and to give back to help other people.

BRAD LIDGE

2. Need a Lift?

*The wisdom of the prudent is to give thought to their ways,
but the folly of fools is deception. Fools mock at making
amends for sin, but goodwill is found among the upright.*
PROVERBS 14:8–9

On April 26, 2008, two college women's softball teams squared off in Ellensburg, Washington. Central Washington and Western Oregon universities were both contenders for the league championship, and whichever team won that day would have had a definite edge. Going into the game, there was only one thing on the minds of the coaches, players, and fans—*win*. But that was about to change. For one small moment in time, winning was going to be put into its proper place.

In the top of the second inning, with two runners on base, Western Oregon's Sara Tucholsky stepped up to the plate. Sara, who stood just 5 feet 2 inches tall, had never hit a home run before. "I'm a line drive hitter," she claimed. But on the second pitch, to everyone's surprise, Tucholsky connected and sent the ball over the center field fence. There were only about a hundred people in attendance that day, and half of them cheered madly, anticipating a victory.

Sara rounded first, but when she approached second base, she realized she had not touched first base, so she turned to go back. That's when the anterior cruciate ligament (ACL) in her right knee snapped. In excruciating pain, she fell to the ground. But she knew she had to get back to first base, so she crawled for what seemed like hours. As she reached the base, she hugged it with one hand and grabbed her right knee with the other. No one knew what to do.

Quickly, Sara's coach, Pam Knox, approached the umpire, Jacob McChesney, and asked what the ruling was if Sara was not able to round the bases. He told her, "A two-run single." The rule states that after hitting a home run, a player must touch all the bases, in order, and cannot be assisted by anyone from her own team. This was bad news for Western Oregon, as they would lose a run, but it was even worse news for Tucholsky; her dream of hitting a home run would forever remain just a dream.

Central Washington's Mallory Holtman, who had hit more home runs than any player in conference history, overheard the ruling and approached the umpire. She asked if it was within the rules for players from the opposing team to carry Sara around the bases. Though puzzled by the request, McChesney told Holtman that it wasn't against the rules. Without hesitation, Holtman and her teammate Liz Wallace asked Tucholsky if they could pick her up and carry her around the bases. Sara said, "Yes."

Holtman replied, "You hit the home run; you deserve it." They picked up Sara so she was in a sitting position, and when they reached each base, they gently lowered her so she could touch the base with her left foot.

When they reached home plate, no cheers went up. Instead, tears came down. The entire crowd, the coaches, and the players were elevated to a state of emotion they had never experienced before. There was something more going on here than softball. There was something more important happening than two teams competing for the conference championship. For that magical moment, no one thought about winning.

Ironically, Western Oregon won the game 4–2 and went on to win the conference championship and head to the nationals. Central Washington stayed home and read about it in the papers.

Mallory Holtman and Liz Wallace taught the rest of the players, the coaches, the umpire, and the crowd an important lesson that day: practice to win, play to win, but never forget that sports are coached by real people, umpired by real people, and played by real people. And if you have to choose between winning and people, well, here's what Sara Tucholsky's coach had to say: "It's a great moment when someone has character to step up and do the right thing at the right time."

That's the lesson everyone there learned that day. Will this story be buried under the dirt between the chain-link fences of that small-town softball field? Not if one of us gives it life by telling the story. Someone dear to me gave me this story. I've given it to you. Now it's your turn.

SWEN NATER

3. Knowing the Score

> *Be careful that you do not forget the LORD your God,*
> *failing to observe his commands, his laws and his decrees.*
> DEUTERONOMY 8:11

When my team, the San Antonio Spurs, won the NBA championship in 1999, it was gratifying on so many levels. For one thing, I think Avery Johnson and I were able to show people that having a strong religious faith doesn't mean you can't be a tough competitor.

I can't overstate how important my faith has been to me as an athlete and as a person. It has helped me deal with so many things, including matters of ego and pride.

For instance, I can't deny that it felt weird to see my teammate Tim Duncan standing on the podium after being awarded the 1999 Finals Most Valuable Player trophy. I was thinking, *Man, never have I come to the end of a tournament and not been the one holding up that trophy.* It was hard, but I thought about the biblical story of David and Goliath. David helped King Saul win the battle, but the king wasn't happy because everyone knew he had killed thousands of men while David had killed tens of thousands. King Saul couldn't enjoy the victory because he was thinking about David getting more credit than he got.

I was blessed that God finally gave me the ability to just enjoy the victory no matter who gets the credit. Tim killed the tens of thousands. That's great. I was happy for him.

Whenever I went out on the basketball floor, people expected me to perform at a certain level. However, I also felt—and still feel—a responsibility to God to perform at a certain level as a husband and a father and as a follower of Christ. Those are things that take an investment of time.

As a player, I had to spend time in the gym shooting and lifting weights to prepare myself. At home, I have to spend time investing in my children and my wife. My worth as a person comes from what I do for God and from being able to go to Him and say, "God, are You proud of me? Am I doing what You called me to do?" My self-worth comes from pleasing Him. The thing that keeps driving me nuts is that I don't have to trust in what I can do alone. I can trust in what God can do with me and through me.

Near the end of my playing career, I had to sit down and have a one-on-one talk with the Lord. I asked, "What do You want me to do—spend more time here with this team and this community, or are You ready to have me move on to something else?" I felt God answering me by saying, "David, I'm preparing you for some other things. I'll let you enjoy this basketball season one more year, but I really have some other things I want you to do."

God now works through my life to bless others. He takes a hand wherever He can find one and then just does what He likes with it. Sometimes He takes a bishop's hand and lays it on the child's head in benediction; He takes the hand of a mother to guide her child; and sometimes He takes the hand of an old creature like me to give a bit of comfort to a neighbor. But they are all hands touched by His Spirit—and His Spirit is everywhere looking for hands to use.

How do I perceive myself? I am a father and a husband and a man blessed with an unbelievable responsibility to honor God.

It's a far bigger responsibility than I ever felt toward my fans. It's far more than what I felt toward the people paying me or even toward my teammates.

Even though my playing days are years behind me, I still have a responsibility to come out and work and make myself better. . .not for my own glory, but for His.

DAVID ROBINSON

4. Coming Clean

The mind governed by the flesh is death, but the mind
governed by the Spirit is life and peace.
ROMANS 8:6

In the spring of 2008, I faced one of the most challenging times of my professional baseball career. There are times when we as individuals feel we are living life as well as we can and serving God to the best of our abilities. We believe things are progressing smoothly as they relate to our faith walks, and then we get whacked on the side of the head by a "major-league" problem. A natural response is to ask, "God, what are You trying to do here?"

In 2002, I was on the disabled list with tendonitis in my elbow. Brian McNamee, my trainer after 1999, went to Tampa, Florida, to assist me in rehabilitating. Six years later, in the spring of 2008, Brian testified before Congress for the Mitchell Report that he recollected injecting me with human growth hormones on two to four occasions

HGH is a synthetic hormone that acts the same way as the chemical the pituitary glands secrete. It is meant to stimulate growth of muscle mass and to speed the healing process. It is not a steroid and was not banned in Major league Baseball until

2005, and I admitted to using the substance.

I am happy that Brian McNamee told the truth about me. My appearance before the congressional committee gave me the opportunity to declare the truth concerning my involvement with HGH. I didn't take it to get an edge—I took it to expedite the healing of my elbow.

God blessed my Major league Baseball career. I earned five World Series rings. When it came to my use of HGH, I knew that I had to be brutally honest and come clean about it, because I was having trouble sleeping at night. Sure, there was a time when no one would've known that I used HGH, except for my father, the Lord, and me. I could have easily ignored the matter and nobody else would have known.

I have used this learning experience on occasions when I've had to share with churches and kids about the issues of substance abuse. Those challenging times proved to me again how wonderful God is, no matter what I'm going through. Our God is always working on me to make me what He wants me to be.

God has taught me to do the right thing, no matter what. I try to treat people the right way—with respect—and to serve people and love them. Everything I have done for God's glory has come back to me tenfold. Day after day, God reveals just how wonderful and omnipotent He is.

ANDY PETTITTE

5. A True Leader

Be strong and take heart, all you who hope in the LORD.
PSALM 31:24

Probably the most inspirational story I know about all the players I have coached over forty-four years would be about one of the finest human beings I have ever met, Don Redden.

Don came from a small town in northern Louisiana and made a major impact on our basketball team and our school, Louisiana State University. He was handsome, talented, bright, caring, disciplined, and a lovely Christian human being. Even though Don was not as talented as Tim Tebow, in every other way he was the Tim Tebow of college basketball. He was the captain of our 1986 team, a team that no one gave a chance of making the NCAA tournament. Yet, this remarkable young man carried our team on his shoulders and did something absolutely marvelous. We not only made the tournament in 1986, but we became the lowest seed in the history of college basketball to make it to the Final Four.

During the NCAA tournament, I noticed that Don had colored in a small cross on each toe of his basketball shoes. One day at practice I asked him the significance of the crosses, and his reply was, "Coach, whenever I get tired late in a ball game and bend over for a rest, I see these crosses and it reminds me who I am really playing the game for, and that's God."

Don graduated in 1986 and was coaching a young team in Baton Rouge, Louisiana, when this handsome, well-muscled athlete unexpectedly died of a heart attack. What a loss for his family and the boys he coached, but what a win for him. He was strong in the Lord during his time here on earth, and as a result, he won the greatest victory of all—heaven.

DALE BROWN

6. In Christ Alone

For the Spirit God gave us does not make us timid,
but gives us power, love and self-discipline.
2 TIMOTHY 1:7

He will go down in the annals of sports as the man who engineered not only one of the greatest comebacks in collegiate football history while at the University of Maryland, but also one of the greatest comebacks in the history of the National Football League.

For Frank Reich, former backup quarterback of the Buffalo Bills, that game, played on a cold winter's day in Buffalo, will be remembered more for the spiritual effect it had on his life and the lives of millions of football fans throughout America.

What can be spiritual about a football game? Not much, but when the victor has won the contest by overcoming the most unbelievable circumstances, like being down 35–3 in the third quarter, the term "miracle comeback" seemed to find its way on the sports pages across the country.

Led by four touchdown passes thrown by Reich and a flawless performance by the rest of the team, the Buffalo Bills made pro football history on January 3, 1993, when Steve Christie's kick sailed through the uprights in overtime to give Buffalo a dramatic 41–38 victory over the Houston Oilers in the American Football Conference's wild card game and capped the greatest comeback in NFL history.

So now the term "miracle comeback" starts to make sense.

However, the real miracle was not the game itself but what happened immediately afterward in the Bills' locker room. With hordes of media people clamoring around him, waiting to hear what the key to Reich's success was in leading his team to victory, this mild-mannered leader proceeded to give one of the boldest witnesses for Jesus Christ ever given by a Christian athlete. These were the words Reich spoke to the media that day:

"There's a song that gave me strength all week that I must have listened to a hundred times this week and I just want to read the words to you. It's by Michael English, and he's a Christian musician," Reich said as he pulled out a crumpled piece of paper and proceeded to read these words:

"In Christ alone
I place my trust. . ."

The song goes on to describe Jesus Christ as the only source of strength and hope.

"You know," said Reich, "there wasn't any way for me possibly to get up there and say anything else other than what I did. I just felt like those had to be the first words out of my mouth because that was the most important thing to me at that time, not the game or anything else."

Frank believed that God was really telling him to share that song. "I never could have believed that in my wildest dreams that this is what God had intended," he said. As a result of his boldness in his witness for Jesus Christ, secular radio stations across the country began playing "In Christ Alone."

"There were times in my career when I've talked about what Jesus Christ has meant in my life and the relationship that I have with Him, but so many other times it never got printed or never got talked about. This time was different. This time the cameras and tape recorders kept rolling. . .and what they heard is that Jesus Christ alone is our source of strength and hope," Frank explained.

Reich's story is about the miracle-working power of the Holy Spirit and what it means to have a relationship with Jesus Christ and to serve Him. Frank has been an encouragement to millions of Christians and non-Christians alike. He understands that football can be a very humbling experience—win or lose. "God has certainly reminded me that just because you were the quarterback of that game, you're no better than anybody else; you're no different than anybody else, you still need Me as much as anybody else needs Me," explained the Lebanon, Pennsylvania, native.

Realizing that he is just a vessel God uses and that the Lord controls all of his steps on and off the field, Frank's humility is one of the strengths of his character. Handling the tremendous victory after the Houston game was quite different than coping with the devastating defeat in Super Bowl XXVII at the hands of the Dallas Cowboys just a few weeks later.

"I like to talk about that Super Bowl more than I like to talk about any other game. With the Houston game, people can look at that, and maybe they have a hard time relating because of the unique circumstances and results of this particular football game. With the Super Bowl, in dealing with defeat, you know people are dealing with defeat in their lives all the time. Believe me, I wanted to win that game as bad as anybody and I really felt like we were going to win that game. But now that I've had time to reflect on the game and reflect on that entire season, I began to understand what God had intended—to trust Him no matter what the circumstances. It was just a matter of a couple of weeks when I experienced the highest high and the lowest low in my field," said Reich.

It was a phone call from Frank's new friend, Michael English, who reminded him that God was a God of the mountains and He's a God of the valleys.

What did that Super Bowl loss teach Frank Reich? It taught him about finding ultimate victory through a relationship with Jesus Christ. No matter the circumstances on the football field (workplace), in the home, or in the community, it is our relationship with Christ that gives us the power to persevere until the end.

Today Reich is back in the NFL, this time as an assistant coach. When Reich is not coaching, he finds himself in demand as a motivational speaker. He also makes time to return to Buffalo every spring, where he and his wife, Linda, host the Athletes in Action's Call to Courage Awards Breakfast, which honors a professional and high school football player who exemplifies outstanding character, commitment, and community both on and off the playing field. Reich has presented the Call to Courage Award to some of the game's most outstanding athletes of faith, such as Kurt Warner, Chad Pennington, Jon Kasay, Trent Dilfer, Curtis Martin, Don Davis, Jon Kitna, and Bob Christian.

For Frank Reich, the song "In Christ Alone" has become an anthem of hope both in victory and defeat. He realizes that in Jesus Christ we find strength in the bad times and the ability to keep humble during the good times.

JOSEPH R. CIFFA

7. The Man Who Brought Church to Baseball

*Through Jesus, therefore, let us continually offer to God a
sacrifice of praise—the fruit of lips that openly profess his name.*
HEBREWS 13:15

When I was a youngster growing up in Wilmington, Delaware, one of the monthly highlights for our family was the postman's delivery of the monthly *Reader's Digest*. My favorite article? "The Most Unforgettable Character I've Met." Let me tell you about my nomination for that honor. His name—Watson Spoelstra. Everyone just called him Waddy.

Waddy grew up in the Detroit area and loved sports his entire life. He was never good enough as an athlete to think about going pro, so he got into the sports business as a writer. Waddy made a name for himself covering the Detroit Lions and Tigers, along with college sports, back in the 1950s and '60s.

Waddy and his wife, Jean, had two children—John, a future sports executive, and Ann. When Ann was a teenager, she was struck with a brain aneurism. At the same time, Waddy's life was spinning out of control. He was fighting a losing battle with alcohol and heading down a path of self-destruction.

One day, with Ann's life hanging in the balance, Waddy wandered into the hospital's Catholic chapel. His prayer to God was, "If You do something about her, I'll let You do something about me." Many an alcoholic has bargained like that with God, only to dismiss it after the prayer is answered. Not Waddy. Ann was healed, and her father was ready to do the Lord's work.

At this point of the story, Waddy was covering the Detroit Lions. In July 1958, the Lions had acquired Bill Glass, a defensive end from Baylor University. Bill is a good friend of mine and told me, "Waddy had come to the Lord six months before I got to Detroit. I was attending divinity school in the off-season, so he knew I was a Christian.

"One day, Waddy said to me, 'I need to grow spiritually.' We met almost daily for Bible study and prayer. He had no biblical background at all, but he was spiritually hungry and grew like a weed. Waddy was a voracious reader and so anxious to learn.

"We kept our relationship secret because neither one of us wanted the team to think I was buttering up a sportswriter. We were together in Detroit for four years until I was traded to the Cleveland Browns. In fact, Waddy called me to tell me about the trade. Before I left, I helped him find a good church to attend in Michigan.

"Waddy remained my friend until his death on July 20, 1999. He had a beautiful, warm heart, so tears came easily to him. As he aged, he talked more and more about heaven. One day he said, 'Bill, I can't wait to sit on the celestial curbstone and talk with you for a few thousand years.'"

I first met Waddy in the early 1970s, when I was serving as general manager of the Chicago Bulls. Waddy was still covering the Tigers, and I visited him at the Chicago White Sox ballpark. One day he said, "Pat, I've got a mission before me that is more important than the newspaper business. Ballplayers and coaches can't get to church during the season, so I want to launch a chapel program and bring church to them on the road."

Waddy told me he planned to share this idea with baseball commissioner Bowie Kuhn. I encouraged Waddy to go forward with his plan. Some weeks later, I heard Waddy's voice on the phone: "The commissioner has given us a grant of $10,000 to launch the chapel movement!"

That was the beginning, and over the next twenty-five years Waddy nurtured and prayed over the baseball ministry, which today continues to impact the lives of hundreds of players and their families.

Waddy loved people and was the best encourager I've ever known. He gave most of his encouragement through handwritten notes on pads of yellow paper.

About a year before his death, Waddy wrote my wife and me one of his famous notes. It turned out to be the last note among dozens I received from him. I had it framed, and it hangs in my office to this day:

> *Dear Pat and Ruth—*
>
> *Each day I ask the Lord to elevate my joy meter—and he does. Our Lord is so faithful.*
>
> *I'm trying to write more notes. I've put in four months of hip rehab and have two to go. I use a walker to reach the dining room.*
>
> *Jack Kinder [a Christian business leader] comes up with Satan's strategy to mess us up. Three stages: 1) Sell no Heaven; 2) Sell no Hell; 3) If that fails, sell no hurry.*
>
> *We pray for you and your family. We love you.*
>
> *Waddy*
>
> *PS—A wise man says, "If you care enough to write with poor penmanship, others will decipher it."*

In the summer of 2008, Waddy's grandson, Erik, was named the head coach of the NBA's Miami Heat. I can just picture his proud grandpa beaming from that celestial curbstone. In one of his first games as a head coach for Miami, Erik and the Heat come to town to play the team I currently work for, the Orlando Magic.

I removed Waddy's framed note from my office and took it to the arena. Before the game, I visited Erik's office in the visitors' locker area. "Erik," I said, "this is the last note I got from your grandfather. I wanted you to read it."

After Erik finished, he looked at me and couldn't speak. I saw tears forming in his eyes. I said, "Waddy has left a legacy for all of us. We have a lot to live up to."

"Yes, we do," said Erik. "Yes, we do."

PAT WILLIAMS

8. Faith and Tomato Juice

[Jesus said,] "According to your faith let it be done to you."
MATTHEW 9:29

My father, Bill Musselman, was born in Wooster, Ohio. His father was an auto mechanic and his mother worked at a potato chip factory. He understood early that if he worked hard enough at school and sports, he could make something of himself. At age twenty-five he became the head basketball coach at Ashland College, where he ignited the arena with his team's pregame warm-up. He left Ashland to coach at the University of Minnesota, where he led the Gophers to their first Big Ten Championship in fifty-three years. He went on to coach in the American Basketball Association, Continental Basketball Association, and the National Basketball Association, where he was the head coach for the San Diego Sails, the Minnesota Timberwolves, and the Cleveland Cavaliers.

He had a contagious intensity, a wicked sense of humor, and an iron will that refused to ever give up. Most of all, he had a remarkable faith in life, especially when things got difficult.

When I think of the Psalms, I always think of songs of joy or celebration, but in a large portion of psalms there is a great deal of lamenting. You often find individuals who, prior to the joy, faced great moments of despair, unending challenges, and giant failures. Despite the challenges, these people never lost faith.

In what would have been the middle of my father's life (if he would have lived past fifty-eight), he faced his own challenges. I remember walking into his one-room apartment and seeing his belongings in cardboard boxes after he had been fired as a head coach in the NBA. In that apartment, amid those boxes, I saw him rebuild his life. I remember visiting and getting up at 2:00 a.m. to get a drink of water and finding him with a small light on, studying old basketball tapes. After games or on his nights off, he would sit at a local truck stop diner until 1:00 a.m., eating chicken noodle soup and drinking his sixth tomato juice and talking about ways he could make his CBA team champions. He didn't know if he would ever be invited back to the NBA, but he never gave up and never lost faith in God's plan.

As I look back at my father's life, it is his failures followed by his faith that I admire most. Yes, I was proud of him as I sat courtside at a Lakers-Timberwolves game, but I was proudest of him in that apartment. I was proudest of his inability to lose faith.

I remember when I had a major failure in my life and called my dad nervously to tell him. I was actually more than nervous—I was quite petrified. We grew up in a very strict home with high expectations, so I was shaking when I made the call.

When I told him what had happened, he was silent for a moment and then replied, "Do you know how many times I have screwed up in my life? How many times I have failed, been fired, or made the wrong choice? You could never fail as much as

I have. Do you understand that? You tried and you will try again, and you will succeed because you are not wired to give up. You have to have faith."

Ironically, there was something quite magical in hearing him tell me how badly he had failed in his life. I had only thought of him as being a success. At that moment, with those words that were so contrary to what I was expecting, he gave me the freedom to fail and know that he, my mother, my brother, and God would still love me. He gave me the secret ingredient to success—the right to fail—and the knowledge that the only failure in life is losing faith in the journey.

Looking back, I realize it was not my father's successes that give me strength during my sleepless nights; it was his resilience coupled with his faith that guide me and give me hope.

The psalmists knew that without faith they were working on a foundation of quicksand, but that with faith anything was possible. My father knew this, too, and after four CBA championships, a trip back to the NBA, and plenty more late-night bowls of soup and too many tomato juices to count, I learned the value of faith.

NICOLE MUSSELMAN BOYKIN

9. Love Your Neighbor "Daly"

And he has given us this command: Anyone who loves God must also love his brother and sister.

1 JOHN 4:21

My family and I were unpacking boxes during our move into our new home in Jamaica Plains, Massachusetts, when we heard a knock at the door. *Who could that be?* I thought. *We don't know anyone here yet.*

A distinguished-looking man stood at the door facing me. "Your next-door neighbor has tried to rally the neighborhood to keep you out," he said. "I've challenged him, and I'm ready to take him on."

This man's words stunned me, even more than his unsolicited support. But I understood what he was talking about. It was 1971, less than ten years since Martin Luther King Jr.'s "I Have a Dream" speech, and while the civil rights movement was passing into history, the racial tensions that marked that era were slow to heal. From my window, I could see the man next door building a fence between our homes, even though it was pouring rain outside. And while I'd hoped things might be different here, I suppose I also understood why that fence was going up.

What I didn't understand was why this man at my door was so ready to take up my battle. But then, I didn't yet know Chuck Daly, basketball coach at Boston College.

On that day, Chuck definitely had the home-court advantage. Since I'd spent eleven years playing in the NBA with the Cincinnati Royals, the Boston Celtics, and the Milwaukee Bucks, he knew something about me. But little did either of us know in that moment what the future held for Chuck. He would go on to become a Hall of Fame NBA coach, leading the down-on-their-luck Detroit Pistons to the top of the pack two seasons in a row, in 1989 and 1990. Two years later, he would become the coach of the USA Dream Team, leading an amazing ensemble of athletic talent to a sweep in the basketball competition in that year's Summer Olympics in Barcelona, Spain.

But for now, he was a neighbor who had come to my defense at a time when I sorely needed it. That, I would learn, was Chuck Daly.

In the succeeding years, our relationship progressed from neighbors to friends, and I came to know Chuck as a man who lived by the philosophy that few things, outside of tonight's game, were really that important. If you were Chuck's friend, he was your ally.

"Not a problem" was one of his famous "Chuckisms." It's how he saw the conflict with that divisive neighbor all those years ago. It was a philosophy he proved each and every time anyone he knew and loved needed help. And Chuck knew and loved a lot of people. Many of them were there at his funeral service thirty-eight years later, in May 2009.

For Chuck, there were no gray lines between right and wrong. He was a man of solid principle who put shoe leather to his faith—just the kind of man you want to be your coach, your friend. . .and especially your neighbor.

WAYNE EMBRY

10. Payne Relief

*Each of you should give what you have decided in your heart to give,
not reluctantly or under compulsion, for God loves a cheerful giver.*
2 CORINTHIANS 9:7

I was blessed to have been one of golfing great Payne Stewart's disciplers the last six months of his life. I helped him understand a broader meaning of various scriptures, of what God's Word says about the sanctity of life, and to understand the basic disciplines that best encourage development of spiritual maturity.

On October 15, 1999, just ten days before Payne soared in a private jet to meet Jesus in the air, our First Orlando Foundation honored him at our annual fund-raising dinner/auction benefiting our First Center for Pregnancy. He was presented the First Annual Legacy Award for his outstanding leadership in helping make a dream of The First Academy (TFA) come true (a new athletic facility, later named the Payne Stewart Athletic Complex). Then Orlando mayor Glenda Hood honored Payne that night with a key to the city and a proclamation declaring

October 15 as Payne Stewart Day in the city of Orlando. However, the highlight of the night came when Payne approached the podium with monster tears running down his cheeks to receive his crystal eagle trophy. His first comments were that the young women who gave their testimonies regarding changing their minds about abortion and bringing their precious children up on the platform "should be the honorees tonight instead of me."

Payne called me in April 1999 and asked me to show him the architectural renderings of our proposed TFA athletic fields. He suggested I give him the names of twelve couples I felt might be interested in helping fund the project. Payne said, "You give me their names and phone numbers, and I'll personally call and invite them to my home for a barbeque and I'll do the cooking. After we eat, you bring out the drawings and tell us how much it will cost." Payne was pumped!

He continued, "Randall, after you state the cost, I am going to say, 'Okay, friends, Tracey and I are going to give a half million dollars for construction. How much will you give?'"

Because of Payne's willingness to step forward and trust God to use him to prompt others to give, we received a $3.2 million commitment in Payne and Tracey's backyard. They were a generous, giving couple. Right after Payne Stewart's exciting victory at the U.S. Open in Pinehurst, he brought me the yellow flag from the eighteenth hole and autographed it for us to auction off to benefit the athletic complex—it brought $45,000.

Today the Payne Stewart Athletic Complex hosts high school football, baseball, softball, and multiple state and regional track and field events. It also serves as a practice facility for college football teams invited to Orlando bowl events and for Major league Baseball spring tryouts.

Thank you, Lord, for allowing us to have Payne for a season.

RANDALL JAMES

11. Schooled in Heavy Lifting

*"Then you will have success if you are careful to observe
the decrees and laws that the LORD gave Moses for Israel.
Be strong and courageous. Do not be afraid or discouraged."*
1 CHRONICLES 22:13

In 1956, power lifter Paul Anderson weighed well over 350 pounds. His neck size was twenty-four inches, his biceps were over twenty-four inches, his chest fifty-eight inches, and his thighs thirty-six inches. In the best condition and form of his life, Paul was ready for the 1956 Olympic Games in Melbourne, Australia. All the experts of the day believed he merely had to show up to win the Olympic gold medal.

Paul and his teammates arrived in Melbourne eighteen days before the lifting competition. Shortly after his arrival, Paul began to feel feverish and unsteady, but he could not pinpoint the reason. Less than two weeks before the competition, he awoke in the middle of the night burning with fever. A doctor treated him, but the fever raged for twelve days and his body weight dropped by thirty pounds. He felt miserable and weak. Since no one could determine what was wrong with him, there was talk of sending him back to the States.

Three days before the competition, the doctors told Paul that they could not allow a man in his condition to compete. But Paul asked them to postpone their final decision until the last possible moment, and they agreed. Without the doctors' consent, Paul put himself on four aspirins every three hours. The aspirins brought the fever down, and by the morning of the day he was scheduled to lift—November 25, 1956—his temperature was nearly normal. The medical professionals were still concerned but said they would not forbid Paul from competing if he would agree to take all responsibility.

The super-heavyweights were scheduled to lift at 8:00 p.m., but the meet was far behind schedule. Paul's first lift took place around 1:00 a.m. The effects of the aspirins had worn off and his fever had returned. Feeling dizzy and cold, he perspired profusely. Paul held on with each lift but was trailing an Argentine lifter in the point count. At 3:30 a.m., he approached the platform for his final lift. He had three chances to successfully make this lift. He would have to break the existing Olympic record and win the gold.

On his first attempt, he tried to drive the bar overhead but never got it past his chin. The bar crashed to the floor and the arena was silent except for the echo.

On his second attempt, he rushed to the bar and pulled it to his chest. The weight felt heavier than before, the bar rumbled to the floor, and he stomped away, bitterly disappointed. Paul waved his teammates away as they rushed to encourage him.

Paul's mind raced as he contemplated the possibilities of losing. He used his officially allotted rest period of three minutes to walk up a long, dark corridor. Paul felt as if God was reminding him of everything He had ever done for him. God had made him what he was. Everything Paul had accomplished had been because God had let him survive Bright's disease as a child. God had given him loving Christian parents. In spite of these countless blessings, Paul had ignored God.

He found it impossible to pray. He tried twice, but his heart was hardened from ignoring God for so long. At this lowest point in his life, a point to which many people must come before they realize a need for God, Paul recognized how unworthy he was of Christ's love. He then returned for his third attempt at the lift.

The arena was silent. When Paul pulled the weight to his chest, he knew immediately that it was futile. He couldn't put it overhead. Now he was desperate. In a split second, he found that he could be sincere with God. As quickly as the words raced through his heart and mind, he told the Lord he was aware of all that had been given him and he had returned nothing. Paul continued by pledging to God that he wanted to be part of His kingdom from here on out; he was making a real commitment. Then Paul realized his immediate need and said, "I'm not trying to make a deal, Lord. No deals, but I must have Your help to get this weight overhead." Paul had made a true commitment to serve God for the rest of his life.

He gave the final push and drove the bar overhead, and it stayed. The crowd went wild as Paul returned the bar to the floor. He suddenly was the Olympic gold medalist. The smile on his face that early morning was not as much for the joy of victory or for the relief that the ordeal was over, but for his new relationship with Christ. What he had really won was not an Olympic championship, measured by poundage, but the strength of God's Holy Spirit.

Throughout the remainder of Paul's life, he would share his faith by saying that it was a tremendous thrill to win the Olympic gold medal for his country and to stand on the winner's platform as the national anthem was played and the American flag was raised. He would continue on by sharing that the *greatest* thrill in his life was knowing Jesus Christ as his personal Savior. He would say, "If I, Paul Anderson, the world's strongest man, cannot make it through one day without Jesus Christ, how can you?"

In 1961, Paul and his wife, Glenda founded the Paul Anderson Youth Home in Vidalia, Georgia. Still in operation today, the home, coupled with its accredited high school, ministers to troubled young men from the ages of sixteen to twenty-one. Unwavering Christian principles and unconditional love, seasoned with discipline and consistency, make up the framework of the home, which was built on the foundation of the Lord Jesus Christ.

PAULA ANDERSON SCHAEFER

12. A "Holy" Donut

*Jesus said, "See that you do not despise on one of
these little ones. For I tell you that their angels in
heaven always see the face of my Father in heaven."*
MATTHEW 18:10

I was born in late May 1974, at a time when my dad, Pat Williams, was serving as general manager of the Atlanta Hawks of the NBA. Later that summer, he accepted the general manager's position with the Philadelphia 76ers. By August I had arrived in my new home.

In addition to his basketball duties, my dad took on the responsibility of coordinating the Philadelphia Phillies Sunday morning chapel services when the team played at home. He had spent the first seven years of his pro sports career in the Phillies organization, so he enjoyed resuming a part-time relationship with the team of his youth.

In the summer of 1977, Dad started taking me to the ballpark early on Sunday mornings, and I would sit through the service—as a three-year old—getting to meet all the stars of the National League. I got to know Mike Schmidt, Gary Carter, Don Sutton, and many other famous players.

One Sunday the Los Angeles Dodgers were in town, and my dad decided he would be the speaker that morning rather than bringing in an outside pastor or Bible teacher. Players from both teams gathered for a fifteen-minute period of Bible teaching and prayer; it was just a nice, warm time of inspiration and fellowship.

Tommy Lasorda was managing the Dodgers at the time, and he was very receptive to the chapel program. My dad went up to him and introduced me, and Tommy said, "Let's just have the meeting right here in my office." The players started wandering in, and I noticed they each had a big cup of coffee and the whitest, most tempting powdered donuts you have ever seen. Since I was a kid at the time, those donuts really caught my eye.

That morning my dad spoke on the topic of Jesus and His strength in serving other people (trust me, I have no memory of that message, because all I was thinking about were those donuts). My father had just gotten warmed up when I chirped loudly, "Daddy, I want a donut."

Immediately, he turned his head to the left and gave me that *look*. The lure of the donuts was too great. Again, I barked (only louder), "Daddy, I want a donut!"

At this point, there was a palpable tension in that room. What was going to happen next? Very quietly, Tommy Lasorda got up, took me by the arm, and tiptoed out of the room with me. We disappeared while my dad preached on. A minute later, we tiptoed back in and I had in my hand one of those big, white, cream-filled donuts.

My father preached in peace and never heard another word from me. His message that morning was about being a servant to others. I don't think he planned on Tommy Lasorda living it out in front of all of his players. Talk about a real live sermon illustration! I'm not discounting my dad's message, but I think Tommy's act of service to a little three-year-old was remembered for a lot longer.

JIMMY WILLIAMS

13. The Minister of Defense

*"Call to me and I will answer you and tell you
great and unsearchable things you do not know."*
JEREMIAH 33:3

As the Minister of Defense and I walked through the door, a wave of recognition rippled through the restaurant. At 6 feet 5 inches tall and weighing 295 pounds, Green Bay Packers' defensive end Reggie White had *presence*. People greeted him as he walked by, and he signed a few autographs on his way to the table.

Reggie ordered a plate of Buffalo wings—"hot and spicy, but not *too* hot and spicy." Then he explained to me his vision for the book he wanted to write—a book about football, faith, and racial reconciliation.

On January 8, 1996, just a few months before our meeting, someone had firebombed the Inner City Church in Knoxville, Tennessee, where Reggie was one of the pastors (hence the nickname the Minister of Defense. The torching of Reggie's church had focused national attention on the issue of church burnings across the South in the mid-1990s.

Reggie had helped found the Inner City Church just three years earlier, and it had quickly become a thriving, vibrant multiracial congregation. "When I got the call," he told me, "that someone had burned the church, I thought, *We must be doing something right for the devil to come against us like that.*"

After lunch, Reggie took me to his home, and we jumped right into the project, hammering out the book that would later be called *Reggie White: In the Trenches*. As we talked, he told me one jaw-dropping story after another.

The most amazing event he related began with the December 3, 1995, game against the Cincinnati Bengals. With 6:43 left to play, the Bengals had possession, trailing 17–10. Bengals quarterback Jeff Blake took the snap, and Reggie came around the corner. He saw the tackle moving to cut-block him, so he leaped over the diving blocker. As he landed, Reggie heard a loud *pop* in his left knee. Instantly, the leg cramped up—he couldn't run. He took a few hops on his right foot—then crashed to the turf and couldn't get up.

Blake launched a pass—which Packers cornerback LeRoy Butler intercepted. The interception sealed the game—but the fans went silent after seeing No. 92 injured on the ground.

After the team doctor looked Reggie over, two teammates, Butler and Sean Jones, helped him off the field. The doctor later determined that Reggie had torn a hamstring, the tendon in the hollow behind his left knee. When the hamstring tore, the muscle bunched up in a knot behind his thigh. The doctor told him he needed surgery.

"I'm not gonna have surgery," Reggie replied. "I'm gonna play."

But when he tried out the leg in practice, he had no strength or speed. He missed the Packers' next game, against Tampa Bay, ending his 166-game streak as a starter. The Packers lost 13–10.

Reggie told the team doctor, "I guess I need that operation after all."

A few days later, at a team meeting, one of Reggie's teammates, Mark Ingram, told him, "Reggie, my mother has a real strong faith in God, and last night she said, 'The devil hasn't beaten Reggie White. Something big is about to happen.'" Reggie thanked his teammate for the encouragement, but he was sure there was nothing ahead of him but the surgeon's knife and a long recovery.

Shortly before Christmas, Reggie was playing with his kids when he realized his leg felt stronger. The more he flexed his leg, the better it felt. He called his weight coach and said, "Meet me at the workout center." With the help of the coach, Reggie ran sprints and practiced hitting the sled. The leg felt great. "Man," he said, "let's tell Mike."

So Reggie and the weight coach went to Coach Mike Holmgren's house. It was late at night. Reggie had just reached the front step when the door swung open and there was Holmgren. Both men jumped.

"Reggie! You scared me!" Holmgren said. He had chosen that exact moment to go outside and turn off the Christmas lights. "What are *you* doing here? I thought you were Santa Claus!"

"Well, Coach," Reggie said, "Maybe I am—'cause I'm ready to play at New Orleans!"

The next day, Reggie called a press conference and told reporters that God had healed him. He recalled, "TV stations broke in and told their audiences that Reggie White had been healed. ESPN ran two video clips back-to-back, the one where I said, 'I'm not going to play no more this year,' and the one where I said, 'God healed me and I'm going to New Orleans.'"

Reggie and the Packers beat the Saints 34–23. Up in the stands, a pair of Green Bay fans raised a sign that read: WE BELIEVE.

After Reggie told me that story, I asked him, "With all the problems and suffering in the world, why did God decide to heal a football player?"

He pondered the question then said, "God didn't do this for my sake. I never prayed for God to heal me—I didn't believe He would do that for me. God usually doesn't take us *out* of our trials. He takes us *through* them. But a lot of people prayed for me to be healed. I think God answered their prayers so that their faith would be impacted."

Reggie never had the surgery to reattach the hamstring. He went on to play three more seasons with the Packers, including appearances in back-to-back Super Bowls. In Super Bowl XXXI, against the Patriots, he collected three sacks and a Super Bowl ring.

Working with the Minister of Defense on his book was one of the great privileges of my life. I could list dozens of lessons I learned from Reggie, but I'll list only three:

1. *Work hard to be the best*. Reggie showed me his private

training room behind his house. He got on the Stairmaster, set it to maximum resistance, and put himself through a grueling workout. I felt the earth tremble beneath my feet. Though training camp was still weeks away, Reggie was dedicated to staying in shape all year 'round. Hard work gets you to your goals.

2. *Live boldly*. On my last day in Knoxville, Reggie told me, "I want to make a prediction in the book: We're going to win the Super Bowl."

"That's a bold prediction," I said. "What if you're wrong?"

"Jim," he said, "after we lost the National Football Conference title game last season, we all promised we'd win it all this season. We're gonna keep that promise."

The book came out in September 1996 with Reggie's bold prediction. Five months later, the Packers beat the Patriots in Super Bowl XXXI, just as Reggie promised. The lesson: high-achieving people set big, bold goals.

3. *God always answers prayer—but not always in the way we expect*. Reggie told me, "Sometimes I prayed for selfish stuff and God said no to those prayers—and later I was glad He did. Sometimes I prayed and prayed, and there was no answer, and I got frustrated and thought, *God isn't paying any attention to me*. Later, I found out He was answering my prayer, but first He wanted to teach me something. He doesn't always answer the way I want Him to, but He always answers."

On the morning of December 26, 2004, I turned on the TV but kept the sound muted. Then I noticed Reggie's picture on the screen. I reached for the remote control to turn up the sound—and then I saw the words on the screen: REGGIE WHITE, 1961–2004.

I had to sit down. I couldn't believe it. The news anchor explained that Reggie had died in his sleep due to a lung ailment. He was forty-three years old. It was incomprehensible. If ever a man seemed physically indestructible, it was Reggie White. I prayed for Reggie's wife, Sara, and for his children, Jeremy and Jecoliah.

Reggie White was a walking miracle, and even though it's hard to understand why he's gone, I know he placed his faith in the Resurrection and the Life. Reggie walked closely with his Lord in this life, and I know he's with his Lord right now.

JIM DENNEY

14. Branch and Bragan

"Do not seek revenge or bear a grudge against anyone among your people, but love your neighbor as yourself. I am the LORD."
LEVITICUS 19:18

I consider Branch Rickey to be the greatest person from the sports world. He and Billy Graham are the two most important individuals I have met in my ninety-two years on this earth.

During his lifetime, Mr. Rickey earned four degrees, one of which was in law, and he also received thirteen honorary degrees. He was also the baseball coach at the University of Michigan while he was in law school.

During his tenure at Michigan, the team had the opportunity to play Notre Dame in a South Bend weekend series. The best player on the Michigan squad was a black centerfielder who was denied admittance by the hotel where the visiting team was staying. When Mr. Rickey learned that the hotel would not allow a black to register he said, "Put him in with me." The hotel accommodated his request. Mr. Rickey vowed at that moment that if he ever had the opportunity to help a minority race, he would do so.

Branch Rickey played a total of four years in the major leagues and managed ten years. Before entering professional baseball, he told his mother he would not participate in any game played on a Sunday. He lived out that promise.

In 1943 I was honored when Branch Rickey, by then the Brooklyn Dodgers general manager, recruited me. I played for Brooklyn for five seasons. In 1946, Mr. Rickey directed his scouts to search for a black player who had major league potential. It turned out that Jackie Robinson was the best of those players the scouts observed. Mr. Rickey signed the UCLA graduate and former US Army officer to a Triple-A contract for the 1946 season. Playing for Montreal, Robinson responded in spectacular form and was named the Most Valuable Player in the International League that year.

In 1947 the Dodgers trained in Cuba—one of the reasons was to limit media coverage of the team and of Jackie. Robinson wore his Montreal uniform all spring, in spite of the fact that he appeared to be the best player in camp. After spring training, the Dodgers returned to Brooklyn. A welcome home luncheon was held for the team at the St. George Hotel.

Mr. Rickey made two announcements to the crowd gathered there: Number one, baseball commissioner Happy Chandler had suspended then Brooklyn manager Leo Durocher for a year for gambling, so Burt Shotton would be the new Dodgers manager. Number two, Jackie Robinson would open the season for the Brooklyn Dodgers at first base. The Dodgers went on to win the National League championship that year.

The color line was crossed, and Jackie Robinson came to prove himself as an outstanding player and a person of great character. Eventually, Mr. Rickey's role in making his dream a reality was applauded around the world, and Jackie Robinson went on to be numbered among the heroes of humanity.

BOBBY BRAGAN

Pat Williams's footnote: Bobby Bragan mailed this story to me on the afternoon of January 21, 2010. That evening, at age ninety-two, Bobby Bragan passed away in Fort Worth, Texas. This story represents the last written communication from my dear friend Bobby.

Bobby told me about his reaction to Jackie Robinson joining the Dodgers. "When we went on our first road trip together, I determined to have nothing to do with Jackie. But when the second road trip started, I was one of those lobbying to sit next to Jackie on the train. Jackie Robinson, the person and the ballplayer, changed my views and changed my life."

15. The A-MAYS-ing Auctioneer

Each of you should give what you have decided in your heart to give, not reluctantly or under compulsion, for God loves a cheerful giver.
2 CORINTHIANS 9:7

I was excited when baseball legend Bobby Bragan called me and invited me to be the principle speaker at his big fund-raising banquet on December 6, 2005, in Fort Worth, Texas. In that inimitable southern drawl, Bobby said, "And after your speech, I want ya to introduce our honored guest."

"Who's the honored guest, Bobby?" I inquired.

"Willie Mays."

I gulped and said, "One of my boyhood idols."

Bobby informed me, "He doesn't like to speak, so I'm gonna have you interview him."

Wow, what an assignment!

I felt that my keynote speech before 750 Texans went well that night, but there was one more event to go—my interview of Willie Mays.

As I went to the microphone to introduce Willie, I suddenly felt a tap on my shoulder. The shy, withdrawn, distant Willie Mays wanted the microphone. I was stunned. And so was the audience. The next series of events left that crowd speechless.

Willie said in that high-pitched voice of his, "All of you have been so nice to me down here in Texas. You've made me feel right at home, but I'm worried about one thing. I don't think we've raised enough money for Bobby Bragan's college scholarship fund."

At this point, he started taking off his tie and held it out in front of the crowd, "Tell you what, I'm gonna auction off my tie." Then, he took off his sport coat, "And I'm gonna auction this off, too." The next thing you know, off came his wristwatch, shoes, his dress shirt. . . fortunately, he kept his pants on.

"Everything I'm wearing tonight you can take home with you. I will meet you in the lobby of my hotel tomorrow morning." And just like that, Willie was running the auction.

Finally, Willie unveiled the highlight of the night: "Oh, and one more thing. Come out to San Francisco this summer for a Giants game. I will have four seats for you in my box."

Now the dinner crowd was really buzzing. You would have thought Willie had been an auctioneer his entire life. He worked that crowd like an old pro. The next thing you know, some businessman committed twenty thousand dollars and won the grand prize. It was an amazing sight.

Later that night, after I had gone to my room, I thought that Willie had demonstrated a lesson that Jesus taught centuries ago. Serving other people and making a difference in their lives out of a heart of love is really the evidence of the Christian life. Willie had not preached a sermon that night, but he certainly had lived one.

PAT WILLIAMS

16. Peacock Today, Feather Duster Tomorrow

*The wisdom of the prudent is to give thought to their ways,
but the folly of fools is deception. Fools mock at making
amends for sin, but goodwill is found among the upright.*
PROVERBS 14:8–9

My father, Joe Lapchick, is credited with helping the National Basketball Association integrate in 1950, when, as coach of the New York Knicks, he signed Nat "Sweetwater" Clifton. He never considered himself a pioneer, but he prided himself on always doing the right thing. There were so many ethical lessons he taught me, his players, and his fellow coaches. But more than anything else, he taught me about race and racism when he explained his playing days with the original Celtics. Back then, there were no integrated teams. That is hard to imagine now that 80 percent of players in the NBA are people of color.

No white team could beat the Celtics, and no black team could beat the legendary Harlem Rens, but they filled arenas everywhere they played against each other. Traveling with the Rens, my dad learned the poisonous effects of segregation. The Celtics would stay in the best hotels while they watched their friends on the Rens board a luxury bus bought by Bobby Douglas, their owner. Douglas knew that most hotels would not allow his black players an overnight stay. My father and his teammates ate at the best restaurants while they sadly watched the Rens bring food onto their bus because too many restaurants would not serve them.

On several occasions, the Celtics pulled into a gas station behind the Rens's bus and watched the owner of the station approach the bus with a rifle because he was not about to serve them from his lily-white pumps.

Race riots broke out in five Celtics-Rens matchups because so many white fans did not want to watch blacks and whites playing on the same court. Owners eventually built nets or cages around the court so angry fans could not get to the players.

My dad and Tarzan Cooper, both Hall of Famers, would not shake hands before every game. Rather, they would embrace each other so fans could clearly see that for the Rens and the Celtics, it was not just about good basketball, but their friendship offered a preview of what America could become if racism was stopped.

These things prepared my dad to sign Clifton in 1950. I recall looking outside my bedroom window and seeing my dad's image hanging from a tree and people picketing. I was five and did not know what it meant. I now know that some people were angry with him for signing Clifton. But he withstood the pressure because his faith and his family taught him to always do the right thing. Yet there were some who hated Joe Lapchick because of the stand he took for equality and the removal of racial barriers.

Dad passed away in 1970. Gus Alfieri, a former player, wrote a biography about him, and a documentary, *Lapchick and Clifton*, was released. Finally, the Joe Lapchick Character Award was created, an enduring tribute to his vision and character created four decades after his passing.

Alfieri tells the story about Dad that famed basketball coach Lou Carnesecca related to him. Lou said, "Joe was a humble man, and he hated *geniuses* who thought they were better than everybody else. Lapchick loved beating those types and had a subtle way of bringing them down to earth. He often did it to me.

"As we were leaving a banquet, Joe handed me a card and said, 'Here. Take this and put it in your wallet. Carry it with you all the time, and when you get to thinking that you're pretty smart, take it out and read it.' The card said, 'Peacock today, feather duster tomorrow.'"

It makes me proud when people tell me that my father was a great coach or a great player. I respond simply by relating that he was even better as a father. I was so blessed to be raised by this quiet giant of a person.

RICHARD LAPCHICK

17. Finding His Way Home

God has made everything beautiful in its time. He has
also set eternity in the human heart; yet no one can
fathom what God has done from beginning to end.
ECCLESIASTES 3:11

Robin Parkhouse was in no particular hurry as he walked toward the infirmary in a Baltimore prison. He knew he wasn't going anywhere. A foolish chase for quick cash brought him here on October 12, 1985. Overwhelmed by temptation, he had sketched a road map without any direction. He was a lost child.

It wasn't always that way.

Parkhouse was once a young man blessed with athletic ability. A football star at Boone High School in Orlando, Parkhouse signed with the University of Alabama in 1968. He didn't skip a beat playing for the legendary Paul "Bear" Bryant. Parkhouse became a team captain and earned All-Southeastern Conference and All-American honors as a defensive end in 1971. That year Alabama went undefeated and won a conference championship before losing to Nebraska in the Orange Bowl.

Parkhouse's downward spiral began shortly after his college career ended. Not quite good enough to make it in the pros, Parkhouse had bounced around a couple of construction jobs before getting an opportunity to play with the Winnipeg Blue Bombers in the Canadian Football League. That lasted six games before a knee injury. Game over.

A new one was about to begin.

With no prospects and no viable career options, Parkhouse was left "on the shifting sands," as he likes to call it. He partied and drank and got high. It was the thing to do back in the 1970s, especially for somebody with no direction in life. Life was one big unnatural high.

And Parkhouse was setting himself up for a painful dose of reality.

A friend called him with the promise of big money to be made by selling cocaine. Now back in Orlando and without any stable employment, the lure of easy money was impossible for Parkhouse to ignore.

But the "friend" had neglected a few significant details. He had cut a deal and was working with the Drug Enforcement Agency, which was listening in on all their conversations.

Parkhouse went to a hotel in Baltimore to "get the ball rolling," only to feel the rug burn on his face as federal agents pushed him to the floor and snapped handcuffs on his wrists. Narcotics agents seized more than six pounds of cocaine, which authorities said had a street value of $1 million.

This all brought Parkhouse to a Baltimore prison for that fateful journey in 1985. He came across a blue pamphlet with bold black letters. He can still see it clearly to this day and recalls leaning down to pick it up as he walked to the infirmary for a physical. He tucked it in his pocket and then read every single word that night back in his cell. A guy who loved getting high on drugs and alcohol felt a more powerful buzz coursing through his veins. It was the Gospel of John—words that would lead Parkhouse from a broken-down road of secrets and sins to a place of spiritual healing.

Behold the Lamb of God, which taketh away the sin of the world.

Parkhouse's tortured soul was finally free. After reading the pamphlet, he got down on his knees in a dingy jail cell and asked Jesus Christ to come into his heart.

They have been inseparable since.

"I had this sense of freedom that the Lord set me free from the bondage of that lifestyle that I had been dragging around like a ball and chain," Parkhouse said. "I built my own lock and prison. I had this sense that I was free of that, that I wouldn't go back down those roads ever."

He would not. Parkhouse would serve forty-two months in prison before coming home to Orlando—a changed man for good. Now in his sixties, he has been married for four years and is an elder at the First Presbyterian Church of Orlando. It's the same church where his father was an elder many years ago.

His journey has taken him to other places, majestic places like the Pacific Coast Highway in California and near Wyoming's Jackson Hole. He has participated in several charitable bike rides for a group called Kids Across America, which sponsors camps for disadvantaged and inner-city youth.

By his side—just like he was during the troubled times—was his former college teammate and friend, Johnny Musso. "Trouble followed him around, but if anybody knew Robin, they knew he had a soft heart and was a good person," Musso said. "We're locked at the hip."

The bike rides with Musso—anywhere from three hundred to five hundred miles within a week's time—have been challenging for Parkhouse. But it's well worth the ache in his muscles. The important thing is that his heart no longer hurts.

"I want to clearly make the point that it's just by the grace of God that I have a story of redemption," Parkhouse said.

It's been more than a quarter century since that pamphlet showed Parkhouse the way. He is forever free of the prison he had created for himself.

He doesn't know what became of the pamphlet. He left it behind in that Baltimore jail cell, hoping that another lost soul might find his way home.

GEORGE DIAZ

18. "Are You Better Than Michael Jordan?"

"From everyone who has been given much, much will be demanded; and from the one who has been entrusted with much, much more will be asked."

LUKE 12:48

One year after graduating from Eastern University in St. David's, Pennsylvania, I was given the opportunity to play basketball for the New York Nationals. Most people did not know who the Nationals were, and that is because our opponent was much more famous than we were. We traveled from city to city as the opponent of the Harlem Globetrotters.

I will never forget a game that I played for the Nationals in the winter of 2001. The game itself was pretty typical. We played in a big arena, the Globetrotters beat us by a comfortable margin, and after the game there was an autograph session for the fans. Now the autograph signing was for the Globetrotters, but there were always fans that would come over and ask the Nationals for their autographs, too. Sometimes they would ask us to sign their basketball or T-shirt, and sometimes it was just to sign a piece of paper.

This autograph session stands out because of something a young boy said to me. He came up to me and asked me to sign his ball, and while I was signing it, he asked, "Are you better than Michael Jordan?"

I looked up at him, expecting to see a sarcastic smile on his face, but I actually saw something different. He was very serious and was waiting for my answer.

I couldn't understand why he asked me that question. Didn't he just watch the game? We got killed, and I didn't even play very well. How could he possibly think that I might be as good as the greatest player who ever picked up a basketball?

I was tempted to say, "Yes." I mean, this was my only chance to ever have someone think I was actually better than Michael Jordan. But I couldn't do it. I looked at the boy, smiled, and said,

"Buddy, not even close."

Being in the spotlight means that you are being watched. All athletes are in the spotlight. Whether you are playing for a fifth-grade rec team, or a high school varsity team, or are in the pros—you are being watched. Individuals, especially young ones, are drawn to people who are in the spotlight. All athletes have a chance to be a good or a bad example to those who are watching them. The apostle Paul tells us, "Whatever you do, whether in word or deed, do it all in the name of the Lord Jesus" (Colossians 3:17). Let's take that challenge every time we go on the court (or field), knowing that we are setting an example to those around us.

I will probably never meet that boy again, but I will always remember the way he looked at me just because I was an athlete.

To be able to play or coach a sport is a gift from God, but with each gift comes the responsibility to use it the right way.

KEVIN STANDFORD

ACKNOWLEDGMENTS

....

With deep appreciation, I acknowledge the support and guidance of the following people who helped make this book possible.

Special thanks to Alex Martins, Dan DeVos, and Rich DeVos of the Orlando Magic.

Hearty thanks to my friends at Barbour Publishing, especially editor Paul Muckley.

Hats off to two dependable associates—my trusted and valuable colleague Andrew Herdliska, who anchored this book from start to finish, and my ace typist, Fran Thomas.

Heartfelt thanks to Ken Hussar, my coeditor and longtime friend, for his enthusiasm and labors to make this book a reality.

My sincere thanks to Peggy Matthews Rose, whose editorial skills helped shape a number of these stories.

Finally, special thanks to my wife, Ruth, for her thorough and professional proofreading of the manuscript and for her enthusiasm concerning this project.

PAT WILLIAMS

ABOUT THE AUTHORS

Pat Williams is the cofounder and senior vice president of the NBA's Orlando Magic. As one of America's top motivational, inspirational, and humorous speakers, he has addressed thousands of executives in organizations ranging from Fortune 500 companies and national associations to universities and nonprofits. Clients include Allstate, American Express, Cisco, Coca-Cola, Disney, Honeywell, IBM, ING, Lockheed Martin, Nike, PricewaterhouseCoopers, and Tyson Foods, to name a few. Pat is also the author of more than eighty books, his most recent title being *The Mission is Remission*.

Pat served for seven years in the United States Army, spent seven years in the Philadelphia Phillies organization—two as a minor league catcher and five in the front office—and also spent three years in the Minnesota Twins organization. Since 1968, he has been in the NBA as general manager for teams in Chicago, Atlanta, Philadelphia—including the 1983 world champion 76ers—and now the Orlando Magic, which he cofounded in 1987 and helped lead to the NBA finals in 1995. Twenty-three of his teams have gone to the NBA playoffs and five have made the NBA finals. In 1996, a national publication named Pat one of the fifty most influential people in NBA history.

Pat has been an integral part of NBA history, including bringing the NBA to Orlando. He has traded Pete Maravich as well as traded for Julius Erving, Moses Malone, and Anfernee "Penny" Hardaway, and he has won four NBA draft lotteries, including back-to-back winners in 1992 and 1993. He also drafted Charles Barkley, Shaquille O'Neal, Maurice Cheeks, Andrew Toney, and Darryl Dawkins. He signed Billy Cunningham, Chuck Daly, and Matt Guokas to their first professional coaching contracts. Nineteen of his former players have become NBA head coaches, nine have become college head coaches, and seven have become assistant NBA coaches.

Pat and his wife, Ruth, are the parents of nineteen children, ranging in age from twenty-four to thirty-eight, including fourteen adopted from four nations. For one year, sixteen of his children were all teenagers at the same time. Pat and his family have been featured in *Sports Illustrated*, *Reader's Digest*, *Good Housekeeping*, *Family Circle*, the *Wall Street Journal*, *Focus on the Family*, *New Man* magazine, plus all of the major television networks, and *The Maury Povich Show* and Dr. Robert Schuller's *Hour of Power*.

Pat teaches an adult Sunday school class at First Baptist Church of Orlando and hosts three weekly radio shows. He has completed fifty-eight marathons—most recently the 2010 Disney Marathon—and also climbed Mount Rainier in Washington State. He is a weightlifter, Civil War buff, and serious baseball fan. Every winter he plays in major league fantasy camps and has caught Hall of Famers Bob Feller, Bob Gibson, Ferguson Jenkins, Rollie Fingers, Gaylord Perry, Phil Niekro, Tom Seaver, and Goose Gossage.

Pat was raised in Wilmington, Delaware. He earned his bachelor's degree at Wake Forest University and his master's degree at Indiana University. He is a member of the Wake Forest Sports Hall of Fame after catching for the Deacon baseball team, including the 1962 Atlantic Coast Conference Championship team. He is also a member of the Delaware Sports Hall of Fame.

Ken Hussar (pronounced "Huh-zar") has entertained over four thousand audiences with his offbeat humor and funny songs for forty-four years.

Ken retired from the Penn Manor School District in 1997 after thirty-one years as an elementary school teacher. In 1994, he was named the district's Outstanding Elementary Educator.

He worked as a brakeman on the Strasburg Rail Road for twenty-two summers.

He wrote 442 *Short and Snappy* humor columns for the *Lancaster New Era*.

Pat and Ken have compiled *The Ultimate Handbook of Jokes*

for Coaches, Leaders, and Speakers and *The Ultimate Handbook of Motivational Quotations for Coaches, Speakers, and Leaders*. Ken has edited more than sixty of Pat Williams's books.

Ken and his wife, Carolyn, have three grown children and three grandchildren and live in Lancaster County, Pennsylvania.

CONTACT

....

You can contact Pat Williams at:

Pat Williams
c/o Orlando Magic
8701 Maitland Summit Boulevard
Orlando, FL 32810
407-916-2404
pwilliams@orlandomagic.com

Visit Pat Williams online at:
www.PatWilliams.com
www.twitter.com/OrlandoMagicPat
www.Facebook.com/PatWilliams.OrlandoMagic

If you would like to set up a speaking engagement for Pat Williams, please call Andrew Herdliska at 407-916-2401 or e-mail him at aherdliska@orlandomagic.com.

To contact Ken Hussar:
174 Ridings Way
Lancaster, PA 17601
717-898-0024
ridingsway@netzero.net